FATHER AND SON

Edmund Gosse, born in London in 1849, was the son of Philip Gosse, eminent zoologist and fanatical fundamentalist Christian. He was educated privately and between 1867 and 1914 worked as assistant librarian in the British Museum, as a translator at the Board of Trade and as a librarian at the House of Lords. He married Ellen Epps in 1875 and had one son and two daughters.

An admirer of Pre-Raphaelite poetry, he wrote verse and published *On Viol and Flute* in 1873 and *Collected Poems* in 1911. He acquired a reputation as a critic and man of letters. Among his many interests was Scandinavian literature; he was one of the first to introduce Ibsen to English readers and his critiques of Ibsen, translations of his plays and *Life* (1908) earned him a Norwegian Knighthood in 1901. He was also deeply drawn to French literature, bringing Gide in particular to the attention of the British public. His most important critical work was *Life and Letters of John Donne* (1893), which played a substantial role in the revaluation of the Metaphysical Poets; but it is the relationship with his father that is the focus of his best work, *Father and Son*, which is also a brilliant reflection of Victorian social and intellectual life.

His other work includes the lives of Gray, Congreve and Swinburne (a close friend). He was knighted in 1925 and died in May 1928.

Peter Abbs is Reader in Education at the University of Sussex, where he directs the Creative Writing Programme at MA level. He has written widely on culture and aesthetics, and his recent work includes *The Educational Imperative: A Defence of Socratic and Aesthetic Learning* (1994) and *The Polemics of Education: Selected Essays on Art, Culture and Society* (1995). He is also an established poet with five published volumes, most recently *Personae and Other Selected Poems* (1995), which contains a moving 'Father and Son' sequence, and *Angelic Imagination* (1996).

EDMUND GOSSE

FATHER AND SON

A STUDY OF TWO TEMPERAMENTS

edited by
Peter Abbs

**DER GLAUBE IST WIE DIE LIEBE;
ER LÄSST SICH NICHT ERZWINGEN**
Schopenhauer

PENGUIN BOOKS
IN ASSOCIATION WITH
WILLIAM HEINEMANN LTD

PENGUIN BOOKS

Published by the Penguin Group
Penguin Books Ltd, 80 Strand, London WC2R 0RL, England
Penguin Putnam Inc., 375 Hudson Street, New York, New York 10014, USA
Penguin Books Australia Ltd, 250 Camberwell Road, Camberwell, Victoria 3124, Australia
Penguin Books Canada Ltd, 10 Alcorn Avenue, Toronto, Ontario, Canada M4V 3B2
Penguin Books India (P) Ltd, 11 Community Centre, Panchsheel Park, New Delhi – 110 017, India
Penguin Books (NZ) Ltd, Cnr Rosedale and Airborne Roads, Albany, Auckland, New Zealand
Penguin Books (South Africa) (Pty) Ltd, 24 Sturdee Avenue, Rosebank 2196, South Africa

Penguin Books Ltd, Registered Offices: 80 Strand, London WC2R 0RL, England

www.penguin.com

First published by William Heinemann Ltd 1907
Published in Penguin English Library 1983
Reprinted in Penguin Classics 1986
Reprinted in Penguin Books 1989

024

Introduction, Notes and Select Bibliography copyright © Peter Abbs, 1983
All rights reserved

Set in Monotype Bembo
Printed in England by Clays Ltd, St Ives plc

ISBN-13: 978–0–14–018276–7

www.greenpenguin.co.uk

MIX
Paper from
responsible sources
FSC
www.fsc.org FSC™ C018179

Penguin Books is committed to a sustainable
future for our business, our readers and our planet.
This book is made from Forest Stewardship
Council™ certified paper.

CONTENTS

CONTENTS

GOSSE'S LIFE AND WORKS:
A CHRONOLOGY

This chronology is strictly confined to main events, awards and publications. A thorough eight-page list of Edmund Gosse's published writings can be found as an appendix in Evan Charteris' *The Life and Letters of Sir Edmund Gosse*. See also Ann Thwaite's *Edmund Gosse: a Literary Landscape*.

1849 Birth of a son, Edmund Gosse, to Philip and Emily Gosse at 13, Trafalgar Terrace, Mortimer Road, Hackney, London.

1853 Family move to 58 Huntingdon Street, Islington.

1857 Emily Gosse dies of cancer.

1858 Philip Gosse and Edmund move to Marychurch in Devonshire.

1859 Public baptism of Edmund.

1860 Philip Gosse marries Eliza Brightwen.

1867 Edmund begins work in the cataloguing department of the British Museum. He begins to associate with the Pre-Raphaelites.

1870 First book published: *Madrigals, Songs and Sonnets*.

1871 First visit to Scandinavia.

1873 Publication of poems *On Viol and Flute*.

1875 Marriage to Nellie Epps. Becomes translator for the Board of Trade (until 1904).

1879 *Studies in the Literature of Northern Europe*, Edmund Gosse's first book of criticism.

1882 *Gray*, first critical biography.

1883 *Seventeenth Century Studies*.

1884 Clark Lecturer in English Literature at Trinity College,

Cambridge (until 1890). Lecture trip to America (November 1884–January 1885).

1888 *Life of William Congreve.* Philip Gosse's death (23 August).

1890 *The Life of Philip Henry Gosse F R S.*

1893 *Questions and Issues*, essays on contemporary literature including Mallarmé and French Symbolism.

1896 *Critical Kit-Kats.*

1899 *The Life and Letters of John Donne*, a biographical study which helped to revive Donne's reputation.

1904 *Jeremy Taylor.* Appointed as Librarian to the House of Lords (until September 1914).

1905 *French Profiles,*
Coventry Patmore,
Sir Thomas Browne,
British Portrait Painters.

1907 Made Fellow of Royal Society of Literature,
Father and Son,
Henrik Ibsen.

1911 *Collected Poems.*

1912 *Portraits and Sketches.*

1913 Elected Vice-President, Royal Society of Literature. *Father and Son* honoured by the French Academy. Made an Officer of the Legion d'Honneur.

1916 President of Modern Language Society.

1917 *The Life of Algernon Charles Swinburne.*

1919 Became literary essayist for *The Sunday Times. Some Diversions of a Man of Letters.*

1921 President of the English Association.

1922 *Aspects and Impressions.*

1925 Knighted. *Silhouettes.* Made Commander of the Legion d'Honneur.

1927 *Leaves and Fruit.*

1928 Died in London on 16 May.

INTRODUCTION

I

Father and Son was first published anonymously in the autumn of 1907. Although some of the initial reactions expressed a sense of alarm at what was discerned as a lack of filial respect the book was, for the most part, well received and before Gosse's death in 1928 was widely regarded as a minor classic. Indeed, within twelve months of its first publication there had been four further editions of the work and Edmund Gosse, habitually cautious and preoccupied with his own literary standing, was soon ready to shed his anonymity.

It is significant that *Father and Son* was more warmly received in the United States of America (where it was published in the same year), for in America the concern for propriety was so much less than in England and the Victorian division between the public and private realm was less tightly drawn, more open to negotiation between author and his reading public. It was not considered an offence to 'speak out' or improper to reveal the inevitable tensions between generations as they manifest themselves in family relationships in, for example, the prolonged and not always conscious struggle between vulnerable, resistant sons and invulnerable and powerful fathers. In a private letter dated 2 February 1908 the American Shakespearean scholar Howard Furness had written to Gosse:

At two sittings I read every word of it. It is a very great book. The best you have written and the most enduring; with it you will celebrate your century. English literature cannot afford to let such a book die.

Independently of its records of a rapidly vanishing faith it is told with an evident truth as unflinching as it is tender.[1]

Furness' remarks were, no doubt, more accurate than he had intended, for *Father and Son* was to be the only book of Gosse's to survive the sudden eclipse of his prodigious reputation which followed upon his death. But the immediate recognition of the work is clearly recorded in Furness' response as it is in another letter sent to Gosse on 16 January 1910 by the American novelist William Howells:

I read slowly and faithfully and I have got only to the point of your mother's death. But what a world I have passed through! There is a universal truth to child life in it all, and the specialized truth is most wonderful and pitiful. I have fairly ached along the story. In all the autobiographical books I have read I remember nothing equalling it.[2]

In a further letter, written five days later, Howells confirmed the truth of his first reactions, praised the diction of the book as 'exquisite in its tender precision' and, with not uncharacteristic American euphoria, claimed:

The pathetic tale could not be better worded if a syndicate of masters rose from their graves to do it; say Milton, Dante and Shakespeare. Truly a most beautiful book.[3]

Gosse never received quite such adulation from his English critics but the reputation of the book grew steadily in this country and its achievement was widely acknowledged. George Bernard Shaw declared it to be 'one of the immortal pages in English literature'[4] and even the young and pugnacious Ezra Pound, in a destructive review of Gosse as representative of official and otiose British culture, yet conceded: 'Gosse has written one excellent book: *Father and Son*.'[5] In 1927, a year before the death of Gosse at the age of seventy-nine, Harold Nicolson also drew attention to the book, naming it 'a masterpiece' in which 'the author had been able to combine the maximum of scientific interest with the maximum of literary form'.[6] We will have reason to consider this judgement at a later point but whatever its critical value it further buttressed the reputation of the book. For as the years passed and as Gosse's vast opus of essays, sketches, poems, plays and biographies turned yellow and gathered layers of library dust *Father and Son* remained in print and found, generation after generation, an appreciative audience of readers. As Furness had said, it was the best Gosse had written and the most enduring.

It is somewhat difficult for us now living in the latter frayed part of the twentieth century, where private lives are ready material for vicarious public consumption, to envisage the kind of courage Gosse required to write the work and why, until the fourth impression of the book, he chose to publish under the protection of anonymity. Harold Nicolson in *The Development of English Biography*, declaring that Victorianism only died in 1921, referred to 'the shock' occasioned by the publication of *Father and Son*. Even Evan Charteris in his biography (1931) of Edmund Gosse hints at the degree of the alarm by the kind of defence he proffers:

Those who take the view that *Father and Son* disregards reticence and respect will see ... what forbearance Gosse exercised and how much he has toned down in that book ... Few have kept the fifth commandment so closely.[7]

Such a commendation is made only when considerable doubt has been cast upon the matter. (And yet, tellingly, the statement itself is unintentionally ambiguous; if the author has 'toned down' his true feelings then, perhaps, indeed he had not inwardly honoured his parents.) For the time in which it was written *Father and Son* was a courageous work although, as we shall see, its courage was frequently inhibited by countervailing pressures which forced the existential truth to work often under the surface of the text and even against its ostensible and scientifically described aims. Yet in its struggle to confront family relationships descriptively rather than rhetorically; in its attempt (though impeded) to delineate honestly the tensions between father and son; in its partial desire to offer a portrait of an eminent Victorian in terms of human fallibility and, indeed, gullibility; in its unexpected and, perhaps, unintended concluding manifesto announcing the right of the individual 'to fashion his inner life for himself' even against the dictates of tradition and parental values, and certainly against the injunctions of puritanical patriarchs, in all of these things *Father and Son* was a somewhat subversive work for those capable of discerning its full implications.

Edmund Gosse wrote in a perceptive review of Lytton Strachey's *Eminent Victorians*, one of the next major works in non-fiction to break away from the tradition of eulogy and rhetoric in the description of individual life:

> Their (Victorian biographers) fault lay, not in their praise, which was much of it deserved, but in their deliberate attempt in the interests of what was Nice and Proper – gods of the Victorian Age – to conceal what any conventional person might think not quite becoming. There were to be no shadows in the picture, no stains or rugosities on the smooth bust of rosy wax.[8]

Gosse titled his evaluation of *Eminent Victorians* 'The Agony of the Victorian Age'. Agony is a strong word, particularly so for Gosse, and it is one that does not frequently appear in his writings. He meant it. The agony of the Victorians resided in the schizoid split between public and private, between the large formal gesture and the intimate personal actuality. It expressed itself at every level of Victorian life and seemed at its most hypocritical in the area of sexuality. For Lytton Strachey the contradiction manifested itself dramatically in the literary form of biography where Victorian biographers privately knew one thing about the eminent figures they portrayed and publicly wrote another. Although Gosse cautiously welcomed *Eminent Victorians* and later in 1927 dedicated his last book, *Leaves and Fruit*, to its author 'with affectionate admiration', he too was a Victorian living out of 'the agony' of a divided consciousness.

To give one example, Gosse wrote the life of Algernon

Charles Swinburne (published in 1917) but, at the same time, compiled a *Confidential Paper on Swinburne's Moral Irregularities* which until quite recently was 'reserved from public use' in the British Museum. He must have felt that the official life could not fully impinge upon the complex actuality of the man; there was public knowledge and there was private knowledge and even in the delicate interpretive act of critical biography discretion kept them apart.

Gosse's ambivalence, his conflicting desires to preserve social decorum and yet seek existential truth, provide us with a key to unlock his own autobiography. In *Father and Son* we sense an unresolved war between compliance and authenticity. This struggle lies not only at the centre of his childhood and adolescence, but also (though less obviously) in the very style and organization of the book. Reading the book one occasionally senses in a phrase, a sequence of sentences, even a whole paragraph, a complexity of contorted emotion of which, one suspects, the author himself was largely unconscious. For Gosse reveals more than he ever proposes in his analytical introduction. To fully comprehend the text and to be able to place it both within and beyond its historical context, the reader has to be prepared to live simultaneously with at least two versions of the work. The first version is the consciously determined one, written with sufficient respect for the Victorian gods of Niceness, Propriety – and one must quickly add a third – Objective Science.

The second version has a different dynamic; it spontaneously emerges at points only to be repressed – to function at deep unconscious levels in the verbal organization of the work – until it finally manifests itself in powerful unambiguous terms in the closing Epilogue. The first version is ironic, detached, scientific, neutral, urbane, sociological. It has great biographical and historical value. The second is exposed, passionate, labile, inward and deep. It has the power to move and disturb. It has true poetic and autobiographical energy. The first version is written from the wary Victorian intelligence; it has a shrewd eye to the audience, a concern for tact and decorum, and has come to believe, like Darwin and Spencer, in the pure objectivity of Science. The second version is the unsettling subjective voice of the more honest but dispossessed modern, of authenticity struggling outside communal values and inherited judgements, ready, at least in principle, to fashion its own inner life. But this is to anticipate later analysis . . .

That *Father and Son* in its style and narrative records both the Victorian and the modern sensibility goes some way to account for the enduring importance of the volume. And yet little has been written about the book. It has received no sustained critical interpretation. It has been not exactly ignored, for it has been given many passing references in literary and historical writings, but nor has it been closely examined. Its wealth of ambiguity, of contradiction, its seesaw dialectic between conscious intention and actual revelation has not been fully delineated or its significance demonstrated. There have been a few perceptive forays, of which Virginia Woolf's spiky essay 'Edmund Gosse' in Volume IV of her *Collected Essays*, and David Grylls' brilliantly probing analysis in *Guardians and Angels*, are by far the best. Many essays, like V. S. Pritchett's in *The Living Novel*, are merely anecdotal, others inertly descriptive. There has been a similar paucity of material on the man. Osbert Sitwell's account of Edmund Gosse is slight, self-advertising and 'literary'. James Woolf's study, *Sir Edmund Gosse*, while giving some information is devoid of intelligence. The main source for biographical material was Evan Charteris' *The Life and Letters of Sir Edmund Gosse*, published in 1931, although there is a well-documented account of Gosse's lecture trip to America in 1884 and of his literary relationship with that country in *Transatlantic Dialogue: Selected American Correspondence of Edmund Gosse*. Now we have Ann Thwaite's closely documented *Edmund Gosse: a Literary Landscape* (1984) which biographically, if not critically, does much to fill the gap. Yet the comparative lack of literary interest in Gosse's work calls for some explanation.

Part of the reason must lie in the eclipse of Edmund Gosse's reputation. In 1920 Gosse was one of the most influential figures in English cosmopolitan literary life, at the heart of a complex web of relationships which included Henry James, Thomas Hardy and André Gide. By 1940 he was all but forgotten. If his poetry or criticism had possessed the power of Coleridge's or Arnold's, doubtless his autobiography would, as a consequence, have received close critical attention. However, his poetry rarely transcended the sticky mannerisms of the Pre-Raphaelites and his criticism, while comprehensive in range and lucid in style, tended to be limited by the superficial approach of belle-lettrism. The titles of the books, *Some Diversions of a Man of Letters*, *Critical Kit-Kats* and *Gossip in a Library*, convey the inveterate disposition of the armchair critic. The words 'charming', 'entertaining', 'exquisite', 'tasteful', 'adorned', litter the pages and tend to obscure any more probing insight which, at times, *is* seriously at work. We must not forget that Gosse found in literature a refuge from the chilling demands of his puritanical background – *Father and Son* is, in large measure, the record of that momentous personal discovery – and that, for this very reason, he was somewhat reluctant to be deeply disturbed by it or, in turn, to be disturbing in his judgements of it. In the light of his background, it is not surprising to find in personal correspondence if not in public disclosure that Gosse hated 'the cocaine and morphine'[9] of Dostoyevsky, that he could not tolerate Tolstoy as social prophet and disturber of the status quo, and that E. M. Forster's *Howards End* outraged him for 'introducing into fiction a high-born maiden who has had a baby'.[10] He called the book 'sensational and dirty and affected'.[11] Against this, however, must be recorded his early recognition of such major writers as Ibsen, Whitman and Gide.

The weakness of Gosse lay in his aestheticism. Charteris says that Gosse believed: 'If the reaction to a literary work was pleasure, they had an adequate basis for criticism without any sizing up of moral values.'[12] But this hedonistic approach to literature floundered badly as civilization encountered the irrational slaughter of the First World War; it had no way of engaging with the upheaval because aestheticism itself was ultimately more a symptom of the malaise than interpretation or corrective. In the changing conditions, Edmund Gosse's lightness of touch became not so much sensitivity as a lack of pressure; the super-refinement, in the crisis of civilization, became a mode of superficiality. As the critics, F. R. Leavis, Ezra Pound and T. S. Eliot made, in the struggle for standards and meanings, a trenchant stand against the Pre-Raphaelites, Gosse's voice grew thinner and thinner until it became a disappearing whisper. One work remained: *Father and Son*; and because it was solitary it missed the scrutiny it merited.

There is, though, a further reason for the critical neglect of *Father and Son*. It relates to the genre. Autobiography has, until recently, eluded serious study. In England there is still no developed method for evaluating autobiography, no tested tradition of interpretation. We have innumerable works on poetry, on drama and the novel but only a handful of books inquiring into the distinct form of autobiography. As I have described this lack of tradition in the *New Pelican Guide to Literature* (volume 8) I will not elaborate upon the point here. However, there can be little doubt that *Father and Son* has suffered as a result of the failure to establish in our culture a critical method and a fitting discourse for autobiographical writing.

I want now to place *Father and Son* in the historical context of autobiographical writing and then to outline a particular approach to the work.

II

In autobiography the natural, forward, linear motion of consciousness is interrupted as an individual turns back upon his own life to understand his own inner development. Autobiography is a form of creative introspection, an examination and recreation of outer circumstances and relationships in terms of inner motives and psychological growth. It is not surprising, therefore, that the first major autobiography in the Western world was written by St Augustine at the beginning of the Christian period. Christianity engendered a delicate and intense preoccupation with the state of the individual soul. It encouraged the analysis of action in the light of underlying motive. It worked for personal salvation in the great scheme of things. The Greeks would have regarded such an intensely personal preoccupation as philosophically excessive and as psychologically unhealthy, but for the Christian it was the fundamental means for securing the very meaning of existence. And out of this Christian commitment to personal salvation arose the literary form of autobiography.

In *The Confessions* St Augustine, in his desire to grasp and deepen his conversion to Christian belief, recreates his own journey to faith, beginning with early childhood and moving chronologically forward. He is not concerned so much with history and the detail of outer circumstance as with the inner and hidden structure of feelings and motives, the obscure but powerful agents of moral action. He makes himself the daring psychologist of his own psyche, stripping away coat after coat of varnish to examine the pattern of the underlying grain. Thus the work, dedicated directly to God, is a confession in which he examines and re-creates his own past and does so in order to move forward, with a new lightness of mood, into an affirmative future based on faith. *The Confessions* is, at once, a transposition of the sacrament of confession into literary form and an early anticipation of the modern psycho-analytical encounter, where the person, struggling for a sense of psychological wholeness, explores his past in a sustained and protected conversation not with God but with the supporting therapist. The habit of writing confessions, though without the informing introspective genius of St Augustine, continued through the centuries but it was not till Rousseau wrote his *Confessions* in 1765 that there was a further major development in the genre.

In his *Confessions* Rousseau, unlike St Augustine, defiantly placed himself at the centre of the stage. His concern was not with salvation so much as self-realization. He will confess his crimes not to crave forgiveness but as a means to understand and unequivocally render his own nature. The psychological and the personal elements, always present in the traditional Confessions, come dramatically to the foreground and become ends in themselves. Human understanding, individual realization, self affirmation: these, rather than eternal life and remission of sins, are, in Rousseau, the impelling forces. As a result there is a momentous change in mood and conception; the note of the genre changes, becomes more intimate, more varied, more complex. Rousseau writes:

> I shall not try to make it uniform; I shall use whatever style seems best to fit the given episode, and I will change it according to my mood, without a qualm. I shall say what I have to say in the way I feel about it, without effort or embarrassment, not worrying about being consistent ... The style, uneven but natural, now rapid and now diffuse, now sensible and now extravagant, now grave and now gay, will itself be part of my story.[13]

Rousseau is prepared to reveal, without defence or apology, his own peculiarities, his own sexual proclivities, his own misdemeanours. He brings his private life into the public realm as a manifesto, as an existential challenge and as a literary masterpiece. Although he still named his work 'confessions', it is, more truly, an autobiography in the modern and proper sense of the word. After Rousseau, autobiography – the actual word being first coined by Southey in 1809 – comes of age; and in the century following, many of the major European writers and thinkers wrote autobiographies for public readership.

And yet, Rousseau did not have a direct influence on the nature of Victorian autobiography. The reasons for this we have already partly touched on. The public demanded heroic images and if they could not be given these, then they expected discretion, decorum and silence. No autobiographer in Victorian England leaps into the public realm and challenges it with the personal and subversive truths of his own inner existence Rousseau's *Confessions*, although secretly admired by a few, were commonly viewed as self indulgent, unwholesome and corrupting to the moral order. In a symposium of essays, *Approaches to Victorian Autobiography*, Phyllis Grosskurth claims:

> The typical Victorian autobiographer was acutely aware of his audience. A mutual complicity shaped the genre, and language became a screen to shelter the vulnerable egos of writers and readers alike [14]

When we examine *Father and Son* (published only a few years after the Victorian period had technically closed) we will need to bear this judgement in mind; we will, at times, need to lift the language screen to see what inner drama lies behind it, what emotions it is consciously or unconsciously intended to conceal. It is vital to our understanding of the book to comprehend the conditions in which Victorian autobiography (and biography) was expected to function.

In editing a version of Count Carlo Gozzi's autobiography during the Victorian period, John Addington Symonds decided to expunge 'those passages and phrases which might have caused offence to some of my readers'.[15] Edmund Gosse himself in a review of a new translation of Montaigne's essays (essays which in their own way formed during the early Renaissance a magnificent assertion of autobiographical understanding) wrote:

> Montaigne, living in an age when speech was free, frequently touches upon subjects of delicacy. He is never morbid or offensive, but he is sometimes outspoken. At such moments, without any emphasis, Mr Ives simply allows his author to retain his own native speech until he ceases to be discreet. No method could be more praiseworthy.[16]

The implication is that the Victorian age is not free; subjects of delicacy have to be veiled. We constantly stumble across a sense of restriction in the matter of personal communication. Of Walter Pater, Gosse writes 'his faith [in the human race] was never positive, nor would he trust it to read his secret

thoughts'.[17] Herbert Spencer in his *Autobiography* asserted
simply that it would 'be out of taste to address the public as
though it consisted of personal friends'.[18] While Anthony
Trollope, in his autobiographical account of his life and work
published in 1883, cautioned: 'That I or any man should tell
everything of himself I hold to be impossible. Who could
endure to own the doing of a mean thing?'[19] As for intimate
relationships: 'My marriage was like the marriage of other
people and of no special interest to any one except my wife
and me.'[20] Any intrusion into private space was considered
indiscreet and, ideally, the private should conform to the public
expectation, to the virtuous and heroic and productive. In the
Victorian period, autobiography, developed to a pitch of
inwardness by Rousseau, became the medium for masked
truths and guarded reflections. Indeed, autobiography was in
danger of becoming more external memoir than the exposed
exploration and recreation of the elusive self.

Edmund Gosse's *Father and Son*, like its counterparts, Mill's
Autobiography (1873) and Mark Rutherford's *Autobiography*
(1881), is not written directly in the tradition of Rousseau or
the earlier style of St Augustine. It belongs to its own age and
country. Like a well-trained Englishman, Gosse has only to
assert himself and he apologizes. If he proclaims, then he qualifies the proclamation out of existence. If he uncharacteristically
expresses a powerful feeling he seeks immediately the first
escape route he can find: all very English and, in particular,
the inveterate disposition of the Victorian mind.

In her short study of Edmund Gosse, Virginia Woolf wrote
perceptively:

Fear always seems to dog his footsteps. He dips his fingers with
astonishing agility and speed into character, but if he finds something
hot or gets hold of something large, he drops it and withdraws with
the agility of a scalded cat ... We know all that can be known by
someone who is always a little afraid of being found out.

But if Gosse's masterpiece and his portraits suffer from his inner
regard for caution, much of the fault must be laid upon his age.[21]

Virginia Woolf defines the lack in the text and then places the text in context; the author does not only influence the public, the same public that he writes for can deeply influence him not only in what he presents but in how he does it. But, in a sense, contrary to Virginia Woolf's judgement, the reader, particularly from another age, can know more than the author intends, can detect what he may be unwilling to tell, can read the private underground of the text as well as the polite public surface, and can find the autobiography within the autobiography. Before we embark on such analysis I must first establish that the work *is* autobiography, for the claim has been challenged and, moreover, in the last chapter of *Father and Son*, Gosse himself denied it.

In *The Development of English Biography*, a study to which we have already referred, Harold Nicolson claimed:

> The book is not ... a conventional biography; still less is it an autobiography. It is something entirely original; it is triumphant experiment in a new formula; it is a clinical examination of states of mind over a detached and limited period.[22]

One can, of course, see what Nicolson means. Both the title of the book and the subtitle, 'A study of two temperaments', would seem to substantiate the judgement that the book is not biography or autobiography, but an experimental form combining both. In his own Preface Gosse states that the work is a *document* diagnosing Puritanism and *a study* of intellectual and moral development. More, then, a formal documentary, than an intimate autobiography? (Doesn't Gosse himself call it 'a slice of life'?) This view is not to be dismissed, for the historical value of the text lies precisely in this realm. We will examine this conception of the book later. I only wish here to show that the book is significantly more than this and that its inherent shape and inspiration is, in fact, that of autobiography.

First, we have the evidence that Charteris provides concerning its genesis. According to Charteris, Gosse decided to write *Father and Son* at the suggestion of George Moore, a literary

21

friend. Moore, having read Edmund Gosse's conventional biography of his father, urged him to rewrite the story, but making the conflict between father and son central. Apparently, he pressed this notion of another work many times, but Edmund Gosse did not respond with animation until Moore suggested he should adopt the first person singular, the autobiographical mode *par excellence*. Such a work should not, Moore insisted, be based upon factual records but upon the recall of his own memory, it was to be the son's view and it was to span the critical period between birth and his arrival in London at the age of seventeen. Once Gosse had perceived a personal and direct way of handling the material, he worked intensively and had completed *Father and Son* within a short period of time. The generative impulse was an autobiographical one; the first person singular was the key to the writing of the book.

Secondly, and as importantly, the text itself reads predominantly as autobiography. It is true that the book claims to offer us a study of two temperaments, but that study is not dispassionate and is always given from the son's perspective. The father we see is the father the son sees. We never experience any of the conflict from *inside* the father's position. He remains a more or less static figure who is judged according to the son's categories. The son, in contrast, grows continuously until he finds and defends his own emancipation. At the front of the book Gosse placed his epigraph: *Der Glaube ist wie die Liebe; er lasst sich nicht erzwingen*: 'Faith is like love: it does not let itself be forced.' That epigraph is not disinterested and impartial. It embodies, as the whole book does, the son's judgement of the father; it is the inexorable conclusion that the autobiographical narrative imposes.

There is, as Nicolson contends, an important historical and biographical element in *Father and Son*. There is a kind of objectivity. There are claims for scientific exactitude. It is also true that Gosse himself disowns the autobiographical form. And yet, without a doubt, the central story we are given is that of the son from his birth to the point of his departure from the family at seventeen. And the son is the writer of the book. Such a narrative can only be called autobiography.

Now let us turn to the work itself.

III

At the present hour, when fiction takes forms so ingenious and so specious, it is perhaps necessary to say that the following narrative, in all its parts, and so far as the punctilious attention of the writer has been able to keep it so, is scrupulously true.[23]

So opens the Preface to *Father and Son*. The insistence on clinical observation and exactitude runs like a steel girder through the Introduction. The word 'document' is italicized and is followed quickly by the words 'record' and 'diagnosis'. The reader is presented with the image of the writer as naturalist conscientiously noting all the details of the particular specimen and setting it against the background of the environment. The author–scientist is determined not to have his perceptions corrupted by sentimental feelings or the possible bias of self-admiration or self-pity. Indeed in the first edition of the book, the Preface draws attention to the author's anonymity:

As regards the anonymous writer himself, whether the reader does or does not recognize an old acquaintance, met with in quite other fields, is a matter of no importance. Here no effort has been made to conceal or identify.[24]

The work, it is insisted, is quite other than that of his 'other fields', his poetry and literary appreciation. (But the dogmatic assertiveness of the text fails to smother an obvious dilemma. Why, if there is 'no effort to conceal or identify' is the book published, in the first instance, anonymously?)

The first paragraphs of Chapter I continue in the same detached manner; it is as if the author is looking down on the two protagonists from a high vantage point, quite forgetting that he himself is one of them:

> Of the two human beings here described . . . There came a time The struggle began soon. But to familiarize my readers with the condition of the two persons . . . and with the outlines of their temperaments . . . it is needful to open with some account . . .[25]

The method, then, is that of objective description. The writer works within the paradigm of the inductive sciences. One can see why Harold Nicolson concluded that the book was not conventional biography and still less autobiography. There are explanations for Gosse's intentions. There is, for example, the literary influence of the French critic Sainte-Beuve about whom Gosse said 'I am the disciple of one man and of one man only – Sainte-Beuve. No one else has been my master.'[26] Sainte-Beuve had demanded that the critic should work as 'a good naturalist in the vast domain of the human spirit'[27] in order to classify the different orders and species of the human mind. Sainte-Beuve had also talked of the 'unbridgeable differences between intellectual types, differences of blood, of temperament'.[28]

In these two notions of critic as naturalist and of the innate temperaments of individuals forming different species to be understood and classified, we can detect powerful influences on the formal construction and underlying conception of *Father and Son*. The notion of science must have been particularly attractive to Gosse for, by the end of the nineteenth century, many were claiming with increasing success that science was the sole way in which to arrive at any certainty in matters of truth. A commonsense inductive approach to life was beginning to prevail; arguments were to be resolved by reference to evidence and facts. As a study of the father *Father and Son* is, in part, the analysis of a man who could not, because of the power of 'the turbid volume of superstition',[29] recognize the truth of the evidence under his very finger tips. The father 'took one step in the service of truth, and then he drew back in an agony, and accepted the servitude of error'.[30] What is missing in *Father and Son*, however, is any conscious recognition of different realms of meaning; thus the scientific is seen as true and the inductive approach adopted as the method of the book. Such a method allowed the author, seemingly in good faith, to exclude the full emotional detonation of the narrative. In a diagnosis and a record one keeps subjective elements under control. Thus Gosse found a way of appealing to the three main prejudices of his time: a desire for decorum and tact in private and emotional matters coupled with an inordinate belief in the power of the fact and the promise of progress.

As a documentary record we know, from other sources, that most of the facts are accurate. In the manner of a scrupulous biographer Gosse drew on all the accounts he could gather. He drew on the intimate diaries of his mother; on letters his father had written him; on an account entitled *A Memorial of the Last Days on Earth of Emily Gosse* which his father had circulated after her death. Furthermore Gosse had already published in 1890 a long formal biography of his father *The Life of Philip Henry Gosse, FRS* and therefore had a wealth of documented material to hand. We can discern the conscious approach of *Father and Son*: it is to be the work of a literary naturalist reconstructing, detail by detail, scrupulous fact by scrupulous fact, the social milieu and then to plot within it the forms of individual and innate behaviour. The impartial reconstruction requires that the author hold back any unruly squads of feeling and any imperious judgements of the heart. For this reason – at least at a conscious level – Gosse seems determined to be fair-minded, ready to qualify his own position, prepared to be judicious in the smallest matters. He also stands back from himself. In many of the early childhood memories, we sense the superior adult inspecting the folly of the once-child:

My theological misdeeds culminated, however, in an act so puerile and preposterous that I should not venture to record it if it did not throw some glimmerings of light on the subject which I have proposed to myself in writing these pages.[31]

'Puerile', 'preposterous'; the words suggest that the adult would hardly sink to consider the misdeeds were it not for the scientific urge to record all relevant facts. One would hardly think in such passages that the author had once been that very child. The quite remarkable experiment in worship is dismissed as 'this ridiculous act'.

The neutrality and remoteness which Gosse establishes in the Preface as the condition for the inquiry ensures a fidelity to outer detail, to encompassing context, to the actual chronological sequence of events. It gives the book an historical value. It paints in miniature a sharply drawn portrait of an age; it presents for our edification the behaviour of a provincial middle-class Puritan family; it conveys, above all, a sense of the traumatic scientific and religious ferment of the mid nineteenth century. (Darwin's *Origin of Species* was published in 1859.) Anyone wishing to understand the psychological and theological dynamics of that upheaval could not go to a more valuable account than that given in Chapter V of *Father and Son*. Yet if this was all the book offered it would not be the classic it is. There is another energy in the writing which is not accounted for in Gosse's clinical Preface. Indeed so crucial is this energy to the full understanding of the work that we are led to ask whether, in fact, the Preface is one of those linguistic screens referred to by Phyllis Grosskurth behind which writer and reader alike could shelter their vulnerable egos. Is the Preface a kind of defence against the half-hidden existential meaning of the book, a defence of which Gosse himself was strangely unaware? This question takes us into a deeper reading of the text.

Although Gosse's style glides rather than penetrates, although it has a subtle propensity to skirt round and out of disconcerting experiences, although it easily digresses and qualifies, yet occasionally the reader confronts an emotion which is presented without defence. Of the death of his mother when the son is only seven, Gosse writes:

We had no cosy talk; often she was too weak to do more than pat my hand: her loud and almost constant cough terrified and harassed me. I felt, as I stood awkwardly and shyly, by her high bed, that I had shrunken into a very small and insignificant figure, that she was floating out of my reach, that all things, but I knew not what nor how, were coming to an end. She herself was not herself; her head that used to be held so erect, now rolled or sank upon the pillow; the sparkle was all extinguished from those bright, dear eyes. I could not understand it; I meditated long, long upon it all in my infantile darkness, in the garret, or in the little slip of a cold room where my bed was now placed; and a great, blind anger against I knew not what awakened in my soul.[32]

This is a most moving autobiographical evocation of pure feeling; everything about the inner experience is caught: the feeling of smallness, of loneliness, of desolation, of emptiness, of anger. It is rendered subjectivity, without the mask of irony, without the pretensions of scientific documentation. And it is this kind of subjectivity running underground through the text, erupting at unexpected points and explosively in the Epilogue, which calls for a second reading of the work. What we must try to do is to locate the unintended but latent significance of the narrative even where it contradicts the conscious and manifest intentions of the autobiographer.

In a typical passage at the opening of a paragraph in Chapter IX Gosse morally praises his father.

My father was very generous. He used to magnify any little effort that I made with stammering tongue . . . The whole thing, however, was artificial and was part of his restless inability to let well alone.[33]

Manifestly the intention is to honour the father, as would be expected by the audience, but the actual outcome is to negate the generosity. If it was 'artificial' and part of his inability to let well alone, in what lay the generosity? The high rhetoric of biography is used and quietly emptied of significance. Grylls, who has made the most perceptive study of *Father and Son* and who has analysed many of these curious contortions in which the manifest meaning is contradicted by the latent, writes:

His appraisals are expressed with civility and wit; he favours for his occasional strictures a tone of mild expostulation. And yet . . . here and there we sense something more intense; a discrepancy of judgement, a telling lapse of tone, a hint that not everything about his past has been so successfully subdued. We sense, surviving over the years, an animus against the father.[34]

The force of the autobiographical and subjective experience rises up and works somewhat subversively against the scientific intentions of the work. Feelings do not have the unambiguous and static nature of facts. Or, to put it another way, there are no 'facts' in family relationships which are not made up of the deep and dialectical flow of feelings, exposed, irrational, multi-layered and labile.

Let us take another example. In the Epilogue Gosse defensively declares that his father was 'no fanatical monomaniac' and then, only a few pages later, insists that the allegation he has dogmatically rejected, is, precisely, the one which best fits. Considering his father's position, he writes with a directness which marks the Epilogue and isolates it from the main text:

> There is something horrible, if we will bring ourselves to face it, *in the fanaticism* that can do nothing with this pathetic and fugitive existence of ours but treat it as if it were the uncomfortable ante-chamber to a palace which no one has explored and of the plan of which we know absolutely nothing.[35]

His father is not fanatical on one page but is so, by implication, on another (and indeed further back in the text, his volume *Omphalos* is dubbed as 'fanatical'). Such contradictions in the author make strange 'facts' indeed, facts which disclose more than the son, no doubt, ever intended.

At the beginning of the Epilogue Edmund Gosse's intention, once again, seems transparently clear:

> This narrative, however, must not be allowed to close with the son in the foregound of the piece. If it has a value, that value consists in what light it may contrive to throw upon the unique and noble figure of my father.[36]

But does he execute what he promises? Once again, no. Not only in the very same paragraph is the father's nobility negated by the references to his psychological cruelty (keeping 'his Biblical bearing rein ... incessantly busy') but, even more shockingly, the Epilogue concentrates on the son's response and ends triumphantly with his manifesto of emancipation:

> No compromise, it is seen, was offered; no proposal of a truce would have been acceptable. It was a case of 'Everything or Nothing'; and thus desperately challenged, the young man's conscience threw off once for all the yoke of his 'dedication', and as respectfully as he could, without parade or remonstrance, he took a human being's privilege to fashion his inner life for himself.[37]

The manifest intention of the work is to end with the Victorian panegyric to the eminent patriarch: unique and noble. At this critical and falsifying moment in the book I suggest that the unconscious thrust of the whole volume broke through the surface and made itself dramatically visible. The deeper purpose of the book was to justify the son's act of freedom. I also suspect that the emotional ambivalence was so great in Gosse that he failed to notice the shocking contradiction between the first and the last paragraph of the Epilogue. Yet, emotionally, dynamically, autobiographically, it is the necessary and moving culmination of the book. Our second reading of the text places the author's conscious intentions to one side and claims that the book is not primarily a study of two temperaments with an inductive approach to knowledge, but rather that it is the autobiographical account of how one of those temperaments, following the innate tendencies of its own nature, frees itself from submission to the other.

Such a definition of the main, if buried, purpose of the work, suggests a further but related way of interpreting the text. It can be read, as many other autobiographies, as a quest for individuation. *Father and Son* shows, perhaps more consistently than anything else, those stages of inner growth which make possible the eventual emancipation from the all-encompassing puritanical environment. 'Certain leading features in each human soul are inherent to it and cannot be accounted for by suggestion or training,'[38] Gosse maintains. Thus the son discovers his distinct sense of identity through a cumulative series of incidents which bring a sense of self coinciding with self and the experience of 'rapture'.

These incidents *happen*. They are not engineered; they have no place in the planned environment, though they implicitly hold within them the promise of the future. The book is full of such resonant moments: the very early response to Uncle E. and to the smell of tobacco, the discovery of the two selves in the garden, the reading of the sensational novel in the attic, the witnessing of Punch and Judy, the first awed response to the sea, the listening to his father's reading of Virgil, the discovery of *Tom Cringle's Log*, the reading of the funereal poets in the garden, the exposure to *The Tempest*, the buying of the poetry books, the violent attraction to the pagan statues. All of these moments confirm, enhance and extend the son's sense of self. Against this emergent if highly vulnerable sense of self operated the organized pressures of the Puritan environment and the indomitable will power of his father. The struggle is, then, that between authenticity and compliance. Edmund Gosse moves uneasily between the two; now adapting to the dictates of the father; now responding, with lyrical delight, to the surfacing elements of his own nature; now cunningly adopting the mask of 'unctuous conformity' to secure his own ends; now losing his own identity completely in the external environment. From this perspective, the book is about the struggle of the self, in a hostile environment, to become itself. The Epilogue is the manifesto for the dim struggle recorded in the book. If our first reading takes the Preface as its starting point; then our second reading puts its interpretive weight upon the closing section.'

In a letter written to Sydney Holland and dated 15 January 1908 Gosse, reflecting on the purpose of *Father and Son*, wrote:

To tell the truth, what I should like to think my book might be – if the idea is not one of too great temerity – is a call to people to face the fact that the old faith is now impossible to sincere and intelligent minds, and that we must courageously face the difficulty of following entirely different ideals in moving towards the higher life But what ideals, or (what is more important) what discipline can we substitute for the splendid metallic rigour of an earlier age?

There must be found some guiding power, influencing artists, financiers, the meditative and imaginative, the self-centred, and the speculative alike.[39]

It is typical that in the letter Gosse is unable to elaborate fully upon the nature of this 'guiding power'. Could he have meant the guiding principle of individuation? Did he mean that individuals must now find the meaning of their own lives within their own existence, within the strange dynamics and inner necessity of self-realization? What other 'guiding power' exists in the book? (Again, we notice how the claim in the letter conflicts with the Preface of *Father and Son*.) In the same year Gosse wrote to Robert Ross:

I detest nothing so much as the *cliché* in mankind And more and more personal liberty becomes a passion, almost a fanaticism with me Less and less can I endure the idea of punishing a man – who is not cruel – because he is unlike other men. Probably if the hideous new religion of Science does not smother all liberty, we are in the darkness before the dawn of a humane and intelligent recognition of the right to differences.[40]

Our second reading of *Father and Son* suggests that the book is very much about 'the right to differences' and that it offers a somewhat screened autobiographical account of the individuation process in action.

Fortunately, we do not have to choose between the two readings: the historical and the autobiographical. Both possess a kind of validity; both have their place. However, as readers, we can also move along the line of friction between them and come to understand more about the author and his society than, perhaps, was ever intended.

PREFACE

At the present hour, when fiction takes forms so ingenious and so specious, it is perhaps necessary to say that the following narrative, in all its parts, and so far as the punctilious attention of the writer has been able to keep it so, is scrupulously true. If it were not true, in this strict sense, to publish it would be to trifle with all those who may be induced to read it. It is offered to them as a *document*, as a record of educational and religious conditions which, having passed away, will never return. In this respect, as the diagnosis of a dying Puritanism, it is hoped that the narrative will not be altogether without significance.

It offers, too, in a subsidiary sense, a study of the development of moral and intellectual ideas during the progress of infancy. These have been closely and conscientiously noted, and may have some value in consequence of the unusual conditions in which they were produced. The author has observed that those who have written about the facts of their own childhood have usually delayed to note them down until age has dimmed their recollections. Perhaps an even more common fault in such autobiographies is that they are sentimental, and are falsified by self-admiration and self-pity. The writer of these recollections has thought that if the examination of his earliest years was to be undertaken at all, it should be attempted while his memory is still perfectly vivid and while he is still unbiased by the forgetfulness or the sensibility of advancing years.

At one point only has there been any tampering with precise fact. It is believed that, with the exception of the Son, there is but one person mentioned in this book who is still alive.

Nevertheless, it has been thought well, in order to avoid any appearance of offence, to alter the majority of the proper names of the private persons spoken of.

It is not usual, perhaps, that the narrative of a spiritual struggle should mingle merriment and humour with a discussion of the most solemn subjects. It has, however, been inevitable that they should be so mingled in this narrative. It is true that most funny books try to be funny throughout, while theology is scandalized if it awakens a single smile. But life is not constituted thus, and this book is nothing if it is not a genuine slice of life. There was an extraordinary mixture of comedy and tragedy in the situation which is here described, and those who are affected by the pathos of it will not need to have it explained to them that the comedy was superficial and the tragedy essential.

September 1907

CHAPTER I

This book is the record of a struggle between two temperaments, two consciences and almost two epochs. It ended, as was inevitable, in disruption. Of the two human beings here described, one was born to fly backward, the other could not help being carried forward. There came a time when neither spoke the same language as the other, or encompassed the same hopes, or was fortified by the same desires. But, at least, it is some consolation to the survivor, that neither, to the very last hour, ceased to respect the other, or to regard him with a sad indulgence.

The affection of these two persons was assailed by forces in comparison with which the changes that health or fortune or place introduce are as nothing. It is a mournful satisfaction, but yet a satisfaction, that they were both of them able to obey the law which says that ties of close family relationship must be honoured and sustained. Had it not been so, this story would never have been told.

The struggle began soon, yet of course it did not begin in early infancy. But to familiarize my readers with the conditions of the two persons (which were unusual) and with the outlines of their temperaments (which were, perhaps innately, antagonistic), it is needful to open with some account of all that I can truly and independently recollect, as well as with some statements which are, as will be obvious, due to household tradition.

My parents were poor gentlefolks; not young; solitary, sensitive, and although they did not know it, proud. They both belonged to what is called the Middle Class, and there was this further resemblance between them that they each descended

35

from families which had been more than well-to-do in the eighteenth century, and had gradually sunken in fortune. In both houses there had been a decay of energy which had led to decay in wealth. In the case of my Father's family it had been a slow decline; in that of my Mother's, it had been rapid. My maternal grandfather was born wealthy, and in the opening years of the nineteenth century, immediately after his marriage, he bought a little estate in North Wales, on the slopes of Snowdon. Here he seems to have lived in a pretentious way, keeping a pack of hounds and entertaining on an extravagant scale. He had a wife who encouraged him in this vivid life, and three children, my Mother and her two brothers. His best trait was his devotion to the education of his children, in which he proclaimed himself a disciple of Rousseau.[1] But he can hardly have followed the teaching of 'Émile' very closely, since he employed tutors to teach his daughter, at an extremely early age, the very subjects which Rousseau forbade, such as history, literature and foreign languages.

My Mother was his special favourite, and his vanity did its best to make a blue-stocking of her. She read Greek, Latin and even a little Hebrew, and, what was more important, her mind was trained to be self-supporting. But she was diametrically opposed in essential matters to her easy-going, luxurious and self-indulgent parents. Reviewing her life in her thirtieth year, she remarked in some secret notes: 'I cannot recollect the time when I did not love religion.' She used a still more remarkable expression: 'If I must date my conversion from my first wish and trial to be holy, I may go back to infancy; if I am to postpone it till after my last wilful sin, it is scarcely yet begun.' The irregular pleasures of her parents' life were deeply distasteful to her, as such were to many young persons in those days of the wide revival of Conscience, and when my grandfather, by his reckless expenditure, which he never checked till ruin was upon him, was obliged to sell his estate, and live in penury, my Mother was the only member of the family who did not regret the change. For my own part, I believe I should have liked my reprobate maternal grandfather, but his conduct was certainly very vexatious. He died, in his eightieth year, when I was nine months old.

It was a curious coincidence that life had brought both my parents along similar paths to an almost identical position in respect to religious belief. She had started from the Anglican standpoint, he from the Wesleyan, and each, almost without counsel from others, and after varied theological experiments, had come to take up precisely the same attitude towards all divisions of the Protestant Church, that, namely, of detached and unbiased contemplation. So far as the sects agreed with my Father and my Mother, the sects were walking in the light; wherever they differed from them, they had slipped more or less definitely into a penumbra of their own making, a darkness into which neither of my parents would follow them. Hence, by a process of selection, my Father and my Mother alike had gradually, without violence, found themselves shut outside all Protestant communions, and at last they met only with a few extreme Calvinists like themselves, on terms of what may almost be called negation – with no priest, no ritual, no festivals, no ornament of any kind, nothing but the Lord's Supper and the exposition of Holy Scripture drawing these austere spirits into any sort of cohesion. They called themselves 'the Brethren', simply; a title enlarged by the world outside into 'Plymouth Brethren'.[2]

It was accident and similarity which brought my parents together at these meetings of the Brethren. Each was lonely, each was poor, each was accustomed to a strenuous intellectual self-support. He was nearly thirty-eight, she was past forty-two, when they married. From a suburban lodging, he brought her home to his mother's little house in the north-east of London without a single day's honeymoon. My Father was a zoologist, and a writer of books on natural history; my Mother also was a writer, author already of two slender volumes of religious verse – the earlier of which, I know not how, must have enjoyed some slight success, since a second edition was printed – afterwards she devoted her pen to popular works of edification. But how infinitely removed in their aims, their habits, their ambitions from 'literary' people of the present day, words are scarcely adequate to describe. Neither knew nor cared about any manifestation of current literature. For each there had been no poet later than Byr n, and neither had read a romance since, in childhood, they ad dipped into the Waverley Novels [3] as they appeared in succe ion. For each the various forms of imaginative and scientific literature were merely means of improvement and profit, which kept the student 'out of the world', gave him full employment, and enabled him to maintain himself. But pleasure was found nowhere but in the Word of God, and to the endless discussion of the Scriptures each hurried when the day's work was over.

In this strange household the advent of a child was not welcomed, but was borne with resignation. The event was thus recorded in my Father's diary:

E. delivered of a son. Received green swallow from Jamaica.

This entry has caused amusement, as showing that he was as much interested in the bird as in the boy. But this does not follow; what the wording exemplifies is my Father's extreme punctilio. The green swallow arrived later in the day than the son, and the earlier visitor was therefore recorded first; my Father was scrupulous in every species of arrangement.

Long afterwards, my Father told me that my Mother suffered much in giving birth to me, and that, uttering no cry, I appeared to be dead. I was laid, with scant care, on another bed in the room, while all anxiety and attention were concentrated on my Mother. An old woman who happened to be there, and who was unemployed, turned her thoughts to me, and tried to awake in me a spark of vitality. She succeeded, and she was afterwards complimented by the doctor on her cleverness. My Father could not – when he told me the story – recollect the name of my preserver. I have often longed to know who she was. For all the rapture of life, for all its turmoils, its anxious desires, its manifold pleasures, and even for its sorrow and suffering, I bless and praise that anonymous old lady from the bottom of my heart.

It was six weeks before my Mother was able to leave her room. The occasion was made a solemn one, and was attended by a species of Churching. Mr Balfour, a valued minister of the denomination, held a private service in the parlour, and 'prayed for our child, that he may be the Lord's'. This was the opening act of that 'dedication' which was never henceforward forgotten, and of which the following pages will endeavour to describe the results. Around my tender and unconscious spirit was flung the luminous web, the light and elastic but impermeable veil, which was hoped would keep me 'unspotted from the world'.

Until this time my Father's mother had lived in the house and taken the domestic charges of it on her own shoulders. She now consented to leave us to ourselves. There was no question that her exodus was a relief to my Mother, since my paternal grandmother was a strong and masterful woman, buxom, choleric and practical, for whom the interests of the mind did not exist. Her daughter-in-law, gentle as she was, and ethereal in manner and appearance – strangely contrasted (no doubt), in her tinctures of gold hair and white skin, with my grandmother's bold carnations and black tresses – was yet possessed of a will like tempered steel. They were better friends apart, with my grandmother lodged hard by, in a bright room, her household gods and bits of excellent eighteenth-century furniture around her, her miniatures and sparkling china arranged on shelves.

Left to my Mother's sole care, I became the centre of her solicitude. But there mingled with those happy animal instincts which sustain the strength and patience of every human mother and were fully present with her – there mingled with these certain spiritual determinations which can be but rare. They are, in their outline, I suppose, vaguely common to many religious mothers, but there are few indeed who fill up the sketch with so firm a detail as she did. Once again I am indebted to her secret notes, in a little locked volume, seen until now, nearly sixty years later, by no eye save her own. Thus she wrote when I was two months old:

We have given him to the Lord; and we trust that He will really manifest him to be His own, if he grow up; and if the Lord take him early, we will not doubt that he is taken to Himself. Only, if it please the Lord to take him, I do trust we may be spared seeing him suffering in lingering illness and much pain. But in this as in all things His will is better than what we can choose. Whether his life be prolonged or not, it has already been a blessing to us, and to the saints, in leading us to much prayer, and bringing us into varied need and some trial.

The last sentence is somewhat obscure to me. How, at that tender age, I contrived to be a blessing 'to the saints' may surprise others and puzzles myself. But 'the saints' was the habitual term by which were indicated the friends who met on Sunday Mornings for Holy Communion, and at many other times in the week for prayer and discussion of the Scriptures, in the small hired hall at Hackney, which my parents attended. I suppose that the solemn dedication of me to the Lord, which was repeated in public in my Mother's arms, being by no means a usual or familiar ceremony even among the Brethren, created a certain curiosity and fervour in the immediate services, or was imagined so to do by the fond, partial heart of my Mother. She, however, who had been so much isolated, now made the care of her child an excuse for retiring still further into silence. With those religious persons who met at the Room, as the modest chapel was called, she had little spiritual and no intellectual sympathy. She noted:

I do not think it would increase my happiness to be in the midst of the saints at Hackney. I have made up my mind to give myself up to Baby for the winter, and to accept no invitations. To go when I can to the Sunday morning meetings and to see my own Mother.

The monotony of her existence now became extreme, but she seems to have been happy. Her days were spent in taking care of me, and in directing one young servant. My Father was

40

for ever in his study, writing, drawing, dissecting; sitting, no doubt, as I grew afterwards accustomed to see him, absolutely motionless, with his eye glued to the microscope, for twenty minutes at a time. So the greater part of every week-day was spent, and on Sunday he usually preached one, and sometimes two extempore sermons. His work-day labours were rewarded by the praise of the learned world, to which he was indifferent, but by very little money, which he needed more. For over three years after their marriage, neither of my parents left London for a single day, not being able to afford to travel. They received scarcely any visitors, never ate a meal away from home, never spent an evening in social intercourse abroad. At night they discussed theology, read aloud to one another, or translated scientific brochures from French or German. It sounds a terrible life of pressure and deprivation, and that it was physically unwholesome there can be no shadow of a doubt. But their contentment was complete and unfeigned In the midst of this, materially, the hardest moment of their lives, when I was one year old, and there was a question of our leaving London, my Mother recorded in her secret notes:

We are happy and contented, having all things needful and pleasant, and our present habitation is hallowed by many sweet associations. We have our house to ourselves and enjoy each other's society If we move we shall no longer be alone. The situation may be more favourable, however, for Baby, as being more in the country. I desire to have no choice in the matter, but as I know not what would be for our good, and God knows, so I desire to leave it with Him, and if it is not His will we should move, He will raise objections and difficulties, and if it is His will He will make Henry [my Father] desirous and anxious to take the step, and then, whatever the result, let us leave all to Him and not regret it.

No one who is acquainted with the human heart will mistake this attitude of resignation for weakness of purpose. It was not poverty of will, it was abnegation, it was a voluntary act. My Mother, underneath an exquisite amenity of manner, concealed a rigour of spirit which took the form of a constant self-denial.

For it to dawn upon her consciousness that she wished for something, was definitely to renounce that wish, or, more exactly, to subject it in everything to what she conceived to be the will of God.

This is perhaps the right moment for me to say that at this time, and indeed until the hour of her death, she exercised, without suspecting it, a magnetic power over the will and nature of my Father. Both were strong, but my Mother was unquestionably the stronger of the two; it was her mind which gradually drew his to take up a certain definite position, and this remained permanent although she, the cause of it, was early removed. Hence, while it was with my Father that the long struggle which I have to narrate took place, behind my Father stood the ethereal memory of my Mother's will, guiding him, pressing him, holding him to the unswerving purpose which she had formed and defined. And when the inevitable disruption came, what was unspeakably painful was to realize that it was not from one, but from both parents that the purpose of the child was separated.

My Mother was a Puritan in grain, and never a word escaped her, not a phrase exists in her diary, to suggest that she had any privations to put up with. She seemed strong and well, and so did I; the one of us who broke down was my Father. With his attack of acute nervous dyspepsia came an unexpected small accession of money, and we were able, in my third year, to take a holiday of nearly ten months in Devonshire. The extreme seclusion, the unbroken strain, were never repeated, and when we returned to London, it was to conditions of greater amenity and to a less rigid practice of 'the world forgetting by the world forgot'. That this relaxation was more relative than positive, and that nothing ever really tempted either of my parents from their cavern in an intellectual Thebaïd,[4] my re-collections will amply prove. But each of them was forced by circumstances into a more or less public position, and neither could any longer quite ignore the world around.

It is not my business here to re-write the biographies of my parents Each of them became, in a certain measure, celebrated, and each was the subject of a good deal of contemporary discussion. Each was prominent before the eyes of a public of his or her own, half a century ago. It is because their minds were vigorous and their accomplishments distinguished that the contrast between their spiritual point of view and the aspect of a similar class of persons today is interesting and may, I hope, be instructive. But this is not another memoir of public individuals, each of whom has had more than one biographer.[5] My serious duty, as I venture to hold it, is other;[6]

> that's the world's side,
> Thus men saw them, praised them, thought they knew them!
> There, in turn, I stood aside and praised them!
> Out of my own self, I dare to phrase it.

But this is a different inspection, this is a study of

> the other side, the novel
> Silent silver lights and darks undreamed of,

the record of a state of soul once not uncommon in Protestant Europe, of which my parents were perhaps the latest consistent exemplars among people of light and leading.

The peculiarities of a family life, founded upon such principles, are, in relation to a little child, obvious; but I may be permitted to recapitulate them. Here was perfect purity, perfect intrepidity, perfect abnegation; yet there was also narrowness, isolation, an absence of perspective, let it be boldly admitted, an absence of humanity. And there was a curious mixture of humbleness and arrogance; entire resignation to the will of God and not less entire disdain of the judgement and opinion of man. My parents founded every action, every attitude, upon their interpretation of the Scriptures, and upon the guidance of the Divine Will as revealed to them by direct answer to prayer. Their ejaculation in the face of any dilemma was, 'Let us cast it before the Lord!'

So confident were they of the reality of their intercourse with God, that they asked for no other guide. They recognized no spiritual authority among men, they subjected themselves to no priest or minister, they troubled their consciences about no current manifestation of 'religious opinion'. They lived in an intellectual cell, bounded at its sides by the walls of their own house, but open above to the very heart of the uttermost heavens.

This, then, was the scene in which the soul of a little child was planted, not as in an ordinary open flower-border or carefully tended social *parterre*,[7] but as on a ledge, split in the granite of some mountain. The ledge was hung between night and the snows on one hand, and the dizzy depths of the world upon the other; was furnished with just soil enough for a gentian to struggle skywards and open its stiff azure stars; and offered no lodgement, no hope of salvation, to any rootlet which should stray beyond its inexorable limits.

CHAPTER II

Out of the darkness of my infancy there comes only one flash of memory. I am seated alone, in my baby-chair, at a dinner-table set for several people. Somebody brings in a leg of mutton, puts it down close to me, and goes out. I am again alone, gazing at two low windows, wide open upon a garden. Suddenly, noiselessly, a large, long animal (obviously a greyhound) appears at one window-sill, slips into the room, seizes the leg of mutton and slips out again. When this happened I could not yet talk. The accomplishment of speech came to me very late, doubtless because I never heard young voices. Many years later, when I mentioned this recollection, there was a shout of laughter and surprise: 'That, then, was what became of the mutton! It was not you, who, as your Uncle A. pretended, ate it up, in the twinkling of an eye, bone and all!'

I suppose that it was the startling intensity of this incident which stamped it upon a memory from which all other impressions of this early date have vanished.

The adventure of the leg of mutton occurred, evidently, at the house of my Mother's brothers, for my parents, at this date, visited no other. My uncles were not religious men, but they had an almost filial respect for my Mother, who was several years senior to the elder of them. When the catastrophe of my grandfather's fortune had occurred, they had not yet left school. My Mother, in spite of an extreme dislike of teaching which was native to her, immediately accepted the situation of a governess in the family of an Irish nobleman. The mansion was only to be approached, as Miss Edgeworth [1] would have said, 'through eighteen sloughs, at the imminent peril of one's life', and when one had reached it, the mixture of opulence and squalor, of civility and savagery, was unspeakable. But my Mother was well paid, and she stayed in this distasteful environment, doing the work she hated most, while with the margin of her salary she helped first one of her brothers and then the other through his Cambridge course. They studied hard and did well at the university. At length their sister received, in her 'ultima Thule',[2] news that her younger brother had taken his degree, and then and there, with a sigh of intense relief, she resigned her situation and came straight back to England.

It is not to be wondered at, then, that my uncles looked up to their sister with feelings of especial devotion. They were not inclined, they were hardly in a position, to criticize her modes of thought. They were easy-going, cultured and kindly gentlemen, rather limited in their views, without a trace of their sister's force of intellect or her strenuous temper. E. resembled her in person, he was tall, fair, with auburn curls; he cultivated a certain tendency to the Byronic type, fatal and melancholy. A. was short, brown and jocose, with a pretension to common sense; bluff and chatty. As a little child, I adored my Uncle E., who sat silent by the fireside holding me against his knee, saying nothing, but looking unutterably sad, and occasionally shaking his warm-coloured tresses. With great injustice, on the other hand, I detested my Uncle A., because he used to joke in a manner very displeasing to me, and because he would so far forget himself as to chase, and even, if it will be credited, to tickle me. My uncles, who remained bachelors to the end of their lives, earned a comfortable living, E. by teaching, A. as 'something in the City', and they rented an old rambling house in Clapton, that same in which I saw the greyhound. Their house had a strange, delicious smell, so unlike anything I smelt anywhere else, that it used to fill my eyes with tears of mysterious pleasure. I know now that this was the odour of cigars, tobacco being a species of incense tabooed at home on the highest religious grounds.

It has been recorded that I was slow in learning to speak. I used to be told that having met all invitations to repeat such words as 'Papa' and 'Mamma' with gravity and indifference, I one day drew towards me a volume, and said 'book' with startling distinctness. I was not at all precocious, but at a rather early age, I think towards the beginning of my fourth year, I learned to read. I cannot recollect a time when a printed page of English was closed to me. But perhaps earlier still my Mother used to repeat to me a poem which I have always taken for granted that she had herself composed, a poem which had a romantic place in my early mental history. It ran thus, I think:

> O pretty Moon, you shine so bright!
> I'll go to bid Mamma good-night,
> And then I'll lie upon my bed
> And watch you move above my head.
>
> Ah! there, a cloud has hidden you!
> But I can see your light shine thro';
> It tries to hide you – quite in vain,
> For – there you quickly come again!
>
> It's God, I know, that makes you shine
> Upon this little bed of mine;
> But I shall all about you know
> When I can read and older grow.

Long, long after the last line had become an anachronism, I used to shout this poem from my bed before I went to sleep, whether the night happened to be moon-lit or no.

It must have been my Father who taught me my letters. To my Mother, as I have said, it was distasteful to teach, though she was so prompt and skilful to learn. My Father, on the contrary, taught cheerfully, by fits and starts. In particular, he had a scheme for rationalizing geography, which I think was admirable. I was to climb upon a chair, while, standing at my side, with a pencil and a sheet of paper, he was to draw a chart of the markings on the carpet. Then, when I understood the system, another chart on a smaller scale of furniture in the room, then of a floor of the house, then of the back-garden, then of a section of the street. The result of this was that geography came to me of itself, as a perfectly natural miniature arrangement of objects, and to this day has always been the science which gives me least difficulty. My father also taught me the simple rules of arithmetic, a little natural history, and the elements of drawing; and he laboured long and unsuccessfully to make me learn by heart hymns, psalms and chapters of Scripture, in which I always failed ignominiously and with tears. This puzzled and vexed him, for he himself had an extremely retentive textual memory. He could not help thinking that I was naughty, and would not learn the chapters, until at last he gave up the effort. All this sketch of an education began, I believe, in my fourth year, and was not advanced or modified during the rest of my Mother's life.

Meanwhile, capable as I was of reading, I found my greatest pleasure in the pages of books. The range of these was limited, for story-books of every description were sternly excluded. No fiction of any kind, religious or secular, was admitted into the house. In this it was to my Mother, not to my Father, that the prohibition was due. She had a remarkable, I confess to me still somewhat unaccountable impression that to 'tell a story', that is, to compose fictitious narrative of any kind, was a sin. She carried this conviction to extreme lengths. My Father, in later years, gave me some interesting examples of her firmness. As a young man in America, he had been deeply impressed by 'Salathiel', a pious prose romance by that then popular writer, the Rev. George Croly.[3] When he first met my Mother, he recommended it to her, but she would not consent to open it. Nor would she read the chivalrous tales in verse of Sir Walter Scott, obstinately alleging that they were not 'true'. She would read none but lyrical and subjective poetry. Her secret diary reveals the history of this singular aversion to the fictitious, although it cannot be said to explain the cause of it. As a child, however, she had possessed a passion for making up stories, and so considerable a skill in it that she was constantly being

48

begged to indulge others with its exercise. But I will, on so curious a point, leave her to speak for herself:

When I was a very little child, I used to amuse myself and my brothers with inventing stories, such as I read. Having, as I suppose, naturally a restless mind and busy imagination, this soon became the chief pleasure of my life. Unfortunately, my brothers were always fond of encouraging this propensity, and I found in Taylor, my maid, a still greater tempter. I had not known there was any harm in it, until Miss Shore [a Calvinist governess], finding it out, lectured me severely, and told me it was wicked. From that time forth I considered that to invent a story of any kind was a sin. But the desire to do so was too deeply rooted in my affections to be resisted in my own strength [she was at that time nine years of age], and unfortunately I knew neither my corruption nor my weakness, nor did I know where to gain strength. The longing to invent stories grew with violence; everything I heard or read became food for my distemper. The simplicity of truth was not sufficient for me; I must needs embroider imagination upon it, and the folly, vanity and wickedness which disgraced my heart are more than I am able to express. Even now [at the age of twenty-nine], tho' watched, prayed and striven against, this is still the sin that most easily besets me. It has hindered my prayers and prevented my improvement, and therefore has humbled me very much.

This is, surely, a very painful instance of the repression of an instinct. There seems to have been, in this case, a vocation such as is rarely heard, and still less often wilfully disregarded and silenced. Was my Mother intended by nature to be a novelist? I have often thought so, and her talents and vigour of purpose, directed along the line which was ready to form 'the chief pleasure of her life', could hardly have failed to conduct her to great success. She was a little younger than Bulwer Lytton,[4] a little older than Mrs Gaskell[5] – but these are vain and trivial speculations!

My own state, however, was, I should think, almost unique among the children of cultivated parents. In consequence of the stern ordinance which I have described, not a single fiction was read or told to me during my infancy. The rapture of the

49

child who delays the process of going to bed by cajoling 'a story' out of his mother or his nurse, as he sits upon her knee, well tucked up, at the corner of the nursery fire, – this was unknown to me. Never in all my early childhood, did anyone address to me the affecting preamble, 'Once upon a time!' I was told about missionaries, but never about pirates; I was familiar with humming-birds, but I had never heard of fairies. Jack the Giant-Killer, Rumpelstiltskin and Robin Hood were not of my acquaintance, and though I understood about wolves, Little Red Ridinghood was a stranger even by name. So far as my 'dedication' was concerned, I can but think that my parents were in error thus to exclude the imaginary from my outlook upon facts. They desired to make me truthful; the tendency was to make me positive and sceptical. Had they wrapped me in the soft folds of supernatural fancy, my mind might have been longer content to follow their traditions in an unquestioning spirit.

Having easily said what, in those early years, I did not read, I have great difficulty in saying what I did read. But a queer variety of natural history, some of it quite indigestible by my undeveloped mind; many books of travels, mainly of a scientific character, among them voyages of discovery in the South Seas, by which my brain was dimly filled with splendour; some geography and astronomy, both of them sincerely enjoyed; much theology, which I desired to appreciate but could never get my teeth into (if I may venture to say so), and over which my eye and tongue learned to slip without penetrating, so that I would read, and read aloud, and with great propriety of emphasis, page after page without having formed an idea or retained an expression. There was, for instance, a writer on prophecy called Jukes,[6] of whose works each of my parents was inordinately fond, and I was early set to read Jukes aloud to them. I did it glibly, like a machine, but the sight of Jukes' volumes became an abomination to me, and I never formed the outline of a notion what they were about. Later on, a publication called The Penny Cyclopaedia[7] became my daily, and for a long time almost my sole study; to the subject of this remarkable work I may presently return.

It is difficult to keep anything like chronological order in recording fragments of early recollection, and in speaking of my reading I have been led too far ahead. My memory does not, practically, begin till we returned from certain visits, made with a zoological purpose, to the shores of Devon and Dorset, and settled, early in my fifth year, in a house at Islington, in the north of London. Our circumstances were now more easy; my Father had regular and well-paid literary work; and the house was larger and more comfortable than even before, though still very simple and restricted. My memories, some of which are exactly dated by certain facts, now become clear and almost abundant. What I do not remember, except from having it very often repeated to me, is what may be considered the only 'clever' thing that I said during an otherwise unillustrious childhood. It was not startlingly 'clever', but it may pass. A lady – when I was just four – rather injudiciously showed me a large print of a human skeleton, saying, 'There! you don't know what that is, do you?' Upon which, immediately and very archly, I replied, 'Isn't it a man with the meat off?' This was thought wonderful, and, as it is supposed that I had never had the phenomenon explained to me, it certainly displays some quickness in seizing an analogy. I had often watched my Father, while he soaked the flesh off the bones of fishes and small mammals. If I venture to repeat this trifle, it is only to point out that the system on which I was being educated deprived all things, human life among the rest, of their mystery. The 'bare-grinning skeleton of death' was to me merely a prepared specimen of that featherless plantigrade vertebrate, 'homo sapiens'.

As I have said that this anecdote was thought worth repeating, I ought to proceed to say that there was, so far as I can recollect, none of that flattery of childhood which is so often merely a backhanded way of indulging the vanity of parents. My Mother, indeed, would hardly have been human if she had not occasionally entertained herself with the delusion that her solitary duckling was a cygnet. This my Father did not encourage, remarking, with great affection, and chucking me under the chin, that I was 'a nice little ordinary boy'. My Mother, stung by this want of appreciation, would proceed so far as to declare that she believed that in future times the F.R.S.[8] would be chiefly known as his son's father! (This is a pleasantry frequent in professional families.)

To this my Father, whether convinced or not, would make no demur, and the couple would begin to discuss, in my presence, the direction which my shining talents would take. In consequence of my dedication to 'the Lord's Service', the range of possibilities was much restricted. My Father, who had lived long in the Tropics, and who nursed a perpetual nostalgia for 'the little lazy isles where the trumpet-orchids blow', leaned towards the field of missionary labour. My Mother, who was cold about foreign missions, preferred to believe that I should be the Charles Wesley[9] of my age, 'or perhaps' she had the candour to admit, 'merely the George Whitefield'.[10] I cannot recollect the time when I did not understand that I was going to be a minister of the Gospel.

It is so generally taken for granted that a life strictly dedicated to religion is stiff and dreary, that I may have some difficulty in persuading my readers that, as a matter of fact, in these early days of my childhood, before disease and death had penetrated to our slender society, we were always cheerful and often gay. My parents were playful with one another, and there were certain stock family jests which seldom failed to enliven the breakfast table. My Father and Mother lived so completely in the atmosphere of faith, and were so utterly convinced of their intercourse with God, that, so long as that intercourse was not clouded by sin, to which they were delicately sensitive, they could afford to take the passing hour very lightly. They would even, to a certain extent, treat the surroundings of their religion as a subject of jest, joking very mildly and gently about such things as an attitude at prayer or the nature of a supplication.

They were absolutely indifferent to forms. They prayed, seated in their chairs as willingly as, reversed, upon their knees; no ritual having any significance for them. My mother was sometimes extremely gay, laughing with a soft, merry sound. What I have since been told of the guileless mirth of nuns in a convent has reminded me of the gaiety of my parents during my early childhood.

So long as I was a mere part of them, without individual existence, and swept on, a satellite, in their atmosphere, I was mirthful when they were mirthful, and grave when they were grave. The mere fact that I had no young companions, no story books, no outdoor amusements, none of the thousand and one employments provided for other children in more conventional surroundings, did not make me discontented or fretful, because I did not know of the existence of such entertainments. In exchange, I became keenly attentive to the limited circle of interests open to me. Oddly enough, I have no recollection of any curiosity about other children, nor of any desire to speak to them or play with them. They did not enter into my dreams, which were occupied entirely with grown-up people and animals. I had three dolls, to whom my attitude was not very intelligible. Two of these were female, one with a shapeless face of rags, the other in wax. But, in my fifth year, when the Crimean War broke out, I was given a third doll, a soldier, dressed very smartly in a scarlet cloth tunic. I used to put the dolls on three chairs, and harangue them aloud, but my sentiment to them was never confidential, until our maidservant one day, intruding on my audience, and misunderstanding the occasion of it, said: 'What? a boy, and playing with a soldier when he's got two lady-dolls to play with?' I had never thought of my dolls as confidants before, but from that time forth I paid a special attention to the soldier, in order to make up to him for Lizzie's unwarrantable insult.

The declaration of war with Russia brought the first breath of outside life into our Calvinist cloister. My parents took in a daily newspaper, which they had never done before, and events in picturesque places, which my Father and I looked out on the map, were eagerly discussed. One of my vividest early memories can be dated exactly. I was playing about the house, and suddenly burst into the breakfast-room, where, close to the door, sat an amazing figure, a very tall young man, as stiff as my doll, in a gorgeous scarlet tunic. Quite far away from him, at her writing-table, my Mother sat with her Bible open before her, and was urging the gospel plan of salvation on his acceptance. She promptly told me to run away and play, but I had seen a great sight. This guardsman was in the act of leaving for the Crimea, and his adventures, – he was converted in consequence of my Mother's instruction, – were afterwards told by her in a tract, called 'The Guardsman of the Alma',[11] of which I believe that more than half a million copies were circulated. He was killed in that battle, and this added an extra-ordinary lustre to my dream of him. I see him still in my mind's eye, large, stiff, and unspeakably brilliant, seated, from respect, as near as possible to our parlour door. This apparition gave reality to my subsequent conversations with the soldier doll.

That same victory of the Alma, which was reported in London on my fifth birthday, is also marked very clearly in my memory by a family circumstance. We were seated at breakfast, at our small round table drawn close up to the window, my Father with his back to the light. Suddenly, he gave a sort of cry, and read out the opening sentences from *The Times* announcing a battle in the valley of the Alma. No doubt the strain of national anxiety had been very great, for both he and my Mother seemed deeply excited. He broke off his reading when the fact of the decisive victory was assured, and he and my Mother sank simultaneously on their knees in front of their tea and bread-and-butter, while in a loud voice my Father gave thanks to the God of Battles. This patriotism was the more remarkable, in that he had schooled himself, as he believed, to put his 'heavenly citizenship' above all earthly duties. To those who said: 'Because you are a Christian, surely

54

you are not less an Englishman?' he would reply by shaking his head, and by saying: 'I am a citizen of no earthly State.' He did not realize that, in reality, and to use a cant phrase not yet coined in 1854, there existed in Great Britain no more thorough 'Jingo' than he.

Another instance of the remarkable way in which the interests of daily life were mingled, in our strange household, with the practice of religion, made an impression upon my memory. We had all three been much excited by a report that a certain dark geometer-moth, generated in underground stables, had been met with in Islington. Its name, I think is, 'Boletobia fuliginaria', and I believe that it is excessively rare in England. We were sitting at family prayers, on a summer morning, I think in 1855, when through the open window a brown moth came sailing. My Mother immediately interrupted the reading of the Bible by saying to my Father, 'O! Henry, do you think that can be "Boletobia"?' My Father rose up from the sacred book, examined the insect, which had now perched, and replied: 'No! it is only the common Vapourer, "Orgyia antiqua"!', resuming his seat, and the exposition of the Word, without any apology or embarrassment.

In the course of this, my sixth year, there happened a series of minute and soundless incidents which, elementary as they may seem when told, were second in real importance to none in my mental history. The recollection of them confirms me in the opinion that certain leading features in each human soul are inherent to it, and cannot be accounted for by suggestion or training. In my own case, I was most carefully withdrawn, like Princess Blanchefleur [12] in her marble fortress, from every outside influence whatever, yet to me the instinctive life came as unexpectedly as her lover came to her in the basket of roses. What came to me was the consciousness of self, as a force and as a companion, and it came as the result of one or two shocks, which I will relate.

In consequence of hearing so much about an Omniscient God, a being of supernatural wisdom and penetration who was always with us, who made, in fact, a fourth in our company, I had come to think of Him, not without awe, but with absolute confidence. My Father and Mother, in their serene discipline of me, never argued with one another, never even differed; their wills seemed absolutely one. My Mother always deferred to my Father, and in his absence spoke of him to me, as if he were all-wise. I confused him in some sense with God; at all events I believed that my Father knew everything and saw everything. One morning in my sixth year, my Mother and I were alone in the morning-room, when my Father came in and announced some fact to us. I was standing on the rug, gazing at him, and when he made this statement, I remember turning quickly, in embarrassment, and looking into the fire. The shock to me was as that of a thunderbolt, for what my Father had said 'was not true'. My Mother and I, who had been present at the trifling incident, were aware that it had not happened exactly as it had been reported to him. My Mother gently told him so, and he accepted the correction. Nothing could possibly have been more trifling to my parents, but to me it meant an epoch. Here was the appalling discovery, never suspected before, that my Father was not as God, and did not know everything. The shock was not caused by any suspicion that he was not telling the truth, as it appeared to him, but by the awful proof that he was not, as I had supposed, omniscient.

This experience was followed by another, which confirmed the first, but carried me a great deal further. In our little back-garden, my Father had built up a rockery for ferns and mosses and from the water-supply of the house he had drawn a leaden pipe so that it pierced upwards through the rockery and produced, when a tap was turned, a pretty silvery parasol of water. The pipe was exposed somewhere near the foot of the rockery. One day, two workmen, who were doing some repairs, left their tools during the dinner-hour in the back-garden, and as I was marching about I suddenly thought that to see whether one of these tools could make a hole in the pipe would be attractive. It did make such a hole, quite easily, and then the matter escaped my mind. But a day or two afterwards, when my Father came in to dinner, he was very angry. He had turned the tap, and instead of the fountain arching at the summit, there had been a rush of water through a hole at the foot. The rockery was absolutely ruined.

Of course I realized in a moment what I had done, and I sat frozen with alarm, waiting to be denounced. But my Mother remarked on the visit of the plumbers two or three days before, and my Father instantly took up the suggestion. No doubt that was it; the mischievous fellows had thought it amusing to stab the pipe and spoil the fountain. No suspicion fell on me; no question was asked of me. I sat there, turned to stone within, but outwardly sympathetic and with unchecked appetite.

We attribute, I believe, too many moral ideas to little children. It is obvious that in this tremendous juncture I ought to have been urged forward by good instincts, or held back by naughty ones. But I am sure that the fear which I experienced for a short time, and which so unexpectedly melted away, was a purely physical one. It had nothing to do with the motions of a contrite heart. As to the destruction of the fountain, I was sorry about that, for my own sake, since I admired the skipping water extremely and had had no idea that I was spoiling its display. But the emotions which now thronged within me, and which led me, with an almost unwise alacrity, to seek solitude in the back-garden, were not moral at all, they were intellectual. I was not ashamed of having successfully – and so surprisingly – deceived my parents by my crafty silence; I looked upon that as a providential escape, and dismissed all further thought of it. I had other things to think of.

In the first place, the theory that my Father was omniscient or infallible was now dead and buried. He probably knew very little; in this case he had not known a fact of such importance that if you did not know that, it could hardly matter what you knew. My Father, as a deity, as a natural force of immense prestige, fell in my eyes to a human level. In future, his statements about things in general need not be accepted implicitly. But of all the thoughts which rushed upon my savage and undeveloped little brain at this crisis, the most curious was that I had found a companion and a confidant in myself. There was a secret in this world and it belonged to me and to a somebody who lived in the same body with me. There were two of us, and we could talk with one another. It is difficult to define impressions so rudimentary, but it is certain that it was in this dual form that the sense of my individuality now suddenly descended upon me, and it is equally certain that it was a great solace to me to find a sympathizer in my own breast.

About this time, my Mother, carried away by the current of her literary and her philanthropic work, left me more and more to my own devices. She was seized with a great enthusiasm; as one of her admirers and disciples has written, 'she went on her way, sowing beside all waters'. I would not for a moment let it be supposed that I regard her as a Mrs Jellyby,[13] or that I think she neglected me. But a remarkable work had opened up before her; after her long years in a mental hermitage, she was drawn forth into the clamorous harvest-field of souls. She developed an unexpected gift of persuasion over strangers whom she met in the omnibus or in the train, and with whom she courageously grappled. This began by her noting, with deep humility and joy, that 'I have reason to judge the sound conversion to God of three young persons within a few weeks, by the instrumentality of my conversations with them'. At the same time, as another of her biographers has said, 'those testimonies to the Blood of Christ, the fruits of her pen, began to be spread very widely, even to the most distant parts of the globe'. My father, too, was at this time at the height of his activity. After breakfast, each of them was amply occupied, perhaps until night-fall; our evenings we still always spent together. Sometimes my Mother took me with her on her 'unknown day's employ'; I recollect pleasant rambles through the City by her side, and the act of looking up at her figure soaring above me. But when all was done, I had hours and hours of complete solitude, in my Father's study, in the back-garden, above all in the garret.

The garret was a fairy place. It was a low lean-to, lighted from the roof. It was wholly unfurnished, except for two objects, an ancient hat-box and a still more ancient skin-trunk. The hat-box puzzled me extremely, till one day, asking my Father what it was, I got a distracted answer which led me to believe that it was itself a sort of hat, and I made a laborious but repeated effort to wear it. The skin-trunk was absolutely empty, but the inside of the lid of it was lined with sheets of what I now know to have been a sensational novel. It was, of course, a fragment, but I read it, kneeling on the bare floor, with indescribable rapture. It will be recollected that the idea of fiction, of a deliberately invented story, had been kept from me with entire success. I therefore implicitly believed the tale in the lid of the trunk to be a true account of the sorrows of a lady of title, who had to flee the country, and who was pursued into foreign lands by enemies bent upon her ruin. Somebody had an interview with a 'minion' in a 'mask'; I went downstairs and looked up these words in Bailey's *English Dictionary*, but was left in darkness as to what they had to do with the lady of title. This ridiculous fragment filled me with delicious fears; I fancied that my Mother, who was out so much, might be threatened by dangers of the same sort; and the fact that the narrative came abruptly to an end, in the middle of one of its most thrilling sentences, wound me up almost to a disorder of wonder and romance.

The preoccupation of my parents threw me more and more upon my own resources. But what are the resources of a solitary child of six? I was never inclined to make friends with servants, nor did our successive maids proffer, so far as I recollect, any advances. Perhaps, with my 'dedication' and my grown-up ways of talking, I did not seem to them at all an attractive little boy. I continued to have no companions, or even acquaintances of my own age. I am unable to recollect exchanging two words with another child till after my Mother's death.

The abundant energy which my Mother now threw into her public work did not affect the quietude of our private life. We had some visitors in the day-time, people who came to consult one parent or the other. But they never stayed to a meal, and we never returned their visits. I do not quite know how it was that neither of my parents took me to any of the sights of London, although I am sure it was a question of principle with them. Notwithstanding all our study of natural history, I was never introduced to live wild beasts at the Zoo, nor to dead ones at the British Museum. I can understand better why we never visited a picture-gallery or a concert-room. So far as I can recollect, the only time I was ever taken to any place of entertainment was when my Father and I paid a visit, long anticipated, to the Great Globe in Leicester Square.[14] This was a huge structure, the interior of which one ascended by means of a spiral staircase. It was a poor affair; that was concave in it which should have been convex, and my imagination was deeply affronted. I could invent a far better Great Globe than that in my mind's eye in the garret.

Being so restricted, then, and yet so active, my mind took refuge in an infantile species of natural magic. This contended with the definite ideas of religion which my parents were continuing, with too mechanical a persistency, to force into my nature, and it ran parallel with them. I formed strange superstitions, which I can only render intelligible by naming some concrete examples. I persuaded myself that, if I could only discover the proper words to say or the proper passes to make, I could induce the gorgeous birds and butterflies in my Father's illustrated manuals to come to life, and fly out of the book, leaving holes behind them. I believed that, when, at the Chapel, we sang, drearily and slowly, loud hymns of experience and humiliation, I could boom forth with a sound equal to that of dozens of singers, if I could only hit upon the formula. During morning and evening prayers, which were extremely lengthy and fatiguing, I fancied that one of my two selves could flit up, and sit clinging to the cornice, and look down on

60

my other self and the rest of us, if I could only find the key. I laboured for hours in search of these formulas, thinking to compass my ends by means absolutely irrational. For example, I was convinced that if I could only count consecutive numbers long enough, without losing one, I should suddenly, on reaching some far-distant figure, find myself in possession of the great secret. I feel quite sure that nothing external suggested these ideas of magic, and I think it probable that they approached the ideas of savages at a very early stage of development.

All this ferment of mind was entirely unobserved by my parents. But when I formed the belief that it was necessary, for the success of my practical magic, that I should hurt myself, and when, as a matter of fact, I began, in extreme secrecy, to run pins into my flesh and bang my joints with books, no one will be surprised to hear that my Mother's attention was drawn to the fact that I was looking 'delicate'. The notice nowadays universally given to the hygienic rules of life was rare fifty years ago and among deeply religious people, in particular, fatalistic views of disease prevailed. If any one was ill, it showed that 'the Lord's hand was extended in chastisement', and much prayer was poured forth in order that it might be explained to the sufferer, or to his relations, in what he or they had sinned. People would, for instance, go on living over a cess-pool, working themselves up into an agony to discover how they had incurred the displeasure of the Lord, but never moving away. As I became very pale and nervous, and slept badly at nights, with visions and loud screams in my sleep, I was taken to a physician, who stripped me and tapped me all over (this gave me some valuable hints for my magical practices), but could find nothing the matter. He recommended, – whatever physicians in such cases always recommend, – but nothing was done. If I was feeble it was the Lord's Will, and we must acquiesce.

It culminated in a sort of fit of hysterics, when I lost all self-control, and sobbed with tears, and banged my head on the table. While this was proceeding, I was conscious of that dual individuality of which I have already spoken, since while one part of me gave way, and could not resist, the other part in some extraordinary sense seemed standing aloof, much impressed. I was alone with my Father when this crisis suddenly occurred, and I was interested to see that he was greatly alarmed. It was a very long time since we had spent a day out of London, and I said, on being coaxed back to calmness, that I wanted 'to go into the country'. Like the dying Falstaff, I babbled of green fields. My Father, after a little reflection, proposed to take me to Primrose Hill. I had never heard of the place, and names have always appealed directly to my imagination. I was in the highest degree delighted, and could hardly restrain my impatience. As soon as possible we set forth westward, my hand in my Father's, with the liveliest anticipations. I expected to see a mountain absolutely carpeted with primroses, a terrestrial galaxy like that which covered the hill that led up to Montgomery Castle in Donne's poem.[15] But at length, as we walked from the Chalk Farm direction, a miserable acclivity stole into view – surrounded, even in those days, on most sides by houses, with its grass worn to the buff by millions of boots, and resembling what I meant by 'the country' about as much as Poplar resembles Paradise. We sat down on a bench at its inglorious summit, whereupon I burst into tears, and in a heart-rending whisper sobbed, 'Oh! Papa, let us go home!'

This was the lachrymose epoch in a career not otherwise given to weeping, for I must tell one more tale of tears. About this time, – the autumn of 1855, – my parents were disturbed more than once in the twilight, after I had been put to bed, by shrieks from my crib. They would rush up to my side, and find me in great distress, but would be unable to discover the cause of it. The fact was that I was half beside myself with ghostly fears, increased and pointed by the fact that there had been some daring burglaries in our street. Our servant-maid, who slept at the top of the house, had seen, or thought she saw, upon a moonlight night the figure of a crouching man, silhouetted against the sky, slip down from the roof and leap into her room. She screamed, and he fled away. Moreover, as if this were not enough for my tender nerves, there had been committed a horrid murder, at a baker's shop just round the corner in the Caledonian Road, to which murder actuality was given to us by the fact that my Mother had been 'just thinking' of getting her bread from this shop. Children, I think, were not spared the details of these affairs fifty years ago; at least, I was not, and my nerves were a packet of spilikins.[16]

But what made me scream o' nights was that when my Mother had tucked me up in bed, and had heard me say my prayer, and had prayed aloud on her knees at my side, and had stolen downstairs, noises immediately began in the room. There was a rustling of clothes, and a slapping of hands, and a gurgling, and a sniffing, and a trotting These horrible muffled sounds would go on, and die away, and be resumed; I would pray very fervently to God to save me from my enemies; and sometimes I would go to sleep. But on other occasions, my faith and fortitude alike gave way, and I screamed 'Mama! Mama!' Then would my parents come bounding up the stairs, and comfort me, and kiss me, and assure me it was nothing And nothing it was while they were there, but no sooner had they gone than the ghostly riot recommenced. It was at last discovered by my Mother that the whole mischief was due to a card of framed texts, fastened by one nail to the wall; this did nothing when the bedroom door was shut, but when it was left open (in order that my parents might hear me call), the card began to gallop in the draught, and made the most intolerable noises.

Several things tended at this time to alienate my conscience from the line which my Father had so rigidly traced for it. The question of the efficacy of prayer, which has puzzled wiser heads than mine was, began to trouble me. It was insisted on in our household that if anything was desired, you should not, as my Mother said, 'lose any time in seeking for it, but ask God to guide you to it'. In many junctures of life this is precisely what, in sober fact, they did. I will not dwell here on their theories, which my Mother put forth, with unflinching directness, in her published writings. But I found that a difference was made between my privileges in this matter and theirs, and this led to many discussions. My parents said: 'Whatever you need, tell Him and He will grant it, if it is His will.' Very well; I had need of a large painted humming-top which I had seen in a shop-window in the Caledonian Road. Accordingly, I introduced a supplication for this object into my evening prayer, carefully adding the words: 'If it is Thy will.' This, I recollect, placed my Mother in a dilemma, and she consulted my Father. Taken, I suppose, at a disadvantage, my Father told me I must not pray for 'things like that'. To which I answered by another query, 'Why?' And I added that he said we ought to pray for things we needed, and that I needed the humming-top a great deal more than I did the conversion of the heathen or the restitution of Jerusalem to the Jews, two objects of my nightly supplication which left me very cold.

I have reason to believe, looking back upon this scene, conducted by candle-light in the front parlour, that my Mother was much baffled by the logic of my argument. She had gone so far as to say publicly that no 'things or circumstances are too insignificant to bring before the God of the whole earth'. I persisted that this covered the case of the humming-top, which was extremely significant to me. I noticed that she held aloof from the discussion, which was carried on with some show of annoyance by my Father. He had never gone quite so far as she did in regard to this question of praying for material things. I am not sure that she was convinced that I ought to have been checked; but he could not help seeing that it reduced their favourite theory to an absurdity for a small child to exercise the privilege. He ceased to argue, and told me peremptorily that it was not right for me to pray for things like humming-tops, and that I must do it no more. His authority, of course, was paramount, and I yielded; but my faith in the efficacy of

64

prayer was a good deal shaken. The fatal suspicion had crossed my mind that the reason why I was not to pray for the top was because it was too expensive for my parents to buy, that being the usual excuse for not getting things I wished for.

It was about the date of my sixth birthday that I did something very naughty, some act of direct disobedience, for which my Father, after a solemn sermon, chastised me, sacrificially. by giving me several cuts with a cane. This action was justified, as everything he did was justified, by reference to Scripture – 'Spare the rod and spoil the child'. I suppose that there are some children, of a sullen and lymphatic temperament, who are smartened up and made more wide-awake by a whipping. It is largely a matter of convention, the exercise being endured (I am told) with pride by the infants of our aristocracy, but not tolerated by the lower classes. I am afraid that I proved my inherent vulgarity by being made, not contrite or humble, but furiously angry by this caning. I cannot account for the flame of rage which it awakened in my bosom. My dear, excellent Father had beaten me, not very severely, without ill-temper, and with the most genuine desire to improve me. But he was not well-advised especially so far as the 'dedication to the Lord's service' was concerned. This same 'dedication' had ministered to my vanity, and there are some natures which are not improved by being humiliated. I have to confess with shame that I went about the house for some days with a murderous hatred of my Father locked within my bosom. He did not suspect that the chastisement had not been wholly efficacious, and he bore me no malice; so that after a while, I forgot and thus forgave him. But I do not regard physical punishment as a wise element in the education of proud and sensitive children.

My theological misdeeds culminated, however, in an act so puerile and preposterous that I should not venture to record it if it did not throw some glimmering of light on the subject which I have proposed to myself in writing these pages. My mind continued to dwell on the mysterious question of prayer

It puzzled me greatly to know why, if we were God's children, and if he was watching over us by night and day, we might not supplicate for toys and sweets and smart clothes as well as for the conversion of the heathen. Just at this juncture, we had a special service at the Room, at which our attention was particularly called to what we always spoke of as 'the field of missionary labour'. The East was represented among 'the saints' by an excellent Irish peer,[17] who had, in his early youth, converted and married a lady of colour; this Asiatic shared in our Sunday morning meetings, and was an object of helpless terror to me; I shrank from her amiable caresses, and vaguely identified her with a personage much spoken of in our family circle, the 'Personal Devil'.

All these matters drew my thoughts to the subject of idolatry, which was severely censured at the missionary meeting. I cross-examined my Father very closely as to the nature of this sin, and pinned him down to the categorical statement that idolatry consisted in praying to any one or anything but God himself. Wood and stone, in the words of the hymn, were peculiarly liable to be bowed down to by the heathen in their blindness. I pressed my Father further on this subject, and he assured me that God would be very angry, and would signify His anger, if anyone, in a Christian country, bowed down to wood and stone. I cannot recall why I was so pertinacious on this subject, but I remember that my Father became a little restive under my cross-examination. I determined, however, to test the matter for myself, and one morning, when both my parents were safely out of the house, I prepared for the great act of heresy. I was in the morning-room on the ground-floor, where, with much labour, I hoisted a small chair on to the table close to the window. My heart was now beating as if it would leap out of my side, but I pursued my experiment. I knelt down on the carpet in front of the table and looking up I said my daily prayer in a loud voice, only substituting the address 'O Chair!' for the habitual one.

Having carried this act of idolatry safely through, I waited to see what would happen. It was a fine day, and I gazed up at the slip of white sky above the houses opposite, and expected something to appear in it. God would certainly exhibit his anger in some terrible form, and would chastise my impious and wilful action. I was very much alarmed, but still more excited; I breathed the high, sharp air of defiance. But nothing happened; there was not a cloud in the sky, not an unusual sound in the street. Presently I was quite sure that nothing would happen. I had committed idolatry, flagrantly and deliberately, and God did not care.

The result of this ridiculous act was not to make me question the existence and power of God; those were forces which I did not dream of ignoring. But what it did was to lessen still further my confidence in my Father's knowledge of the Divine mind. My Father had said, positively, that if I worshipped a thing made of wood, God would manifest his anger. I had then worshipped a chair, made (or partly made) of wood, and God had made no sign whatever. My Father, therefore, was not really acquainted with the Divine practice in cases of idolatry. And with that, dismissing the subject, I dived again into the unplumbed depths of the *Penny Cyclopaedia*.[18]

CHAPTER III

That I might die in my early childhood was a thought which frequently recurred to the mind of my Mother. She endeavoured, with a Roman fortitude, to face it without apprehension. Soon after I had completed my fifth year she had written as follows in her secret journal:

Should we be called on to weep over the early grave of the dear one whom now we are endeavouring to train for heaven, may we be able to remember that we never ceased to pray for and watch over him. It is easy, comparatively, to watch over an infant. Yet shall I be sufficient for these things? I am not. But God is sufficient. In his strength I have begun the warfare, in his strength I will persevere, and I will faint not till either I myself or my little one is beyond the reach of earthly solicitude.

That either she or I would be called away from earth, and that our physical separation was at hand, seems to have been always vaguely present in my Mother's dreams, as an obstinate conviction to be carefully recognized and jealously guarded against.

It was not, however, until the course of my seventh year that the tragedy occurred, which altered the whole course of our family existence. My Mother had hitherto seemed strong and in good health; she had even made the remark to my Father, that 'sorrow and pain, the badges of Christian discipleship', appeared to be withheld from her. On her birthday, which was to be her last, she had written these ejaculations in her locked diary:

Lord, forgive the sins of the past, and help me to be faithful in future! May this be a year of much blessing, a year of jubilee! May I be kept lowly, trusting, loving! May I more have blessing than in all former years combined! May I be happier as a wife, mother, sister, writer, mistress, friend!

But a symptom began to alarm her, and in the beginning of May, having consulted a local physician without being satisfied, she went to see a specialist in a northern suburb in whose judgement she had great confidence. This occasion I recollect with extreme vividness. I had been put to bed by my Father, in itself a noteworthy event. My crib stood near a window overlooking the street; my parents' ancient four-poster, a relic of the eighteenth century, hid me from the door, but I could see the rest of the room. After falling asleep on this particular evening, I awoke silently, surprised to see two lighted candles on the table, and my Father seated writing by them. I also saw a little meal arranged.

While I was wondering at all this, the door opened, and my Mother entered the room; she emerged from behind the bed-curtains, with her bonnet on, having returned from her expedition. My Father rose hurriedly, pushing back his chair. There was a pause, while my Mother seemed to be steadying her voice, and then she replied, loudly and distinctly, 'He says it is –' and she mentioned one of the most cruel maladies[1] by which our poor mortal nature can be tormented. Then I saw them fold one another in a silent long embrace, and presently sink together out of sight on their knees, at the farther side of the bed, whereupon my Father lifted up his voice in prayer. Neither of them had noticed me, and now I lay back on my pillow and fell asleep.

Next morning, when we three sat at breakfast, my mind reverted to the scene of the previous night. With my eyes on my plate, as I was cutting up my food, I asked, casually, 'What is –?' mentioning the disease whose unfamiliar name I had heard from my bed. Receiving no reply, I looked up to discover why my question was not answered, and I saw my parents gazing at each other with lamentable eyes. In some way, I know not how, I was conscious of the presence of an

69

incommunicable mystery, and I kept silence, though tortured with curiosity, nor did I ever repeat my inquiry.

About a fortnight later, my Mother began to go three times a week all the long way from Islington to Pimlico, in order to visit a certain practitioner, who undertook to apply a special treatment to her case. This involved great fatigue and distress to her, but so far as I was personally concerned it did me a great deal of good. I invariably accompanied her, and when she was very tired and weak, I enjoyed the pride of believing that I protected her. The movement, the exercise, the occupation, lifted my morbid fears and superstitions like a cloud. The medical treatment to which my poor Mother was subjected was very painful, and she had a peculiar sensitiveness to pain. She carried on her evangelical work as long as she possibly could, continuing to converse with her fellow passengers on spiritual matters. It was wonderful that a woman, so reserved and proud as she by nature was, could conquer so completely her natural timidity. In those last months, she scarcely ever got into a railway carriage or into an omnibus, without presently offering tracts to the persons sitting within reach of her, or endeavouring to begin a conversation with some one of the sufficiency of the Blood of Jesus to cleanse the human heart from sin. Her manners were so gentle and persuasive, she looked so innocent, her small, sparkling features were lighted up with so much benevolence, that I do not think she ever met with discourtesy or roughness. Imitative imp that I was, I sometimes took part in these strange conversations, and was mightily puffed up by compliments paid, in whispers, to my infant piety. But my Mother very properly discouraged this, as tending in me to spiritual pride.

If my parents, in their desire to separate themselves from the world, had regretted that through their happiness they seemed to have forfeited the Christian privilege of affliction, they could not continue to complain of any absence of temporal adversity. Everything seemed to combine, in the course of this fatal year

1856, to harass and alarm them. Just at the moment when illness created a special drain upon their resources, their slender income, instead of being increased, was seriously diminished. There is little sympathy felt in this world of rhetoric for the silent sufferings of the genteel poor, yet there is no class that deserves a more charitable commiseration.

At the best of times, the money which my parents had to spend was an exiguous and an inelastic sum. Strictly economical, proud – in an old-fashioned mode now quite out of fashion – to conceal the fact of their poverty, painfully scrupulous to avoid giving inconvenience to shop-people, tradesmen or servants, their whole financial career had to be carried on with the adroitness of a campaign through a hostile country. But now, at the moment when fresh pressing claims were made on their resources, my Mother's small capital suddenly disappeared. It had been placed, on bad advice (they were as children in such matters), in a Cornish mine, the grotesque name of which, Wheal Maria, became familiar to my ears. One day the river Tamar, in a playful mood, broke into Wheal Maria, and not a penny more was ever lifted from that unfortunate enterprise. About the same time, a small annuity which my Mother had inherited also ceased to be paid.

On my Father's books and lectures, therefore, the whole weight now rested, and that at a moment when he was depressed and unnerved by anxiety. It was contrary to his principles to borrow money, so that it became necessary to pay doctor's and chemist's bills punctually, and yet to carry on the little household with the very small margin. Each artifice of economy was now exercised to enable this to be done without falling into debt, and every branch of expenditure was cut down, clothes, books, the little garden which was my Father's pride, all felt the pressure of new poverty. Even our food, which had always been simple, now became Spartan indeed, and I am sure that my Mother often pretended to have no appetite that there might remain enough to satisfy my hunger. Fortunately my Father was able to take us away in the autumn

71

for six weeks by the sea in Wales, the expenses of this tour being paid for by a professional engagement, so that my seventh birthday was spent in an ecstasy of happiness, on golden sands, under a brilliant sky, and in sight of the glorious azure ocean beating in from an infinitude of melting horizons. Here, too, my Mother, perched in a nook of the high rocks, surveyed the west and forgot for a little while her weakness and the gnawing, grinding pain.

But in October, our sorrows seemed to close in upon us. We went back to London, and for the first time in their married life, my parents were divided. My Mother was now so seriously weaker that the omnibus-journeys to Pimlico became impossible. My Father could not leave his work and so my Mother and I had to take a gloomy lodging close to the doctor's house. The experiences upon which I presently entered were of a nature in which childhood rarely takes a part. I was now my Mother's sole and ceaseless companion; the silent witness of her suffering, of her patience, of her vain and delusive attempts to obtain alleviation of her anguish. For nearly three months I breathed the atmosphere of pain, saw no other light, heard no other sounds, thought no other thoughts than those which accompany physical suffering and weariness. To my memory these weeks seem years; I have no measure of their monotony. The lodgings were bare and yet tawdry; out of dingy windows we looked from a second storey upon a dull small street, drowned in autumnal fog. My Father came to see us when he could, but otherwise, save when we made our morning expedition to the doctor, or when a slatternly girl waited upon us with our distasteful meals, we were alone, – without any other occupation than to look forward to that occasional abatement of suffering which was what we hoped for most.

It is difficult for me to recollect how these interminable hours were spent. But I read aloud in a great part of them. I have now in my mind's cabinet a picture of my chair turned towards the window, partly that I might see the book more distinctly, partly not to see quite so distinctly that dear patient figure rocking on her sofa, or leaning, like a funeral statue, like a muse upon a monument, with her head on her arms against the mantelpiece. I read the Bible every day, and at much length; also, – with I cannot but think some praiseworthy patience, – a book of incommunicable dreariness, called Newton's *Thoughts on the Apocalypse*. Newton bore a great resemblance to my old aversion, Jukes, and I made a sort of playful compact with my Mother that if I read aloud a certain number of pages out of *Thoughts on the Apocalypse*, as a reward I should be allowed to recite 'my own favourite hymns'. Among these there was one which united her suffrages with mine. Both of us extremely admired the piece by Toplady[2] which begins:

> What though my frail eyelids refuse
> Continual watchings to keep,
> And, punctual as midnight renews,
> Demand the refreshment of sleep.

To this day, I cannot repeat this hymn without a sense of poignant emotion, nor can I pretend to decide how much of this is due to its merit and how much to the peculiar nature of the memories it recalls. But it might be as rude as I genuinely think it to be skilful, and I should continue to regard it as a sacred poem. Among all my childish memories none is clearer than my looking up, – after reading, in my high treble,

> Kind Author and Ground of my hope,
> Thee, Thee for my God I avow;
> My glad Ebenezer set up,
> And own Thou hast help'd me till now;
> I muse on the years that are past,
> Wherein my defence Thou hast prov'd,
> Nor wilt Thou relinquish at last
> A sinner so signally lov'd, –

and hearing my Mother, her eyes brimming with tears and her alabastrine fingers tightly locked together, murmur in unconscious repetiton:

In our lodgings at Pimlico I came across a piece of verse which exercised a lasting influence on my taste. It was called 'The Cameronian's Dream', and it had been written by a certain James Hyslop,[3] a schoolmaster on a man-of-war. I do not know how it came into my possession, but I remember it was adorned by an extremely dim and ill-executed wood-cut of a lake surrounded by mountains, with tombstones in the foreground. This lugubrious frontispiece positively fascinated me, and lent a further gloomy charm to the ballad itself. It was in this copy of mediocre verses that the sense of romance first appealed to me, the kind of nature-romance which is connected with hills, and lakes, and the picturesque costumes of old times. The following stanza, for instance, brought a revelation to me:

> 'Twas a dream of those ages of darkness and blood,
> When the minister's home was the mountain and wood;
> When in Wellwood's dark valley the standard of Zion,
> All bloody and torn, 'mong the heather was lying.

I persuaded my Mother to explain to me what it was all about, and she told me of the affliction of the Scottish saints, their flight to the waters and the wilderness, their cruel murder while they were singing 'their last song to the God of Salvation'. I was greatly fired, and the following stanza, in particular, reached my ideal of the Sublime:

> The muskets were flashing, the blue swords were gleaming,
> The helmets were cleft, and the red blood was streaming,
> The heavens grew dark, and the thunder was rolling,
> When in Wellwood's dark muirlands the mighty were falling.

Twenty years later I met with the only other person whom I have ever encountered who had ever heard of 'The Cameronian's Dream'. This was Robert Louis Stevenson,[4] who had been greatly struck by it when he was about my age. Probably the same ephemeral edition of it reached, at the same time, each of our pious households.

As my Mother's illness progressed, she could neither sleep, save by the use of opiates, nor rest, except in a sloping posture, propped up by many pillows. It was my great joy, and a pleasant diversion, to be allowed to shift, beat up, and rearrange these pillows, a task which I learned to accomplish not too awkwardly. Her sufferings, I believe, were principally caused by the violence of the medicaments to which her doctor, who was trying a new and fantastic 'cure', thought it proper to subject her. Let those who take a pessimistic view of our social progress ask themselves whether such tortures could today be inflicted on a delicate patient, or whether that patient would be allowed to exist, in the greatest misery in a lodging with no professional nurse to wait upon her, and with no companion but a little helpless boy of seven years of age. Time passes smoothly and swiftly, and we do not perceive the mitigations which he brings in his hands. Everywhere, in the whole system of human life, improvements, alleviations, ingenious appliances and humane inventions are being introduced to lessen the great burden of suffering.

If we were suddenly transplanted into the world of only fifty years ago, we should be startled and even horror-stricken by the wretchedness to which the step backwards would reintroduce us. It was in the very year of which I am speaking, a year of which my personal memories are still vivid, that Sir James Simpson [5] received the Monthyon prize as a recognition of his discovery of the use of anaesthetics. Can our thoughts embrace the mitigation of human torment which the application of chloroform alone has caused? My early experiences, I confess, made me singularly conscious, at an age when one should know nothing about these things, of that torrent of sorrow and anguish and terror which flows under all footsteps of man. Within my childish conscience, already, some dim inquiry was awake as to the meaning of this mystery of pain –

The floods of the tears meet and gather;
The sound of them all grows like thunder;
O into what bosom, I wonder,

75

Is poured the whole sorrow of years?
For Eternity only seems keeping
Account of the great human weeping;
May God then, the Maker and Father,
May He find a place for the tears!

In my Mother's case, the savage treatment did no good; it had to be abandoned, and a day or two before Christmas, while the fruits were piled in the shop-fronts and the butchers were shouting outside their forests of carcases, my Father brought us back in a cab through the streets to Islington. a feeble and languishing company. Our invalid bore the journey fairly well, enjoying the air, and pointing out to me the glittering evidences of the season, but we paid heavily for her little entertainment, since, at her earnest wish the window of the cab having been kept open, she caught a cold, which became, indeed, the technical cause of a death that no applications could now have long delayed.

Yet she lingered with us six weeks more, and during this time I again relapsed, very naturally, into solitude. She now had the care of a practised woman, one of the 'saints' from the Chapel, and I was only permitted to pay brief visits to her bedside. That I might not be kept indoors all day and every day, a man, also connected with the meeting-house, was paid a trifle to take me out for a walk each morning. This person, who was by turns familiar and truculent, was the object of my intense dislike. Our relations became, in the truest sense, 'forced'; I was obliged to walk by his side, but I held that I had no further responsibility to be agreeable, and after a while I ceased to speak to him, or to answer his remarks. On one occasion, poor dreary man, he met a friend and stopped to chat with him. I considered this act to have dissolved the bond; I skipped lightly from his side, examined several shop-windows which I had been forbidden to look into, made several darts down courts and up passages, and finally, after a delightful morning, returned home, having known my directions perfectly. My official conductor, in a shocking condition of fear, was crouching by the area-rails looking up and down the street He darted upon me, in a great rage, to know 'what I meant by it?' I drew myself up as tall as I could, hissed 'Blind leader of the blind!' at him, and, with this inappropriate but very effective Parthian shot,[6] slipped into the house.

When it was quite certain that no alleviations and no medical care could prevent, or even any longer postpone the departure of my Mother, I believe that my future conduct became the object of her greatest and her most painful solicitude. She said to my Father that the worst trial of her faith came from the feeling that she was called upon to leave that child whom she had so carefully trained from his earliest infancy for the peculiar service of the Lord, without any knowledge of what his further course would be. In many conversations, she most tenderly and closely urged my Father, who, however, needed no urging, to watch with unceasing care over my spiritual welfare. As she grew nearer her end, it was observed that she became calmer, and less troubled by fears about me. The intensity of her prayers and hopes seemed to have a prevailing force; it would have been a sin to doubt that such applications, such confidence and devotion, such an emphasis of will, should not be rewarded by an answer from above in the affirmative. She was able, she said, to leave me 'in the hands of her loving Lord', or, on another occasion, 'to the care of her covenant God'.

Although her faith was so strong and simple, my Mother possessed no quality of the mystic. She never pretended to any visionary gifts, believed not at all in dreams or portents, and encouraged nothing in herself or others which was superstitious or fantastic. In order to realize her condition of mind, it is necessary, I think, to accept the view that she had formed a definite conception of the absolute, unmodified and historical veracity, in its direct and obvious sense, of every statement contained within the covers of the Bible. For her, and for my Father, nothing was symbolic, nothing allegorical or allusive in any part of Scripture, except what was, in so many words,

77

proffered as a parable or a picture. Pushing this to its extreme limit, and allowing nothing for the changes of scene or time or race, my parents read injunctions to the Corinthian converts without any suspicion that what was apposite in dealing with half-breed Achaian colonists of the first century might not exactly apply to respectable English men and women of the nineteenth. They took it, text by text, as if no sort of difference existed between the surroundings of Trimalchion's feast [7] and those of a City dinner. Both my parents, I think, were devoid of sympathetic imagination; in my Father, I am sure, it was singularly absent. Hence, although their faith was so strenuous that many persons might have called it fanatical, there was no mysticism about them. They went rather to the opposite extreme, to the cultivation of a rigid and iconoclastic literalness.

This was curiously exemplified in the very lively interest which they both took in what is called 'the interpretation of prophecy', [8] and particularly in unwrapping the dark sayings bound up in the Book of Revelation. In their impartial survey of the Bible, they came to this collection of solemn and splendid visions, sinister and obscure, and they had no intention of allowing these to be merely stimulating to the fancy, or vaguely doctrinal in symbol. When they read of seals broken and of vials poured forth, of the star which was called Wormwood that fell from Heaven, and of men whose hair was as the hair of women and their teeth as the teeth of lions, they did not admit for a moment that these vivid mental pictures were of a poetic character, but they regarded them as positive statements, in guarded language, describing events which were to happen, and could be recognized when they did happen. It was the explanation, the perfectly prosaic and positive explanation, of all these wonders which drew them to study the Habershons and the Newtons whose books they so much enjoyed. They were helped by these guides to recognize in wild Oriental visions direct statements regarding Napoleon III and Pope Pius IX and the King of Piedmont, historic figures which they conceived as foreshadowed, in language which admitted of plain interpretation, under the names of denizens of Babylon and companions of the Wild Beast.

My Father was in the habit of saying, in later years, that no small element in his wedded happiness had been the fact that my Mother and he were of one mind in the interpretation of Sacred Prophecy. Looking back, it appears to me that this unusual mental exercise was almost their only relaxation, and that in their economy it took the place which is taken, in profaner families, by cards or the piano. It was a distraction; it took them completely out of themselves. During those melancholy weeks at Pimlico, I read aloud another work of the same nature as those of Habershon and Jukes,[9] the *Horae Apocalypticae* of a Mr Elliott.[10] This was written, I think, in a less disagreeable style, and certainly it was less opaquely obscure to me. My recollection distinctly is that when my mother could endure nothing else, the arguments of this book took her thoughts away from her pain and lifted her spirits. Elliott saw 'the queenly arrogance of Popery' everywhere, and believed that the very last days of Babylon the Great were come. Lest I say what may be thought extravagant, let me quote what my Father wrote in his diary at the time of my Mother's death. He said that the thought that Rome was doomed (as seemed not impossible in 1857) so affected my Mother that it 'irradiated' her dying hours with an assurance that was like 'the light of the Morning Star, the harbinger of the rising sun'.

After our return to Islington, there was a complete change in my relation to my Mother. At Pimlico, I had been all-important, her only companion, her friend, her confidant. But now that she was at home again, people and things combined to separate me from her. Now, and for the first time in my life, I no longer slept in her room, no longer sank to sleep under her kiss, no longer saw her mild eyes smile on me with the earliest sunshine. Twice a day, after breakfast and before I went to rest, I was brought to her bedside; but we were never alone, other people, sometimes strange people, were there. We had no cosy talk; often she was too weak to do more than pat my hand: her loud and almost constant cough terrified and harassed me. I felt, as I stood, awkwardly and shyly, by her high bed, that I had shrunken into a very small and insignificant figure, that she was floating out of my reach, that all things, but I knew not what nor how, were coming to an end. She herself was not herself; her head, that used to be held so erect, now rolled or sank upon the pillow; the sparkle was all extinguished from those bright, dear eyes. I could not understand it; I meditated long, long upon it all in my infantile darkness, in the garret, or in the little slip of a cold room where my bed was now placed; and a great, blind anger against I knew not what awakened in my soul.

The two retreats which I have mentioned were now all that were left to me. In the back-parlour some one from outside gave me occasional lessons, of a desultory character. The break-fast-room was often haunted by visitors, unknown to me by face or name, – ladies, who used to pity me and even to pet me, until I became nimble in escaping from their caresses. Everything seemed to be unfixed, uncertain; it was like being on the platform of a railway-station waiting for a train. In all this time, the agitated, nervous presence of my Father, whose pale face was permanently drawn with anxiety, added to my perturbation, and I became miserable, stupid, as if I had lost my way in a cold fog.

Had I been older and more intelligent, of course, it might have been of him and not of myself that I should have been thinking. As I now look back upon that tragic time, it is for him that my heart bleeds – for them both, so singularly fitted as they were to support and cheer one another in an existence which their own innate and cultivated characteristics had made little hospitable to other sources of comfort. This is not to be dwelt on here. But what must be recorded was the extraordin-ary tranquillity, the serene and sensible resignation, with which at length my parents faced the awful hour.[11] Language cannot utter what they suffered, but there was no rebellion, no repin-ing, in their case even an atheist might admit that the over-powering miracle of grace was mightily efficient.

It seems almost cruel to the memory of their opinions that the only words which rise to my mind, the only ones which seem in the least degree adequate to describe the attitude of my parents, had fallen from the pen of one whom, in their want of imaginative sympathy, they had regarded as anathema. But John Henry Newman [12] might have come from the contemplation of my Mother's death-bed when he wrote: 'All the trouble which the world inflicts upon us, and which flesh cannot but feel, – sorrow, pain, care, bereavement, – these avail not to disturb the tranquillity and the intensity with which faith gazes at the Divine Majesty.' It was 'tranquillity', it was not the rapture of the mystic. Almost in the last hour of her life, urged to confess her 'joy' in the Lord, my Mother, rigidly honest, meticulous in self-analysis, as ever, replied: 'I have peace, but not *joy*. It would not do to go into eternity with a lie in my mouth.'

When the very end approached, and her mind was growing clouded, she gathered her strength together to say to my Father, 'I shall walk with Him in white. Won't you take our lamb and walk with me?' Confused with sorrow and alarm, my Father failed to understand her meaning. She became agitated, and she repeated two or three times: 'Take our lamb, and walk with me!' Then my Father comprehended, and pressed me forward; her hand fell softly upon mine and she seemed content. Thus was my dedication, that had begun in my cradle, sealed with the most solemn, the most poignant and irresistible insistence, at the death-bed of the holiest and purest of women. But what a weight, intolerable as the burden of Atlas, to lay on the shoulders of a little fragile child!

CHAPTER IV

Certainly the preceding year, the seventh of my life, had been weighted for us with comprehensive disaster. I have not yet mentioned that, at the beginning of my Mother's fatal illness, misfortune came upon her brothers. I have never known the particulars of their ruin, but, I believe in consequence of A.'s unsuccessful speculations, and of the fact that E. had allowed the use of his name as a surety, both my uncles were obliged to fly from their creditors, and take refuge in Paris. This happened just when our need was the sorest, and this, together with the poignancy of knowing that their sister's devoted labours for them had been all in vain, added to their unhappiness. It was doubtless also the reason why, having left England, they wrote to us no more, carefully concealing from us even their address, so that when my Mother died, my Father was unable to communicate with them. I fear that they fell into dire distress; before very long we learned that A. had died, but it was fifteen years more before we heard anything of E., whose life had at length been preserved by the kindness of an old servant, but whose mind was now so clouded that he could recollect little or nothing of the past; and soon he also died. Amiable, gentle, without any species of practical ability, they were quite unfitted to struggle with the world, which had touched them only to wreck them.

The flight of my uncles at this particular juncture left me without a relative on my Mother's side at the time of her death. This isolation threw my Father into a sad perplexity. His only obvious source of income – but it happened to be a remarkably hopeful one – was an engagement to deliver a long series of lectures on marine natural history throughout the north and centre of England. These lectures were an entire novelty; nothing like them had been offered to the provincial public before; and the fact that the newly-invented marine aquarium was the fashionable toy of the moment added to their attraction. My Father was bowed down by sorrow and care, but he was not broken. His intellectual forces were at their height, and so was his popularity as an author. The lectures were to begin in March; my Mother was buried on 13 February. It seemed at first, in the inertia of bereavement, to be all beyond his powers to make the supreme effort, but the wholesome prick of need urged him on. It was a question of paying for food and clothes, of keeping a roof above our heads. The captain of a vessel in a storm must navigate his ship, although his wife lies dead in the cabin. That was my Father's position in the spring of 1857; he had to stimulate, instruct, amuse large audiences of strangers, and seem gay, although affliction and loneliness had settled in his heart. He had to do this, or starve.

But the difficulty still remained. During these months what was to become of me? My father could not take me with him from hotel to hotel and from lecture-hall to lecture-hall. Nor could he leave me, as people leave the domestic cat, in an empty house for the neighbours to feed at intervals. The dilemma threatened to be insurmountable, when suddenly there descended upon us a kind, but little-known, paternal cousin[1] from the west of England, who had heard of our calamities. This lady had a large family of her own at Bristol; she offered to find room in it for me so long as ever my Father should be away in the north: and when my Father, bewildered by so much goodness, hesitated, she came up to London and carried me forcibly away in a whirlwind of good-nature. Her benevolence was quite spontaneous; and I am not sure that she had not added to it already by helping to nurse our beloved sufferer through part of her illness. Of that I am not positive, but I recollect very clearly her snatching me from our cold and desolate hearthstone, and carrying me off to her cheerful house at Clifton.

Here, for the first time, when half through my eighth year, I was thrown into the society of young people. My cousins were none of them, I believe, any longer children, but they were youths and maidens busily engaged in various personal interests, all collected in a hive of wholesome family energy. Everybody was very kind to me, and I sank back, after the strain of so many months, into mere childhood again. This long visit to my cousins at Clifton must have been very delightful: I am dimly aware that it was: yet I remember but few of its incidents. My memory, so clear and vivid about earlier solitary times, now in all this society becomes blurred and vague. I recollect certain pleasures; being taken, for instance, to a menagerie, and having a practical joke, in the worst taste, played upon me by the pelican. One of my cousins, who was a medical student, showed me a pistol, and helped me to fire it; he smoked a pipe, and I was oddly conscious that both the firearm and the tobacco were definitely hostile to my 'dedication'. My girl-cousins took turns in putting me to bed, and on cold nights, or when they were in a hurry, allowed me to say my prayer under the bedclothes instead of kneeling at a chair. The result of this was further spiritual laxity, because I could not help going to sleep before the prayer was ended.

The visit to Clifton was, in fact, a blessed interval in my strenuous childhood. It probably prevented my nerves from breaking down under the pressure of the previous months. The Clifton family was God-fearing, in a quiet, sensible way, but there was a total absence of all the intensity and compulsion of our religious life at Islington. I was not encouraged – I even remember that I was gently snubbed – when I rattled forth, parrot-fashion, the conventional phraseology of 'the saints'. For a short, enchanting period of respite, I lived the life of an ordinary little boy, relapsing, to a degree which would have filled my Father with despair, into childish thoughts and childish language. The result was that of this little happy breathing-space I have nothing to report. Vague, half-blind remembrances of walks, with my tall cousins waving like trees above me, pleasant noisy evenings in a great room on the ground-floor, faint silver-points of excursions into the country, all this is the very pale and shadowy testimony to a brief interval of healthy, happy child-life, when my hard-driven soul was allowed to have, for a little while, no history.

The life of a child is so brief, its impressions are so illusory and fugitive, that it is as difficult to record its history as it would be to design a morning cloud sailing before the wind. It is short, as we count shortness in after years, when the drag of lead pulls down to earth the foot that used to flutter with a winged impetuosity, and to float with the pulse of Hermes. But in memory, my childhood was long, long with interminable hours, hours with the pale cheek pressed against the window-pane, hours of mechanical and repeated lonely 'games', which had lost their savour, and were kept going by sheer inertness. Not unhappy, not fretful, but long, – long, long. It seems to me, as I look back to the life in the motherless Islington house, as I resumed it in that slow eighth year of my life, that time had ceased to move. There was a whole age between one tick of the eight-day clock in the hall, and the next tick. When the milkman went his rounds in our grey street, with his eldritch [2] scream over the top of each set of area railings, it seemed as though he would never disappear again. There was no past and no future for me, and the present felt as though it were sealed up in a Leyden jar. [3] Even my dreams were interminable, and hung stationary from the nightly sky.

At this time, the street was my theatre, and I spent long periods, as I have said, leaning against the window. I feel now that coldness of the pane, and the feverish heat that was produced, by contrast, in the orbit round the eye. Now and then amusing things happened. The onion-man was a joy long waited for. This worthy was a tall and bony Jersey protestant with a raucous voice, who strode up our street several times a week, carrying a yoke across his shoulders, from the ends of which hung ropes of onions. He used to shout, at abrupt intervals, in a tone which might wake the dead:

Here's your rope . . .
To hang the Pope . . .
And a penn'orth of cheese to choke him.

The cheese appeared to be legendary; he sold only onions. My Father did not eat onions, but he encouraged this terrible fellow, with his wild eyes and long strips of hair, because of his godly attitude towards the 'Papacy', and I used to watch him dart out of the front door, present his penny, and retire, graciously waving back the proffered onion. On the other hand, my Father did not approve of a fat sailor, who was a constant passer-by. This man, who was probably crazed, used to walk very slowly up the centre of our street, vociferating with the voice of a bull,

Wa-a-atch and pray-hay!
Night and day-hay!

This melancholy admonition was the entire business of his life. He did nothing at all but walk up and down the streets of Islington exhorting the inhabitants to watch and pray. I do not recollect that this sailor-man stopped to collect pennies, and my impression is that he was, after his fashion, a volunteer evangelist.

The tragedy of Mr Punch was another, and a still greater delight. I was never allowed to go out into the street to mingle with the little crowd which gathered under the stage, and as I was extremely near-sighted, the impression I received was vague. But when, by happy chance, the show stopped opposite our door, I saw enough of that ancient drama to be thrilled with terror and delight. I was much affected by the internal troubles of the Punch family; I thought that with a little more tact on the part of Mrs Punch and some restraint held over a temper, naturally violent, by Mr Punch, a great deal of this sad misunderstanding might have been prevented.

The momentous close, when a figure of shapeless horror appears on the stage, and quells the hitherto undaunted Mr Punch, was to me the bouquet of the entire performance. When Mr Punch, losing his nerve, points to this shape and says in an awestruck, squeaking whisper, 'Who's that? Is it the butcher?' and the stern answer comes, 'No, Mr Punch!' And then, 'Is it the baker?' 'No, Mr Punch!' 'Who is it then?' (this in a squeak trembling with emotion and terror); and then the full, loud reply, booming like a judgement-bell, 'It is the Devil come to take you down to Hell,' and the form of Punch, with kicking legs, sunken in epilepsy on the floor, – all this was solemn and exquisite to me beyond words. I was not amused – I was deeply moved and exhilarated, 'purged', as the old phrase hath it, 'with pity and terror'.

Another joy, in a lighter key, was watching a fantastic old man who came slowly up the street, hung about with drums and flutes and kites and coloured balls, and bearing over his shoulders a great sack. Children and servant-girls used to bolt out of areas, and chaffer with this gaudy person, who would presently trudge on, always repeating the same set of words –

> Here's your toys
> For girls and boys,
> For bits of brass
> And broken glass,
> (these four lines being spoken in a breathless hurry)
> A penny or a vial-bottell . . .
> (this being drawled out in an endless wail).

I was not permitted to go forth and trade with this old person, but sometimes our servant-maid did, thereby making me feel that if I did not hold the rose of merchandise, I was very near it. My experiences with my cousins at Clifton had given me the habit of looking out into the world – even though it was only into the pale world of our quiet street.

My Father and I were now great friends. I do not doubt that he felt his responsibility to fill as far as might be the gap which

87

the death of my Mother had made in my existence. I spent a large portion of my time in his study, while he was writing or drawing, and though very little conversation passed between us, I think that each enjoyed the companionship of the other. There were two, and sometimes three aquaria in the room, tanks of sea-water, with glass sides, inside which all sorts of creatures crawled and swam; these were sources of endless pleasure to me, and at this time began to be laid upon me the occasional task of watching and afterwards reporting the habits of animals.

At other times, I dragged a folio volume of the *Penny Cyclopaedia*[4] up to the study with me, and sat there reading successive articles on such subjects as Parrots, Parthians, Passion-flowers, Passover and Pastry, without any invidious preferences, all information being equally welcome, and equally fugitive. That something of all this loose stream of knowledge clung to odd cells of the back of my brain seems to be shown by the fact that to this day, I occasionally find myself aware of some stray useless fact about peonies or pemmican or pepper, which I can only trace back to the *Penny Cyclopaedia* of my infancy.

It will be asked what the attitude of my Father's mind was to me, and of mine to his, as regards religion, at this time, when we were thrown together alone so much. It is difficult to reply with exactitude. But so far as the former is concerned, I think that the extreme violence of the spiritual emotions to which my Father had been subjected, had now been followed by a certain reaction. He had not changed his views in any respect, and he was prepared to work out the results of them with greater zeal than ever, but just at present his religious nature, like his physical nature, was tired out with anxiety and sorrow. He accepted the supposition that I was entirely with him in all respects, so far, that is to say, as a being so rudimentary and feeble as a little child could be. My Mother, in her last hours, had dwelt on our unity in God; we were drawn together, she said, elect from the world, in a triplicity of faith and joy. She had constantly repeated the words: 'We shall be one family, one song. One song! one family!' My Father, I think, accepted this as a prophecy, he felt no doubt of our triple unity; my Mother had now merely passed before us, through a door, into a world of light, where we should presently join her, where all things would be radiant and blissful, but where we three would, in some unknown way, be particularly drawn together in a tie of inexpressible beatitude. He fretted at the delay; he would fain have taken me by the hand, and have joined her in the realms of holiness and light, at once, without this dreary dalliance with earthly cares.

He held this confidence and vision steadily before him, but nothing availed against the melancholy of his natural state. He was conscious of his dull and solitary condition, and he saw, too, that it enveloped me. I think his heart was, at this time, drawn out towards me in an immense tenderness. Sometimes, when the early twilight descended upon us in the study, and he could no longer peer with advantage into the depths of his microscope, he would beckon me to him silently, and fold me closely in his arms. I used to turn my face up to his, patiently and wonderingly, while the large, unwilling tears gathered in the corners of his eyelids. My training had given me a preternatural faculty of stillness, and we would stay so, without a word or a movement, until the darkness filled the room. And then, with my little hand in his, we would walk sedately downstairs, to the parlour, where we would find that the lamp was lighted, and that our melancholy vigil was ended. I do not think that at any part of our lives my Father and I were drawn so close to one another as we were in that summer of 1857. Yet we seldom spoke of what lay so warm and fragrant between us, the flower-like thought of our Departed.

The visit to my cousins had made one considerable change in me. Under the old solitary discipline, my intelligence had grown at the expense of my sentiment. I was innocent, but inhuman. The long suffering and the death of my Mother had awakened my heart, had taught me what pain was, but had left me savage and morose. I had still no idea of the relations of human beings to one another; I had learned no word of that philosophy which comes to the children of the poor in the struggle of the street and to the children of the well-to-do in the clash of the nursery. In other words, I had no humanity; I had been carefully shielded from the chance of 'catching' it, as though it were the most dangerous of microbes. But now that I had enjoyed a little of the common experience of childhood, a great change had come upon me. Before I went to Clifton, my mental life was all interior, a rack of baseless dream upon dream. But now, I was eager to look out of the window, to go out in the streets; I was taken with a curiosity about human life. Even, from my vantage of the window-pane, I watched boys and girls go by with an interest which began to be almost wistful.

Still I continued to have no young companions. But on summer evenings I used to drag my Father out, taking the initiative myself, stamping in playful impatience at his irresolution, fetching his hat and stick, and waiting. We used to sally forth at last together, hand in hand, descending the Caledonian Road, with all its shops, as far as Mother Shipton, or else winding among the semi-genteel squares and terraces westward by Copenhagen Street, or, best of all, mounting to the Regent's Canal, where we paused to lean over the bridge and watch flotillas of ducks steer under us, or little white dogs dash, impotently furious, from stem to stern of the great, lazy barges painted in a crude vehemence of vermilion and azure. These were happy hours, when the spectre of Religion ceased to overshadow us for a little while, when my Father forgot the Apocalypse and dropped his austere phraseology, and when our bass and treble voices used to ring out together over some foolish little jest or some mirthful recollection of his past experiences. Little soft oases these, in the hard desert of our sandy spiritual life at home.

There was an unbending, too, when we used to sing together, in my case very tunelessly. I had inherited a plentiful lack of musical genius from my Mother, who had neither ear nor voice, and who had said, in the course of her last illness, 'I shall sing His praise, *at length*, in strains I never could master here below'. My Father, on the other hand, had some knowledge of the principles of vocal music, although not, I am afraid, much taste. He had at least great fondness for singing hymns, in the manner then popular with the Evangelicals, very loudly, and so slowly that I used to count how many words I could read silently, between one syllable of the singing and another. My lack of skill did not prevent me from being zealous at these vocal exercises, and my Father and I used to sing lustily together. The Wesleys, Charlotte Elliott[5] ('Just as I am, without one plea'), and James Montgomery[6] ('For ever with the Lord') represented his predilection in hymnology. I acquiesced, although that would not have been my independent choice. These represented the devotional verse which made its direct appeal to the evangelical mind, and served in those 'Puseyite'[7] days to counteract the High Church poetry founded on *The Christian Year*.[8] Of that famous volume I never met with a copy until I was grown up, and equally unknown in our circle were the hymns of Newman, Faber and Neale.

It was my Father's plan from the first to keep me entirely ignorant of the poetry of the High Church, which deeply offended his Calvinism; he thought that religious truth could be sucked in, like mother's milk, from hymns which were godly and sound, and yet correctly versified; and I was therefore carefully trained in this direction from an early date. But my spirit had rebelled against some of these hymns, especially against those written – a mighty multitude – by Horatius Bonar;[9] naughtily refusing to read Bonar's 'I heard the voice of Jesus say' to my Mother in our Pimlico lodgings. A secret hostility to this particular form of effusion was already, at the age of seven, beginning to define itself in my brain, side by side with an unctuous infantile conformity.

I find a difficulty in recalling the precise nature of the religious instruction which my Father gave me at this time. It was incessant, and it was founded on the close inspection of the Bible, particularly of the epistles of the New Testament. This summer, as my eighth year advanced, we read the 'Epistle to the Hebrews', with very great deliberation, stopping every moment, that my Father might expound it, verse by verse. The extraordinary beauty of the language – for instance, the matchless cadences and images of the first chapter – made a certain impression upon my imagination, and were (I think) my earliest initiation into the magic of literature. I was incapable of defining what I felt, but I certainly had a grip in the throat, which was in its essence a purely aesthetic emotion, when my Father read, in his pure, large, ringing voice, such passages as 'The heavens are the works of Thy hands. They shall perish, but Thou remainest, and they all shall wax old as doth a garment, and as a vesture shalt Thou fold them up, and they shall be changed; but Thou art the same, and Thy years shall not fail.' But the dialectic parts of the Epistle puzzled and confused me. Such metaphysical ideas as 'laying again the foundation of repentance from dead works' and 'crucifying the Son of God afresh' were not successfully brought down to the level of my understanding.

My Father's religious teaching to me was almost exclusively doctrinal. He did not observe the value of negative education, that is to say, of leaving Nature alone to fill up the gaps which it is her design to deal with at a later and riper date. He did not, even, satisfy himself with those moral injunctions which should form the basis of infantile discipline. He was in a tremendous hurry to push on my spiritual growth, and he fed me with theological meat which it was impossible for me to digest. Some glimmer of a suspicion that he was sailing on the wrong tack must, I should suppose, have broken in upon him when we had reached the eighth and ninth chapters of Hebrews, where, addressing readers who had been brought up under the Jewish dispensation, and had the formalities of the Law of Moses in their very blood, the apostle battles with their dangerous conservatism. It is a very noble piece

92

of spiritual casuistry, but it is signally unfitted for the comprehension of a child. Suddenly by my flushing up with anger and saying, 'O how I do hate that Law,' my Father perceived, and paused in amazement to perceive, that I took the Law to be a person of malignant temper from whose cruel bondage, and from whose intolerable tyranny and unfairness, some excellent person was crying out to be delivered. I wished to hit Law with my fist, for being so mean and unreasonable.

Upon this, of course, it was necessary to reopen the whole line of exposition. My Father, without realizing it, had been talking on his own level, not on mine, and now he condescended to me. But without very great success. The melodious language, the divine forensic audacities, the magnificent ebb and flow of argument which make the 'Epistle to the Hebrews' such a miracle, were far and away beyond my reach, and they only bewildered me. Some evangelical children of my generation, I understand, were brought up on a work called 'Line upon Line: Here a Little, and there a Little'.[10] My Father's ambition would not submit to anything suggested by such a title as that, and he committed, from his own point of view, a fatal mistake when he sought to build spires and battlements without having been at the pains to settle a foundation beneath them.

We were not always reading the 'Epistle to the Hebrews', however; not always was my flesh being made to creep by having it insisted upon that 'almost all things are by the Law purged with blood, and without blood is no remission of sin'. In our lighter moods, we turned to the 'Book of Revelation', and chased the phantom of Popery through its fuliginous pages. My Father, I think, missed my Mother's company almost more acutely in his researches into prophecy than in anything else. This had been their unceasing recreation, and no third person could possibly follow the curious path which they had hewn for themselves through this jungle of symbols. But, more and more, my Father persuaded himself that I, too, was

93

initiated, and by degrees I was made to share in all his speculations and interpretations.

Hand in hand we investigated the number of the Beast, which number is six hundred three score and six. Hand in hand we inspected the nations, to see whether they had the mark of Babylon in their foreheads. Hand in hand we watched the spirits of devils gathering the kings of the earth into the place which is called in the Hebrew tongue Armageddon. Our unity in these excursions was so delightful, that my Father was lulled in any suspicion he might have formed that I did not quite understand what it was all about. Nor could he have desired a pupil more docile or more ardent that I was in my flaming denunciations of the Papacy.

If there was one institution more than another which, at this early stage of my history, I loathed and feared, it was what we invariably spoke of as 'the so-called Church of Rome'. In later years, I have met with stout Protestants, gallant 'Down-with-the-Pope' men from County Antrim, and ladies who see the hands of the Jesuits in every public and private misfortune. It is the habit of a loose and indifferent age to consider this dwindling body of enthusiasts with suspicion, and to regard their attitude towards Rome as illiberal. But my own feeling is that they are all too mild, that their denunciations err on the side of the anodyne. I have no longer the slightest wish myself to denounce the Roman communion, but, if it is to be done, I have an idea that the latter-day Protestants do not know how to do it. In Lord Chesterfield's [11] phrase, these anti-Pope men 'don't understand their own silly business'. They make concessions and allowances, they put on gloves to touch the accursed thing.

Not thus did we approach the Scarlet Woman in the 'fifties. We palliated nothing, we believed in no good intentions, we used (I myself used, in my tender innocency) language of the seventeenth century such as is now no longer introduced into any species of controversy. As a little boy, when I thought, with intense vagueness, of the Pope, I used to shut my eyes tight and clench my fists. We welcomed any social disorder in any part of Italy, as likely to be annoying to the Papacy. If there was a custom-house officer stabbed in a fracas at Sassari, we gave loud thanks that liberty and light were breaking in upon Sardinia. If there was an unsuccessful attempt to murder the Grand Duke, we lifted up our voices to celebrate the faith and sufferings of the dear persecuted Tuscans, and the record of some apocryphal monstrosity in Naples would only reveal to us a glorious opening for Gospel energy. My Father celebrated the announcement in the newspapers of a considerable emigration from the Papal Dominions by rejoicing at 'this outcrowding of many, throughout the harlot's domain, from her sins and her plagues'.

No, the Protestant League may consider itself to be an earnest and active body, but I can never look upon its efforts as anything but lukewarm, standing, as I do, with the light of other days around me. As a child, whatever I might question, I never doubted the turpitude of Rome. I do not think I had formed any idea whatever of the character of pretensions or practices of the Catholic Church, or indeed of what it consisted, or its nature, but I regarded it with a vague terror as a wild beast, the only good point about it being that it was very old and was soon to die. When I turned to Jukes or Newton for further detail, I could not understand what they said. Perhaps, on the whole, there was no disadvantage in that.

It is possible that someone may have observed to my Father that the conditions of our life were unfavourable to our health, although I hardly think that he would have encouraged any such advice. As I look back upon this far-away time, I am surprised at the absence in it of any figures but our own. He and I together, now in the study among the sea-anemones and starfishes; now on the canal-bridge, looking down at the ducks; now at our hard little meals, served up as those of a dreamy widower are likely to be when one maid-of-all-work provides them, now under the lamp at the maps we both loved so much, this is what I see: – no third presence is ever with us. Whether it occurred to himself that such a solitude *à deux* was excellent, in the long run, for neither of us, or whether any chance visitor or one of the 'Saints', who used to see me at the Room every Sunday morning, suggested that a female influence might put a little rose-colour into my pasty cheeks, I know not. All I am sure of is that one day, towards the close of the summer, as I was gazing into the street, I saw a four-wheeled cab stop outside our door, and deposit, with several packages, a strange lady, who was shown up into my Father's study and was presently brought down and introduced to me.

Miss Marks, as I shall take the liberty of calling this person, was so long a part of my life that I must pause to describe her. She was tall, rather gaunt, with high cheek-bones; her teeth were prominent and very white; her eyes were china-blue, and were always absolutely fixed, wide open, on the person she spoke to; her nose was inclined to be red at the tip. She had a kind, hearty, sharp mode of talking, but did not exercise it much, being on the whole taciturn. She was bustling and nervous, not particularly refined, not quite, I imagine, what is called 'a lady'. I supposed her, if I thought of the matter at all, to be very old, but perhaps she may have seen, when we knew her first, some forty-five summers. Miss Marks was an orphan, depending upon her work for her living; she would not, in these days of examinations, have come up to the necessary educational standards, but she had enjoyed experience in teaching, and was prepared to be a conscientious and careful governess, up to her lights. I was now informed by my Father that it was in this capacity that she would in future take her place in our household. I was not informed, what I gradually learned by observation, that she would also act in it as housekeeper.

Miss Marks was a somewhat grotesque personage, and might easily be painted as a kind of eccentric Dickens character, a mixture of Mrs Pipchin and Miss Sally Brass.[12] I will confess that when, in years to come, I read 'Dombey and Son', certain features of Mrs Pipchin did irresistibly remind me of my excellent past governess. I can imagine Miss Marks saying, but with a facetious intent, that children who sniffed would not go to heaven. But I was instantly ashamed of the parallel, because my gaunt old friend was a thoroughly good and honest woman, not intelligent and not graceful, but desirous in every way to do her duty. Her duty to me she certainly did, and I am afraid I hardly rewarded her with the devotion she deserved From the first, I was indifferent to her wishes, and, as much as was convenient, I ignored her existence. She held no power over my attention, and if I accepted her guidance along the path of instruction, it was because, odd as it may sound, I really loved knowledge. I accepted her company without objection, and though there were occasional outbreaks of tantrums on both sides, we got on very well together for several years. I did not, however, at any time surrender my inward will to the wishes of Miss Marks.

In the circle of our life the religious element took so preponderating a place, that it is impossible to avoid mentioning, what might otherwise seem unimportant, the theological views of Miss Marks. How my Father had discovered her, or from what field of educational enterprise he plucked her in her prime, I never knew, but she used to mention that my Father's ministrations had 'opened her eyes', from which 'scales' had fallen. She had accepted, on their presentation to her, the entire gamut of his principles. Miss Marks was accustomed, while putting me to bed, to dwell darkly on the incidents of her past, which had, I fear, been an afflicted one. I believe I do her rather limited intelligence no injury when I say that it was prepared to swallow, at one mouthful, whatever my Father presented to it, so delighted was its way-worn possessor to find herself in a comfortable, or, at least, an independent position. She soon bowed, if there was indeed any resistance from the first, very contentedly in the House of Rimmon,[13] learning to repeat, with marked fluency, the customary formulas and shibboleths. On my own religious development she had no great influence.

Any such guttering theological rushlight as Miss Marks might dutifully exhibit faded for me in the blaze of my Father's glaring beacon-lamp of faith.

Hardly was Miss Marks settled in the family, than my Father left us on an expedition about which my curiosity was exercised, but not until later, satisfied. He had gone, as we afterwards found, to South Devon, to a point on the coast which he had known of old. Here he had hired a horse, and had ridden about until he saw a spot he liked, where a villa was being built on speculation. Nothing equals the courage of these recluse men; my Father got off his horse, and tied it to the gate, and then he went in and bought the house on a ninety-nine years' lease. I need hardly say that he had made the matter a subject of the most earnest prayer, and had entreated the Lord for guidance. When he felt attracted to this particular villa, he did not doubt that he was directed to it in answer to his supplication, and he wasted no time in further balancing or inquiring. On my eighth birthday, with bag and baggage complete, we all made the toilful journey down into Devonshire, and I was a town-child no longer.

CHAPTER V

A new element now entered into my life, a fresh rival arose to compete for me with my Father's dogmatic theology. This rival was the Sea. When Wordsworth was a little child, the presence of the mountains and the clouds lighted up his spirit with gleams that were like the flashing of a shield. He has described, in the marvellous pages of the 'Prelude',[1] the impact of nature upon the infant soul, but he has described it vaguely and faintly, with some 'infirmity of love for days disowned by memory', – I think because he was brought up in the midst of spectacular beauty, and could name no moment, mark no 'here' or 'now', when the wonder broke upon him. It was at the age of twice five summers, he thought, that he began to hold unconscious intercourse with nature, 'drinking in a pure organic pleasure' from the floating mists and winding waters. Perhaps, in his anxiety to be truthful, and in the absence of any record, he put the date of this conscious rapture too late rather than too early. Certainly my own impregnation with the obscurely-defined but keenly-felt loveliness of the open sea dates from the first week of my ninth year.

The village, on the outskirts[2] of which we had taken up our abode, was built parallel to the cliff-line above the shore, but half a mile inland. For a long time after the date I have now reached, no other form of natural scenery than the sea had any effect upon me at all. The tors of the distant moor might be drawn in deep blue against the pallor of our morning or our evening sky, but I never looked at them. It was the Sea, always the sea, nothing but the sea. From our house, or from the field at the back of our house, or from any part of the village itself,

there was no appearance to suggest that there could lie anything
in an easterly direction to break the infinitude of red ploughed
fields. But on that earliest morning. how my heart remembers!
we hastened, – Miss Marks, the maid, and I between them, –
along a couple of high-walled lanes, when suddenly, far below
us, in an immense arc of light, there stretched the enormous
plain of waters. We had but to cross a step or two of downs,
when the hollow sides of the great limestone cove yawned at
our feet, descending, like a broken cup, down, down to the
moon of snow-white shingle and the expanse of blue-green
sea.

In these twentieth-century days, a careful municipality has
studded the down with rustic seats and has shut its dangers out
with railings, has cut a winding carriage-drive round the curves
of the cove down to the shore, and has planted sausage-laurels
at intervals in clearings made for that aesthetic purpose. When
last I saw the place, thus smartened and secured, with its hair in
curl-papers and its feet in patent-leathers, I turned from it in
anger and disgust, and could almost have wept. I suppose that
to those who knew it in no other guise, it may still have
beauty. No parish councils, beneficent and shrewd, can obscure
the lustre of the waters or compress the vastness of the sky. But
what man could do to make wild beauty ineffectual, tame and
empty, has amply been performed at Oddicombe.

Very different was it fifty years ago, in its uncouth majesty.
No road, save the merest goat-path, led down its concave
wilderness, in which loose furze-bushes and untrimmed
brambles wantoned into the likeness of trees, each draped in
audacious tissue of wild clematis. Through this fantastic maze
the traveller wound his way, led by little other clue than by the
instinct of descent. For me, as a child, it meant the labour of a
long, an endless morning, to descend to the snow-white
pebbles, to sport at the edge of the cold, sharp sea, and then to
climb up home again, slipping in the sticky red mud, clutching
at the smooth boughs of the wild ash, toiling, toiling upwards
into flat land out of that hollow world of rocks.

On the first occasion, I recollect, our Cockney housemaid, enthusiastic young creature that she was, flung herself down upon her knees, and drank of the salt waters. Miss Marks, more instructed in phenomena, refrained, but I, although I was perfectly aware what the taste would be, insisted on sipping a few drops from the palm of my hand. This was a slight recurrence of what I have called my 'natural magic' practices, which had passed into the background of my mind, but had not quite disappeared. I recollect that I thought I might secure some power of walking on the sea, if I drank of it – a perfectly irrational movement of mind, like those of savages.

My great desire was to walk out over the sea as far as I could, and then lie flat on it, face downwards, and peer into the depths. I was tormented with this ambition, and, like many grown-up people, was so fully occupied by these vain and ridiculous desires that I neglected the actual natural pleasures around me. The idea was not quite so demented as it may seem, because we were in the habit of singing, as well as reading, of those enraptured beings who spend their days in 'flinging down their golden crowns upon the jasper sea'. Why, I argued, should I not be able to fling down my straw hat upon the tides of Oddicombe? And, without question, a majestic scene upon the Lake of Gennesaret had also inflamed my fancy. Of all these things, of course, I was careful to speak to no one.

It was not with Miss Marks, however, but with my Father, that I became accustomed to make the laborious and exquisite journeys down to the sea and back again. His work as a naturalist eventually took him, laden with implements, to the rock-pools on the shore, and I was in attendance as an acolyte. But our earliest winter in South Devon was darkened for us both by disappointments, the cause of which lay, at the time, far out of my reach. In the spirit of my Father were then running, with furious velocity, two hostile streams of influence. I was standing, just now, thinking of these things, where the Cascine ends in the wooded point which is carved out sharply by the lion-coloured swirl of the Arno on the one side and by the pure flow of the Mugnone on the other. The rivers meet, and run parallel, but there comes a moment when the one or the other must conquer, and it is the yellow vehemence that drowns the purer tide.

So, through my Father's brain, in that year of scientific crisis, 1857, there rushed two kinds of thought, each absorbing, each convincing, yet totally irreconcilable. There is a peculiar agony in the paradox that truth has two forms, each of them indisputable, yet each antagonistic to the other. It was this discovery, that there were two theories of physical life, each of which was true, but the truth of each incompatible with the truth of the other, which shook the spirit of my Father with perturbation. It was not, really, a paradox, it was a fallacy, if he could only have known it, but he allowed the turbid volume of superstition to drown the delicate stream of reason. He took one step in the service of truth, and then he drew back in an agony, and accepted the servitude of error.

This was the great moment in the history of thought when the theory of the mutability of species was preparing to throw a flood of light upon all departments of human speculation and action. It was becoming necessary to stand emphatically in one army or the other. Lyell[3] was surrounding himself with disciples, who were making strides in the direction of discovery. Darwin[4] had long been collecting facts with regard to the variation of animals and plants. Hooker and Wallace, Asa Gray and even Agassiz,[5] each in his own sphere, were coming closer and closer to a perception of that secret which was first to reveal itself clearly to the patient and humble genius of Darwin. In the year before, in 1856, Darwin, under pressure from Lyell, had begun that modest statement of the new revelation, that 'abstract of an essay', which developed so mightily into 'The Origin of Species'. Wollaston's 'Variation of Species' had just appeared, and had been a nine days' wonder in the wilderness.

On the other side, the reactionaries, although never dreaming of the fate which hung over them, had not been idle. In 1857 the astounding question had for the first time been propounded with contumely, 'What, then, did we come from an orang-outang?' The famous 'Vestiges of Creation[6] had been supplying a sugar-and-water panacea for those who could not escape from the trend of evidence, and who yet clung to revelation. Owen[7] was encouraging reaction by resisting, with all the strength of his prestige, the theory of the mutability of species.

In this period of intellectual ferment, as when a great political revolution is being planned, many possible adherents were confidentially tested with hints and encouraged to reveal their bias in a whisper. It was the notion of Lyell, himself a great mover of men, that, before the doctrine of natural selection was given to a world which would be sure to lift up at it a howl of execration, a certain body-guard of sound and experienced naturalists, expert in the description of species, should be privately made aware of its tenor. Among those who were thus initiated, or approached with a view towards possible illumination, was my Father. He was spoken to by Hooker, and later on by Darwin, after meetings of the Royal Society in the summer of 1857.

My Father's attitude towards the theory of natural selection was critical in his career, and oddly enough, it exercised an immense influence on my own experience as a child. Let it be admitted at once, mournful as the admission is, that every instinct in his intelligence went out at first to greet the new light. It had hardly done so, when a recollection of the opening chapter of 'Genesis' checked it at the outset. He consulted with Carpenter,[8] a great investigator, but one who was fully as incapable as himself of remodelling his ideas with regard to the old, accepted hypotheses. They both determined, on various grounds, to have nothing to do with the terrible theory, but to hold steadily to the law of the fixity of species. It was exactly at this juncture that we left London, and the slight and occasional but always extremely salutary personal intercourse with men of scientific leaning which my Father had enjoyed at the British Museum and at the Royal Society came to an end. His next act was to burn his ships, down to the last beam and log out of which a raft could have been made. By a strange act of wilfulness, he closed the doors upon himself for ever.

My Father had never admired Sir Charles Lyell. I think that the famous 'Lord Chancellor manner' of the geologist intimidated him, and we undervalue the intelligence of those whose conversation puts us at a disadvantage. For Darwin and Hooker, on the other hand, he had a profound esteem, and I know not whether this had anything to do with the fact that he chose, for his impetuous experiment in reaction, the field of geology, rather than that of zoology or botany. Lyell had been threatening to publish a book on the geological history of Man, which was to be a bomb-shell flung into the camp of the catastrophists My Father, after long reflection, prepared a theory of his own, which, as he fondly hoped, would take the wind out of Lyell's sails, and justify geology to godly readers of 'Genesis'. It was, very briefly, that there had been no gradual modification of the surface of the earth, or slow development of organic forms, but that when the catastrophic act of creation took place, the world presented, instantly, the structural appearance of a planet on which life had long existed.

The theory, coarsely enough, and to my Father's great indignation. was defined by a hasty press as being this – that God hid the fossils in the rocks in order to tempt geologists into infidelity. In truth, it was the logical and inevitable conclusion of accepting, literally, the doctrine of a sudden act of creation, it emphasized the fact that any breach in the circular course of nature could be conceived only on the supposition that the object created bore false witness to past processes, which had never taken place. For instance, Adam would certainly possess hair and teeth and bones in a condition which it must have taken many years to accomplish, yet he was created full-grown yesterday. He would certainly – though Sir Thomas Browne denied it [9] – display an 'omphalos', yet no umbilical cord had ever attached him to a mother

Never was a book cast upon the waters with greater anticipations of success than was this curious, this obstinate, this fanatical volume. My Father lived in a fever of suspense, waiting for the tremendous issue. This 'Omphalos' of his,[10] he thought, was to bring all the turmoil of scientific speculation to a close, fling geology into the arms of Scripture, and make the lion eat grass with the lamb. It was not surprising, he admitted, that there had been experienced an ever-increasing discord between the facts which geology brings to light and the direct statements of the early chapters of 'Genesis'. Nobody was to blame for that. My Father, and my Father alone, possessed the secret of the enigma; he alone held the key which could smoothly open the lock of geological mystery. He offered it, with a glowing gesture, to atheists and Christians alike. This was to be the universal panacea; this the system of intellectual therapeutics which could not but heal all the maladies of the age. But, alas! atheists and Christians alike looked at it, and laughed, and threw it away.

In the course of that dismal winter, as the post began to bring in private letters, few and chilly, and public reviews, many and scornful, my Father looked in vain for the approval of the churches, and in vain for the acquiescence of the scientific societies, and in vain for the gratitude of those 'thousands of thinking persons', which he had rashly assured himself of receiving. As his reconciliation of Scripture statements and geological deductions was welcomed nowhere; as Darwin continued silent, and the youthful Huxley[11] was scornful, and even Charles Kingsley,[12] from whom my Father had expected the most instant appreciation, wrote that he could not 'give up the painful and slow conclusion of five and twenty years' study of geology, and believe that God has written on the rocks one enormous and superfluous lie', – as all this happened or failed to happen, a gloom, cold and dismal, descended upon our morning teacups. It was what the poets mean by an 'inspissated' gloom; it thickened day by day, as hope and self-confidence evaporated in thin clouds of disappointment. My Father was not prepared for such a fate He had been the spoiled darling of

the public, the constant favourite of the press, and now, like
the dark angels of old,

> so huge a rout
> Encumbered him with ruin.

He could not recover from amazement at having offended
everybody by an enterprise which had been undertaken in the
cause of universal reconciliation.

During that grim season, my Father was no lively companion, and circumstance after circumstance combined to drive
him further from humanity. He missed more than ever the
sympathetic ear of my Mother; there was present to support
him nothing of that artful, female casuistry which insinuates
into the wounded consciousness of a man the conviction that,
after all, he is right and all the rest of the world is wrong. My
Father used to tramp in solitude round and round the red
ploughed field which was going to be his lawn, or sheltering
himself from the thin Devonian rain, pace up and down the
still-naked verandah where blossoming creepers were to be.
And I think that there was added to his chagrin with all his
fellow mortals a first tincture of that heresy which was to
attack him later on. It was now that, I fancy, he began, in his
depression, to be angry with God. How much devotion had he
given, how many sacrifices had he made, only to be left storm-
ing round this red morass with no one in all the world to care
for him except one pale-faced child with its cheek pressed to
the window!

After one or two brilliant excursions to the sea, winter, in its
dampest, muddiest, most languid form, had fallen upon us and
shut us in. It was a dreary winter for the wifeless man and the
motherless boy. We had come into the house, in precipitate
abandonment to that supposed answer to prayer, a great deal
too soon. In order to rake together the lump sum for buying it,
my Father had denuded himself of almost everything, and our
sticks of chairs and tables filled but two or three rooms. Half
the little house, or 'villa' as we called it, was not papered,

two-thirds were not furnished. The workmen were still finishing the outside when we arrived, and in that connexion I recall a little incident which exhibits my Father's morbid delicacy of conscience. He was accustomed in his brighter moments – and this was before the publication of his 'Omphalos' – occasionally to sing loud Dorsetshire songs of his early days, in a strange, broad Wessex lingo that I loved. One October afternoon he and I were sitting on the verandah, and my Father was singing; just round the corner, out of sight, two carpenters were putting up the framework of a greenhouse. In a pause, one of them said to his fellow: 'He can zing a zong, zo well's another, though he be a minister.' My Father, who was holding my hand loosely, clutched it, and looking up, I saw his eyes darken. He never sang a secular song again during the whole of his life.

Later in the year, and after his literary misfortune, his conscience became more troublesome than ever. I think he considered the failure of his attempt at the reconciliation of science with religion to have been intended by God as a punishment for something he had done or left undone. In those brooding tramps round and round the garden, his soul was on its knees searching the corners of his conscience for some sin of omission or commission, and one by one every pleasure, every recreation, every trifle scraped out of the dust of past experience, was magnified into a huge offence. He thought that the smallest evidence of levity, the least unbending to human instinct, might be seized by those around him as evidence of inconsistency, and might lead the weaker brethren into offence. The incident of the carpenters and the comic song is typical of a condition of mind which now possessed my Father, in which act after act became taboo, not because each was sinful in itself, but because it might lead others into sin.

I have the conviction that Miss Marks was now mightily afraid of my Father. Whenever she could, she withdrew to the room she called her 'boudoir', a small, chilly apartment, sparsely furnished, looking over what was in process of becoming the vegetable garden. Very properly, that she might have some sanctuary, Miss Marks forbade me to enter this virginal bower, which, of course, became to me an object of harrowing curiosity. Through the key-hole I could see practically nothing; one day I contrived to slip inside, and discovered that there was nothing to see but a plain bedstead and a toilet-table, void of all attraction. In this 'boudoir', on winter afternoons, a fire would be lighted, and Miss Marks would withdraw to it, not seen by us any more between high-tea and the apocalyptic exercise known as 'worship' – in less strenuous households much less austerely practised under the name of 'family prayers'. Left meanwhile to our own devices, my Father would mainly be reading, his book or paper held close up to the candle, while his lips and heavy eyebrows occasionally quivered and palpitated, with literary ardour, in a manner strangely exciting to me. Miss Marks, in a very high cap, and her large teeth shining, would occasionally appear in the doorway, desiring, with spurious geniality, to know how we were 'getting on'. But on these occasions neither of us replied to Miss Marks.

Sometimes in the course of this winter, my Father and I had long cosy talks together over the fire. Our favourite subject was murders. I wonder whether little boys of eight, soon to go upstairs alone at night, often discuss violent crime with a widower-papa? The practice, I cannot help thinking, is unusual; it was, however, consecutive with us. We tried other secular subjects, but we were sure to come round at last to 'what do you suppose they really did with the body?' I was told, a thrilled listener, the adventure of Mrs Manning, who killed a gentleman on the stairs and buried him in quick-lime in the back-kitchen, and it was at this time that I learned the useful historical fact, which abides with me after half a century, that Mrs Manning was hanged in black satin, which thereupon went wholly out of fashion in England. I also heard about Burke and Hare, whose story nearly froze me into stone with horror.

These were crimes which appear in the chronicles. But who

will tell me what 'the Carpet-bag Mystery'[13] was, which my Father and I discussed evening after evening? I have never come across a whisper of it since, and I suspect it of having been a hoax. As I recall the details, people in a boat, passing down the Thames, saw a carpet-bag hung high in air, on one of the projections of a pier of Waterloo Bridge. Being with difficulty dragged down - or perhaps up - this bag was found to be full of human remains, dreadful butcher's business of joints and fragments. Persons were missed, were identified, were again denied - the whole is a vapour in my memory which shifts as I try to define it. But clear enough is the picture I hold of myself, in a high chair, on the lefthand side of the sitting-room fireplace, the leaping flames reflected in the glass-case of tropical insects on the opposite wall, and my Father, leaning anxiously forward, with uplifted finger, emphasizing to me the pros and cons of the horrible carpet-bag evidence

I suppose that my interest in these discussions - and Heaven knows I was animated enough - amused and distracted my Father, whose idea of a suitable theme for childhood's ear now seems to me surprising. I soon found that these subjects were not welcome to everybody, for, starting the Carpet-bag Mystery one morning with Miss Marks, in the hope of delaying my arithmetic lesson, she fairly threw her apron over her ears and told me, from that vantage, that if I did not desist at once, she should scream.

Occasionally we took winter walks together, my Father and I, down some lane that led to a sight of the sea, or over the rolling downs. We tried to recapture the charm of those delightful strolls in London, when we used to lean over the bridges and watch the ducks. But we could not recover this pleasure. My Father was deeply enwoven in the chain of his own thoughts, and would stalk on, without a word, buried in angry reverie. If he spoke to me, on these excursions, it was a pain to me to answer him. I could talk on easy terms with him indoors, seated in my high chair, with our heads on a level, but it was intolerably laborious to look up into the firmament and converse with a dark face against the sky. The actual exercise of walking, too, was very exhausting to me; the bright red mud, to the strange colour of which I could not for a long while get accustomed, becoming caked about my little shoes, and wearying me extremely. I would grow petulant and cross, contradict my Father, and oppose his whims. These walks were distressing to us both, yet he did not like to walk alone, and he had no other friend. However, as the winter advanced, they had to be abandoned, and the habit of our taking a 'constitutional' together was never resumed.

I look back upon myself at this time as upon a cantankerous, ill-tempered and unobliging child. The only excuse I can offer is that I really was not well. The change to Devonshire had not suited me; my health gave the excellent Miss Marks some anxiety, but she was not ready in resource. The dampness of the house was terrible; indoors and out, the atmosphere seemed soaked in chilly vapours. Under my bed-clothes at night I shook like a jelly, unable to sleep for cold, though I was heaped with coverings, while my skin was all puckered with gooseflesh. I could eat nothing solid, without suffering immediately from violent hiccough, so that much of my time was spent lying prone on my back upon the hearthrug, awakening the echoes like a cuckoo. Miss Marks, therefore, cut off all food but milk-sop, a loathly bowl of which appeared at every meal. In consequence the hiccough lessened, but my strength declined with it. I languished in a perpetual catarrh. I was roused to a consciousness that I was not considered well by the fact that my Father prayed publicly at morning and evening 'worship' that if it was the Lord's will to take me to himself there might be no doubt whatever about my being a sealed child of God and an inheritor of glory. I was partly disconcerted by, partly vain of, this open advertisement of my ailments.

Of our dealings with the 'Saints', a fresh assortment of whom met us on our arrival in Devonshire, I shall speak presently. My Father's austerity of behaviour was, I think, perpetually accentuated by his fear of doing anything to offend the consciences of these persons, whom he supposed, no doubt, to be more sensitive than they really were. He was fond of saying that 'a very little stain upon the conscience makes a wide breach in our communion with God', and he counted possible errors of conduct by hundreds and by thousands. It was in this winter that his attention was particularly drawn to the festival of Christmas, which, apparently, he had scarcely noticed in London.

On the subject of all feasts of the Church he held views of an almost grotesque peculiarity. He looked upon each of them as nugatory and worthless, but the keeping of Christmas appeared to him by far the most hateful, and nothing less than an act of idolatry. 'The very word is Popish,' he used to exclaim, 'Christ's Mass!' pursing up his lips with the gesture of one who tastes assafoetida[14] by accident. Then he would adduce the antiquity of the so-called feast, adapted from horrible heathen rites, and itself a soiled relic of the abominable Yule-Tide. He would denounce the horrors of Christmas until it almost made me blush to look at a holly-berry.

On Christmas Day of this year 1857 our villa saw a very unusual sight. My Father had given strictest charge that no difference whatever was to be made in our meals on that day; the dinner was to be neither more copious than usual nor less so. He was obeyed, but the servants, secretly rebellious, made a small plum-pudding for themselves. (I discovered afterwards, with pain, that Miss Marks received a slice of it in her boudoir.) Early in the afternoon, the maids, – of whom we were now advanced to keeping two, – kindly remarked that 'the poor dear child ought to have a bit, anyhow', and wheedled me into the kitchen, where I ate a slice of plum-pudding. Shortly I began to feel that pain inside which in my frail state was inevitable, and my conscience smote me violently. At length I could bear my spiritual anguish no longer, and bursting into the study I called out: 'Oh! Papa, Papa, I have eaten of flesh offered to idols!' It took some time, between my sobs, to explain what had happened. Then my Father sternly said:

'Where is the accursed thing?' I explained that as much as was left of it was still on the kitchen table He took me by the hand, and ran with me into the midst of the startled servants, seized what remained of the pudding, and with the plate in one hand and me still tight in the other, ran till we reached the dust-heap, when he flung the idolatrous confectionery on to the middle of the ashes, and then raked it deep down into the mass. The suddenness, the violence, the velocity of this extraordinary act made an impression on my memory which nothing will ever efface

The key is lost by which I might unlock the perverse malady from which my Father's conscience seemed to suffer during the whole of this melancholy winter. But I think that a disloca-tion of his intellectual system had a great deal to do with it. Up to this point in his career, he had, as we have seen, nourished the delusion that science and revelation could be mutually justified, that some sort of compromise was possible. With great and ever greater distinctness, his investigations had shown him that in all departments of organic nature there are visible the evidences of slow modification of forms, of the type de-veloped by the pressure and practice of aeons. This conviction had been borne in upon him until it was positively irresistible. Where was his place, then, as a sincere and accurate observer? Manifestly, it was with the pioneers of the new truth, it was with Darwin, Wallace and Hooker. But did not the second chapter of 'Genesis' say that in six days the heavens and earth were finished, and the host of them, and that on the seventh day God ended his work which he had made?

Here was a dilemma! Geology certainly *seemed* to be true, but the Bible, which was God's word, *was* true. If the Bible said that all things in Heaven and Earth were created in six days, created in six days they were, – in six literal days of twenty-four hours each. The evidences of spontaneous varia-tion of form, acting, over an immense space of time, upon ever-modifying organic structures, *seemed* overwhelming, but they must either be brought into line with the six-day labour of creation, or they must be rejected. I have already shown how my Father worked out the ingenious 'Omphalos' theory in order to justify himself as a strictly scientific observer who was also a humble slave of revelation. But the old convention and the new rebellion would alike have none of his compromise.

To a mind so acute and at the same time so narrow as that of my Father – a mind which is all logical and positive without breadth, without suppleness and without imagination – to be subjected to a check of this kind is agony. It has not the relief of a smaller nature, which escapes from the dilemma by some foggy formula; nor the resolution of a larger nature to take to its wings and surmount the obstacle. My Father, although half suffocated by the emotion of being lifted, as it were, on the great biological wave, never dreamed of letting go his clutch of the ancient tradition, but hung there, strained and buffeted. It is extraordinary that he – an 'honest hodman of science', as Huxley[15] once called him – should not have been content to allow others, whose horizons were wider than his could be, to pursue those purely intellectual surveys for which he had no species of aptitude. As a collector of facts and marshaller of observations, he had not a rival in that age; his very absence of imagination aided him in this work. But he was more an attorney than philosopher, and he lacked that sublime humility which is the crown of genius. For, this obstinate persuasion that he alone knew the mind of God, that he alone could interpret the designs of the Creator, what did it result from if not from a congenital lack of that highest modesty which replies 'I do not know' even to the questions which Faith, with menacing finger, insists on having most positively answered?

CHAPTER VI

During the first year of our life in Devonshire, the ninth year of my age, my Father's existence, and therefore mine, was almost entirely divided between attending to the little community of 'Saints' in the village and collecting, examining and describing marine creatures from the sea-shore. In the course of these twelve months, we had scarcely any social distractions of any kind, and I never once crossed the bounds of the parish. After the worst of the winter was over, my Father recovered much of his spirits and his power of work, and the earliest sunshine soothed and refreshed us both. I was still almost always with him, but we had now some curious companions.

The village, at the southern end of which our villa stood, was not pretty. It had no rural picturesqueness of any kind. The only pleasant feature of it, the handsome and ancient parish church, with its umbrageous churchyard, was then almost entirely concealed by a congeries of mean shops, which were ultimately, before the close of my childhood, removed. The village consisted of two parallel lines of contiguous houses, all white-washed and most of them fronted by trifling shop-windows; for half a mile this street ascended to the church, and then it descended for another half-mile, ending suddenly in fields, the hedges of which displayed, at intervals, the inevitable pollard elm-tree. The walk through the village, which we seemed to make incessantly, was very wearisome to me. I dreaded the rudeness of the children, and there was nothing in the shops to amuse me. Walking on the inch or two of broken pavement in front of the houses was disagreeable and tiresome, and the foetor which breathed on close days from the open doors and windows made me feel faint. But this walk was obligatory, since the 'Public Room', as our little chapel was called, lay at the farther extremity of the dreary street.

We attended this place of worship immediately on our arrival, and my Father, uninvited but unresisted, immediately assumed the administration of it. It was a square, empty room, built, for I know not what purpose, over a stable. Ammoniac odours used to rise through the floor as we sat there at our long devotions. Before our coming, a little flock of persons met in the Room, a community of the indefinite sort just then becoming frequent in the West of England, pious rustics connected with no other recognized body of Christians, and depending directly on the independent study of the Bible. They were largely women, but there was more than a sprinkling of men, poor, simple and generally sickly. In later days, under my Father's ministration, the body increased and positively flourished. It came to include retired professional men, an admiral, nay, even the brother of a peer. But in those earliest years the 'brethren' and 'sisters' were all of them ordinary peasants. They were jobbing gardeners and journeymen carpenters, masons and tailors, washer-women and domestic servants. I wish that I could paint, in colours so vivid that my readers could perceive what their little society consisted of, this quaint collection of humble, conscientious, ignorant and gentle persons. In chronicle or fiction I have never been fortunate enough to meet with anything which resembled them. The caricatures of enmity and worldly scorn are as crude, to my memory, as the unction of religious conventionality is featureless.

The origin of the meeting had been odd. A few years before we came, a crew of Cornish fishermen, quite unknown to the villagers, were driven by stress of weather into the haven under the cliff. They landed, and, instead of going to a public-house, they looked about for a room where they could hold a prayer-meeting. They were devout Wesleyans; they had come from the open sea, they were far from home, and they had been starved by lack of their customary religious privileges. As they stood about in the street before their meeting, they challenged the respectable girls who came out to stare at them, with the question, 'Do you love the Lord Jesus, my maid?' Receiving dubious answers, they pressed the inhabitants to come in and pray with them, which several did. Ann Burmington, who long afterwards told me about it, was one of those girls, and she repeated that the fishermen said, 'What a dreadful thing it will be, at the Last Day, when the Lord says, "Come, ye blessed", and says it not to you, and then, "Depart ye cursed", and you maidens have to depart.' They were finely-built young men, with black beards and shining eyes, and I do not question that some flash of sex unconsciously mingled with the curious episode, although their behaviour was in all respects discreet. It was, perhaps, not wholly a coincidence that almost all those particular girls remained unmarried to the end of their lives. After two or three days, the fishermen went off to sea again. They prayed and sailed away, and the girls, who had not even asked their names, never heard of them again. But several of the young women were definitely converted, and they formed the nucleus of our little gathering.

My Father preached, standing at a desk; or celebrated the communion in front of a deal table, with a white napkin spread over it. Sometimes the audience was so small, generally so unexhilarating, that he was discouraged, but he never flagged in energy and zeal. Only those who had given evidence of intelligent acceptance of the theory of simple faith in their atonement through the Blood of Jesus were admitted to the communion, or, as it was called, 'the Breaking of Bread'. It was made a very strong point that no one should 'break bread', – unless for good reason shown – until he or she had been baptized, that is to say, totally immersed, in solemn conclave, by the ministering brother. This rite used, in our earliest days, to be performed, with picturesque simplicity, in the sea on the Oddicombe beach, but to this there were, even in those quiet years, extreme objections. A jeering crowd could scarcely be avoided, and women, in particular, shrank from the ordeal.

This used to be a practical difficulty, and my Father, when communicants confessed that they had not yet been baptized, would shake his head and say gravely, 'Ah! ah! you shun the Cross of Christ!' But that baptism in the sea on the open beach *was* a 'cross', he would not deny, and when we built our own little chapel, a sort of font, planked over, was arranged in the room itself.

Among these quiet, taciturn people, there were several whom I recall with affection. In this remote corner of Devonshire, on the road nowhither, they had preserved much of the air of that eighteenth century which the elders among them perfectly remembered. There was one old man, born before the French Revolution, whose figure often recurs to me. This was James Petherbridge, the Nestor of our meeting,[1] extremely tall and attenuated; he came on Sundays in a full, white smock-frock, smartly embroidered down the front, and when he settled himself to listen, he would raise this smock like a skirt, and reveal a pair of immensely long thin legs, cased in tight leggings, and ending in shoes with buckles. As the sacred message fell from my Father's lips the lantern jaws of Mr Petherbridge slowly fell apart, while his knees sloped to so immense a distance from one another that it seemed as though they never could meet again. He had been pious all his life, and he would tell us, in some modest pride, that when he was a lad, the farmer's wife who was his mistress used to say, 'I think our Jem is going to be a Methody, he do so hanker after godly discoursings.' Mr Petherbridge was accustomed to pray orally, at our prayer-meetings, in a funny old voice like wind in a hollow tree, and he seldom failed to express a hope that 'the Lord would support Miss Lafroy' – who was the village school-mistress, and one of our congregation, – 'in her labour of teaching the young idea how to shoot'. I, not understanding this literary allusion, long believed the school to be addicted to some species of pistol-practice.

The key of the Room was kept by Richard Moxhay, the mason, who was of a generation younger than Mr

Petherbridge, but yet 'getting on in years'. Moxhay, I cannot tell why, was always dressed in white corduroy, on which any stain of Devonshire scarlet mud was painfully conspicuous; when he was smartened up, his appearance suggested that somebody had given him a coating of that rich Western white-wash which looks like Devonshire cream. His locks were long and sparse, and as deadly black as his clothes were white. He was a modest, gentle man, with a wife even more meek and gracious than himself. They never, to my recollection, spoke unless they were spoken to, and their melancholy impassiveness used to vex my Father, who once, referring to the Moxhays, described them, sententiously but justly, as being 'laborious, but it would be an exaggeration to say happy, Christians'. Indeed, my memory pictures almost all the 'saints' of that early time as sad and humble souls, lacking vitality, yet not complaining of anything definite. A quite surprising number of them, it is true, male and female, suffered from different forms of consumption, so that the Room rang in winter evenings with a discord of hacking coughs. But it seems to me that, when I was quite young, half the inhabitants of our rural district were affected with phthisis.[2] No doubt, our peculiar religious community was more likely to attract the feeble members of a population, than to tempt the flush and the fair.

Miss Marks, patient pilgrim that she was, accepted this quaint society without a murmur, although I do not think it was much to her taste. But in a very short time it was sweetened to her by the formation of a devoted and romantic friendship for one of the 'sisters', who was, indeed, if my childish recollection does not fail me, a very charming person. The consequence of this enthusiastic alliance was that I was carried into the bosom of the family to which Miss Marks' new friend belonged, and of these excellent people I must give what picture I can. Almost opposite the Room, therefore at the far end of the village, across one of the rare small gardens (in which this first winter I discovered with rapture the magenta stars of a new flower, hepatica) – a shop-window displayed a thin row of plates and dishes, cups and saucers; above it was painted the name of Burmington. This china-shop was the property of three orphan sisters, Ann, Mary Grace, and Bess, the latter lately married to a carpenter, who was 'elder' at our meeting; the other two, resolute old maids. Ann, whom I have already mentioned, had been one of the girls converted by the Cornish fishermen. She was about ten years older than Bess, and Mary Grace came halfway between them. Ann was a very worthy woman, but masterful and passionate, suffering from an ungovernable temper, which at calmer moments she used to refer to, not without complacency, as 'the sin which doth most easily beset me'. Bess was insignificant, and vulgarized by domestic cares. But Mary Grace was a delightful creature.

The Burmingtons lived in what was almost the only old house surviving in the village. It was an extraordinary construction of two storeys, with vast rooms, and winding passages, and surprising changes of level. The sisters were poor, but very industrious, and never in anything like want; they sold, as I have said, crockery, and they took in washing, and did a little fine needlework, and sold the produce of a great, vague garden at the back. In process of time, the elder sisters took a young woman, whose name was Drusilla Elliott, to live with them as servant and companion; she was a converted person, worshipping with a kindred sect, the Bible Christians. I remember being much interested in hearing how Bess, before her marriage, became converted. Mary Grace, on account of her infirm health, slept alone in one room; in another, of vast size, stood a family four-poster, where Ann slept with Drusilla Elliott, and another bed in the same room took Bess. The sisters and their friend had been constantly praying that Bess might 'find peace', for she was still a stranger to salvation. One night, she suddenly called out, rather crossly, 'What are you two whispering about? Do go to sleep,' to which Ann replied: 'We are praying for you.' 'How do you know,' answered Bess, 'that I don't believe?' And then she told them that, that very night, when she was sitting in the shop, she had closed with

God's offer of redemption. Late in the night as it was, Ann and Drusilla could do no less than go in and waken Mary Grace, whom, however, they found awake, praying, she too, for the conversion of Bess. They told her the good news, and all four, kneeling in the darkness, gave thanks aloud to God for his infinite mercy.

It was Mary Grace Burmington who now became the romantic friend of Miss Marks, and a sort of second benevolence to me. She must have been under thirty years of age; she was very small, and she was distressingly deformed in the spine, but she had an animated, almost a sparkling countenance. When we first arrived in the village, Mary Grace was only just recovering from a gastric fever which had taken her close to the grave. I remember hearing that the vicar, a stout and pompous man at whom we always glared defiance, went, in Mary Grace's supposed extremity, to the Burmingtons' shop-door, and shouted: 'Peace be to this house,' intending to offer his ministrations, but that Ann, who was in one of her tantrums, positively hounded him from the doorstep and down the garden, in her passionate nonconformity. Mary Grace, however, recovered, and soon became, not merely Miss Marks' inseparable friend, but my Father's spiritual factotum. He found it irksome to visit the 'saints' from house to house, and Mary Grace Burmington gladly assumed this labour. She proved a most efficient coadjutor; searched out, cherished and confirmed any of those, especially the young, who were attracted by my Father's preaching, and for several years was a great joy and comfort to us all. Even when her illness so increased that she could no longer rise from her bed, she was a centre of usefulness and cheerfulness from that retreat, where she 'received', in a kind of rustic state, under a patchwork coverlid that was like a basket of flowers.

My Father, ever reflecting on what could be done to confirm my spiritual vocation, to pin me down, as it were, beyond any possibility of escape, bethought him that it would accustom me to what he called 'pastoral work in the Lord's service', if I accompanied Mary Grace on her visits from house to house If it is remembered that I was only eight and a half when this scheme was carried into practice, it will surprise no one to hear that it was not crowned with success. I disliked extremely this visitation of the poor. I felt shy, I had nothing to say, with difficulty could I understand their soft Devonian patois, and most of all — a signal perhaps of my neurotic condition - I dreaded and loathed the smells of their cottages. One had to run over the whole gamut of odours, some so faint that they embraced the nostril with a fairy kiss, others bluntly gross, of the 'knock-you-down' order; some sweet, with a dreadful sourness; some bitter, with a smack of rancid hair-oil. There were fine manly smells of the pigsty and the open drain, and these prided themselves on being all they seemed to be: but there were also feminine odours, masquerading as you knew not what, in which penny whiffs, vials of balm and opopanax, seemed to have become tainted, vaguely, with the residue of the slop-pail. It was not, I think, that the villagers were particularly dirty, but those were days before the invention of sanitary science, and my poor young nose was morbidly, nay ridiculously sensitive. I often came home from 'visiting the saints' absolutely incapable of eating the milk-sop, with brown sugar strewn over it, which was my evening meal.

There was one exception to my unwillingness to join in the pastoral labours of Mary Grace. When she announced, on a fine afternoon, that we were going to Pavor and Barton, I was always agog to start. These were two hamlets in our parish, and, I should suppose, the original home of its population. Pavor was, even then, decayed almost to extinction, but Barton preserved its desultory street of ancient, detached cottages. Each, however poor, had a wild garden round it, and, where the inhabitants possessed some pride in their surroundings, the roses and the jasmines and that distinguished creeper, which one sees nowhere at its best but in Devonshire cottage-gardens, – the stately cotoneaster, made the whole place a bower. Barton was in vivid contrast to our own harsh, open, squalid village, with its mean modern houses, its absence of all vegetation. The ancient thatched cottages of Barton were shut in by moist hills, and canopied by ancient trees; they were approached along a deep lane which was all a wonder and a revelation to me that spring, since, in the very words of Shelley: [3]

> There in the warm hedge grew lush eglantine,
>   Green cow-bind and the moonlight-coloured may,
> And cherry blossoms, and white cups, whose wine
>   Was the bright dew yet drained not by the day;
> And wild roses, and ivy serpentine
>   With its dark buds and leaves, wandering astray.

Around and beyond Barton there lay fairyland. All was mysterious, unexplored, rich with infinite possibilities. I should one day enter it, the sword of make-believe in my hand, the cap of courage on my head, 'when you are a big boy', said the oracle of Mary Grace. For the present, we had to content ourselves with being an unadventurous couple – a little woman, bent half double, and a preternaturally sedate small boy – as we walked very slowly, side by side, conversing on terms of high familiarity, in which Biblical and colloquial phrases were quaintly jumbled, through the sticky red mud of the Pavor lanes with Barton as a bourne before us.

When we came home, my Father would sometimes ask me for particulars. Where had we been, whom had we found at home, what testimony had those visited been able to give of the Lord's goodness to them, what had Mary Grace replied in the way of exhortation, reproof or condolence? These questions I hated at the time, but they were very useful to me, since they gave me the habit of concentrating my attention on what was going on in the course of our visits, in case I might be called upon to give a report. My Father was very kind in the matter; he cultivated my powers of expression, he did not snub me when I failed to be intelligent. But I overheard Miss Marks and Mary Grace discussing the whole question under the guise of referring to 'you know whom, not a hundred miles hence'.

fancying that I could not recognize their little ostrich because its head was in a bag of metaphor. I understood perfectly, and gathered that they both of them thought this business of my going into undrained cottages injudicious. Accordingly, I was by degrees taken 'visiting' only when Mary Grace was going into the country-hamlets, and then I was usually left outside, to skip among the flowers and stalk the butterflies.

I must not, however, underestimate the very prominent part taken all through this spring and summer of 1858 by the collection of specimens on the sea-shore. My Father had returned, the chagrin of his failure in theorizing now being mitigated, to what was his real work in life, the practical study of animal forms in detail. He was not a biologist, in the true sense of the term. That luminous indication which Flaubert gives of what the action of the scientific mind should be, *affranchissant l'esprit et pesant les mondes, sans haine, sans peur, sans pitié, sans amour et sans Dieu*,[4] was opposed in every segment to the attitude of my Father, who, nevertheless, was a man of very high scientific attainment. But, again I repeat, he was not a philosopher; he was incapable, by temperament and education, of forming broad generalizations and of escaping in a vast survey from the troublesome pettiness of detail. He saw everything through a lens, nothing in the immensity of nature. Certain senses were absent in him; I think that, with all his justice, he had no conception of the importance of liberty; with all his intelligence, the boundaries of the atmosphere in which his mind could think at all were always close about him; with all his faith in the Word of God, he had no confidence in the Divine Benevolence; and with all his passionate piety, he habitually mistook fear for love.

It was down on the shore, tramping along the pebbled terraces of the beach, clambering over the great blocks of fallen conglomerate which broke the white curve with rufous promontories that jutted into the sea, or, finally, bending over those shallow tidal pools in the limestone rocks which were our proper hunting-ground, – it was in such circumstances as these that my Father became most easy, most happy, most human. That hard look across his brows, which it wearied me to see, the look that came from sleepless anxiety of conscience, faded away, and left the dark countenance still always stern indeed, but serene and unupbraiding. Those pools were our mirrors, in which, reflected in the dark hyaline and framed by the sleek and shining fronds of oar-weed there used to appear the shapes of a middle-aged man and a funny little boy, equally eager, and, I almost find the presumption to say, equally well prepared for business.

If any one goes down to those shores now, if man or boy seeks to follow in our traces, let him realize at once, before he takes the trouble to roll up his sleeves, that his zeal will end in labour lost. There is nothing, now, where in our days there was so much. Then the rocks between tide and tide were submarine gardens of a beauty that seemed often to be fabulous, and was positively delusive, since, if we delicately lifted the weed-curtains of a windless pool, though we might for a moment see its sides and floor paven with living blossoms, ivory-white, rosy-red, orange and amethyst, yet all that panoply would melt away, furled into the hollow rock, if we so much as dropped a pebble in to disturb the magic dream.

Half a century ago, in many parts of the coast of Devonshire and Cornwall, where the limestone at the water's edge is wrought into crevices and hollows, the tide-line was, like Keats' Grecian vase, 'a still unravished bride of quietness'.[5] These cups and basins were always full, whether the tide was high or low, and the only way in which they were affected was that twice in the twenty-four hours they were replenished by cold streams from the great sea, and then twice were left brimming to be vivified by the temperate movement of the upper air. They were living flower-beds, so exquisite in their perfection, that my Father, in spite of his scientific requirements, used not seldom to pause before he began to rifle them, ejaculating that it was indeed a pity to disturb such congregated beauty. The antiquity of these rock-pools, and the infinite succession of the soft and radiant forms, sea-anemones, sea-weeds, shells, fishes, which had inhabited them, undisturbed since the creation of the world, used to occupy my Father's fancy. We burst in, he used to say, where no one had ever thought of intruding before; and if the Garden of Eden had been situate in Devonshire, Adam and Eve, stepping lightly down to bathe in the rainbow-coloured spray, would have seen the identical sights that we now saw, – the great prawns gliding like transparent launches, anthea waving in the twilight its thick white waxen tentacles, and the fronds of the dulse faintly streaming on the water, like huge red banners in some reverted atmosphere.

All this is long over, and done with. The ring of living beauty drawn about our shores was a very thin and fragile one. It had existed all those centuries solely in consequence of the indifference, the blissful ignorance of man. These rock-basins, fringed by corallines, filled with still water almost as pellucid as the upper air itself, thronged with beautiful sensitive forms of life, – they exist no longer, they are all profaned, and emptied, and vulgarized. An army of 'collectors' has passed over them, and ravaged every corner of them. The fairy paradise has been violated, the exquisite product of centuries of natural selection has been crushed under the rough paw of well-meaning, idle-minded curiosity. That my Father, himself so reverent, so conservative, had by the popularity of his books acquired the direct responsibility for a calamity that he had never anticipated became clear enough to himself before many years had passed, and cost him great chagrin. No one will see again on the shore of England what I saw in my early childhood, the submarine vision of dark rocks, speckled and starred with an infinite variety of colour, and streamed over by silken flags of royal crimson and purple.

In reviving these impressions, I am unable to give any exact chronological sequence to them. These particular adventures began early in 1858, they reached their greatest intensity in the summer of 1859, and they did not altogether cease, so far as my Father was concerned, until nearly twenty years later. But it was while he was composing what, as I am told by scientific men of today, continues to be his most valuable contribution to knowledge, his *History of the British Sea-Anemones and Corals*,[6] that we worked together on the shore for a definite purpose, and the last instalment of that still-classic volume was ready for press by the close of 1859.

The way in which my Father worked, in his most desperate escapades, was to wade breast-high into one of the huge pools, and examine the worm-eaten surface of the rock above and below the brim. In such remote places – spots where I could never venture, being left, a slightly timorous Andromeda, chained to a safer level of the cliff – in these extreme basins, there used often to lurk a marvellous profusion of animal and vegetable forms. My Father would search for the roughest and most corroded points of rock, those offering the best refuge for a variety of creatures, and would then chisel off fragments as low down in the water as he could. These pieces of rock were instantly plunged in the salt water of jars which we had brought with us for the purpose. When as much had been collected as we could carry away – my Father always dragged about an immense square basket, the creak of whose handles I can still fancy that I hear – we turned to trudge up the long climb home. Then all our prizes were spread out, face upward, in shallow pans of clean sea-water.

In a few hours, when all dirt had subsided, and what living creatures we had brought seemed to have recovered their composure, my work began. My eyes were extremely keen and powerful, though they were vexatiously near-sighted. Of no use in examining objects at any distance, in investigating a minute surface my vision was trained to be invaluable. The shallow pan, with our spoils, would rest on a table near the window, and I, kneeling on a chair opposite the light, would lean over the surface till everything was within an inch or two of my eyes. Often I bent, in my zeal, so far forward that the water touched the tip of my nose and gave me a little icy shock In this attitude – an idle spectator might have formed the impression that I was trying to wash my head and could not quite summon up resolution enough to plunge – in this odd pose I would remain for a long time, holding my breath and examining with extreme care every atom of rock, every swirl of detritus. This was a task which my Father could only perform by the help of a lens, with which, of course, he took care to supplement my examination. But that my survey was of use, he has himself most handsomely testified in his *Actinologia Britannica*,[7] where he expresses his debt to the 'keen and well-practised eye of my little son'. Nor, if boasting is not to be excluded, is it every eminent biologist, every proud and masterful F.R.S., who can lay his hand on his heart and swear that, before reaching the age of ten years, he had added, not merely a new species, but a new genus to the British fauna. That however, the author of these pages can do, who, on 29 June 1859, discovered a tiny atom, – and ran in the greatest agitation to announce the discovery of that object 'as a form with which he was unacquainted', – which figures since then on all lists of sea-anemones as phellia murocincta, or the walled corklet. Alas! that so fair a swallow should have made no biological summer in after-life.

These delicious agitations by the edge of the salt sea wave must have greatly improved my health, which however was still looked upon as fragile. I was loaded with coats and comforters, and strolled out between Miss Marks and Mary Grace Burmington, a muffled ball of flannel. This alone was enough to give me a look of delicacy, which the 'saints', in their blunt way, made no scruple of commenting upon to my face. I was greatly impressed by a conversation held over my bed one evening by the servants. Our cook, Susan, a person of enormous size, and Kate, the tattling, tiresome parlour-maid who waited upon us, on the summer evening I speak of were standing – I cannot tell why – on each side of my bed. I shut my eyes, and lay quite still, in order to escape conversing with them, and they spoke to one another. 'Ah, poor lamb,' Kate said trivially, *'he's* not long for this world; going home to

Jesus, he is, – m a jiffy, I should say by the look of 'un.' But Susan answered: 'Not so. I dreamed about 'un, and I know for sure that he is to be spared for missionary service.' 'Missionary service?' repeated Kate, impressed. 'Yes,' Susan went on, with solemn emphasis, 'he'll bleed for his Lord in heathen parts, that's what the future have in store for '*im*.' When they were gone, I beat upon the coverlid with my fists, and I determined that whatever happened, I would not, not, *not*, go out to preach the Gospel among horrid, tropical niggers.

CHAPTER VII

In the history of an infancy so cloistered and uniform as mine, such a real adventure as my being publicly and successfully kidnapped cannot be overlooked. There were several 'innocents' in our village, harmless eccentrics who had more or less unquestionably crossed the barrier which divides the sane from the insane. They were not discouraged by public opinion; indeed, several of them were favoured beings, suspected by my Father of exaggerating their mental density in order to escape having to work, like dogs, who, as we all know, could speak as well as we do, were they not afraid of being made to fetch and carry. Miss Mary Flaw was not one of these imbeciles. She was what the French call a *détraquée*;[1] she had enjoyed a good intelligence and an active mind, but her wits had left the rails and were careering about the country. Miss Flaw was the daughter of a retired Baptist minister, and she lived, with I remember not what relations, in a little solitary house high up at Barton Cross, whither Mary Grace and I would sometimes struggle when our pastoral duties were over. In later years, when I met with those celebrated verses in which the philosopher expresses the hope[2]

> In the downhill of life, when I find I'm declining,
> May my lot no less fortunate be
> Than a snug elbow-chair can afford for reclining,
> And a cot that o'erlooks the wide sea

my thoughts returned instinctively, and they still return, to the high abode of Miss Flaw. There was a porch at her door, both for shelter and shade, and it was covered with jasmine: but the charm of the place was a summer-house close by, containing a table, encrusted with cowry-shells, and seats from which one saw the distant waters of the bay. At the entrance to this grot there was always set a 'snug elbow-chair', destined, I suppose, for the Rev. Mr Flaw, or else left there in pious memory of him, since I cannot recollect whether he was alive or dead.

I delighted in these visits to Mary Flaw. She always received us with effusion, tripping forward to meet us, and leading us, each by a hand held high, with a dancing movement which I thought infinitely graceful, to the cowry-shell bower, where she would regale us with Devonshire cream and with small hard biscuits that were like pebbles. The conversation of Mary Flaw was a great treat to me. I enjoyed its irregularities, its waywardness; it was like a tune that wandered into several keys. As Mary Grace Burmington put it, one never knew what dear Mary Flaw would say next, and that she did not herself know added to the charm. She had become crazed, poor thing, in consequence of a disappointment in love, but of course I did not know that, nor that she was crazed at all. I thought her brilliant and original, and I liked her very much. In the light of coming events, it would be affectation were I to pretend that she did not feel a similar partiality for me.

Miss Flaw was, from the first, devoted to my Father's ministrations, and it was part of our odd village indulgence that no one ever dreamed of preventing her from coming to the Room. On Sunday evenings the bulk of the audience was arranged on forms, with backs to them, set in the middle of the floor, with a passage round them, while other forms were placed against the walls. My Father preached from a lectern, facing the audience. If darkness came on in the course of the service, Richard Moxhay, glimmering in his cream-white corduroys, used to go slowly round, lighting groups of tallow candles by the help of a box of lucifers. Mary Flaw always assumed the place of honour, on the left extremity of the front bench, immediately opposite my Father. Miss Marks and Mary Grace, with me ensconced and almost buried between them, occupied the right of the same bench. While the lighting proceeded, Miss Flaw used to direct it from her seat silently, by pointing out to Moxhay, who took no notice, what groups of candles he should light next. She did this just as the clown in the circus directs the grooms how to move the furniture and Moxhay paid no more attention to her than the grooms do to the clown. Miss Flaw had another peculiarity: she silently went through a service exactly similar to ours, but much briefer. The course of our evening service was this. My Father prayed, and we all knelt down: then he gave out a hymn and most of us stood up to sing; then he preached for about an hour, while we sat and listened; then a hymn again, then prayer and the valediction.

Mary Flaw went through this ritual, but on a smaller scale. We all knelt down together, but when we rose from our knees, Miss Flaw was already standing up, and was pretending, without a sound, to sing a hymn: in the midst of our hymn, she sat down, opened her Bible, found a text, and then leaned back, her eyes fixed in space, listening to an imaginary sermon which our own real one soon caught up, and coincided with for about three-quarters of an hour. Then, while our sermon went peacefully on, Miss Flaw would rise, and sing in silence (if I am permitted to use such an expression) her own visionary hymn; then she would kneel down and pray, then rise, collect her belongings, and sweep, in fairy majesty, out of the chapel, my Father still rounding his periods from the pulpit. Nobody ever thought of preventing these movements, or of checking the poor creature in her innocent flightiness, until the evening of the great event.

It was all my own fault. Mary Flaw had finished her imaginary service earlier than usual. She had stood up alone with her hymn-book before her; she had flung herself on her knees alone, in the attitude of devotion; she had risen; she had seated herself for a moment to put on her gloves, and to collect her Bible, her hymn-book and her pocket-handkerchief in her reticule. She was ready to start, and she looked around her with a pleasant air; my Father, all undisturbed, booming away meanwhile over our heads. I know not why the manoeuvres of Miss Flaw especially attracted me that evening, but I leaned out across Miss Marks and I caught Miss Flaw's eye. She nodded, I nodded; and the amazing deed was done, I hardly know how. Miss Flaw, with incredible swiftness, flew along the line, plucked me by the coat-collar from between my paralysed protectresses, darted with me down the chapel and out into the dark, before any one had time to say 'Jack Robinson'.

My Father gazed from the pulpit and the stream of exhortation withered on his lips. No one in the body of the audience stirred; no one but himself had clearly seen what had happened. Vague rows of 'saints' with gaping countenances stared up at him, while he shouted, 'Will nobody stop them?' as we whisked out through the doorway. Forth into the moist night we went, and up the lampless village, where, a few minutes later, the swiftest of the congregation, with my Father at their head, found us sitting on the doorstep of the butcher's shop. My captor was now quite quiet, and made no objection to my quitting her, – 'without a single kiss or a goodbye', as the poet says.

Although I had scarcely felt frightened at the time, doubtless my nerves were shaken by this escapade, and it may have had something to do with the recurrence of the distressing visions from which I had suffered as a very little child. These came back, with a force and expansion due to my increased maturity. I had hardly laid my head down on the pillow, than, as it seemed to me, I was taking part in a mad gallop through space. Some force, which had tight hold of me, so that I felt myself an atom in its grasp, was hurrying me on, over an endless slender bridge, under which on either side a loud torrent rushed at a vertiginous depth below. At first our helpless flight, – for I was bound hand and foot like Mazeppa,[3] – proceeded in a straight line, but presently it began to curve, and we raced and roared along, in what gradually became a monstrous vortex, reverberant with noises, loud with light, while, as we proceeded, enormous concentric circles engulfed us, and wheeled above and about us. It seemed as if we, – I, that is, and the undefined force which carried me, – were pushing feverishly on towards a goal which our whole concentrated energies were bent on reaching, but which a frenzied despair in my heart told me we never could reach, yet the attainment of which alone could save us from destruction. Far away, in the pulsation of the great luminous whorls, I could just see that goal, a ruby-coloured point waxing and waning, and it bore, or to be exact it consisted of, the letters of the word CARMINE.

This agitating vision recurred night after night, and filled me with inexpressible distress. The details of it altered very little, and I knew what I had to expect when I crept into bed. I knew that for a few minutes I should be battling with the chill of the linen sheets, and trying to keep awake, but that then, without a pause, I should slip into that terrible realm of storm and stress in which I was bound hand and foot, and sent galloping through infinity. Often have I wakened, with unutterable joy, to find my Father and Miss Marks, whom my screams had disturbed, standing one on each side of my bed. They could release me from my nightmare, which seldom assailed me twice a night, but how to preserve me from its original attack passed their understanding. My Father, in his tenderness, thought to exorcize the demon by prayer. He would appear in the bedroom, just as I was first slipping into bed, and he would kneel at my side. The light from a candle on the mantel-shelf streamed down upon his dark head of hair while his face was buried in the coverlid, from which a loud voice came up, a little muffled, begging that I might be preserved against all the evil spirits that walk in darkness and that the deep might not swallow me up.

This little ceremony gave a distraction to my thoughts, and may have been useful in that way. But it led to an unfortunate circumstance. My Father began to enjoy these orisons at my bedside, and to prolong them. Perhaps they lasted a little too long, but I contrived to keep awake through them, sometimes

by a great effort. On one unhappy night, however, I gave even
worse offence than slumber would have given. My Father was
praying aloud, in the attitude I have described, and I was half
sitting, half lying in bed, with the clothes sloping from my
chin. Suddenly a rather large insect, dark and flat, with more
legs than a self-respecting insect ought to need, appeared at the
bottom of the counterpane, and slowly advanced. I think it
was nothing worse than a beetle. It walked successfully past
my Father's sleek black ball of a head, and climbed straight up
at me, nearer, nearer, till it seemed all a twinkle of horns and
joints. I bore it in silent fascination till it almost tickled my
chin, and then I screamed 'Papa! Papa!' My Father rose in great
dudgeon, removed the insect (what were insects to him!) and
then gave me a tremendous lecture.

The sense of desperation which this incident produced I shall
not easily forget. Life seemed really to be very harassing when
to visions within and beetles without there was joined the
consciousness of having grievously offended God by an act of
disrespect. It is difficult for me to justify to myself the violent
jobation which my Father gave me in consequence of my
scream, except by attributing to him something of the human
weakness of vanity. I cannot help thinking that he liked to hear
himself speak to God in the presence of an admiring listener.
He prayed with fervour and animation, in pure Johnsonian
English, and I hope I am not undutiful if I add my impression
that he was not displeased with the sound of his own devotions.
My cry for help had needlessly, as he thought, broken in upon
this holy and seemly performance. 'You, the child of a naturalist,' he remarked in awesome tones, '*you* to pretend to feel
terror at the advance of an insect?' It could but be a pretext, he
declared, for avoiding the testimony of faith in prayer. 'If your
heart were fixed, if it panted after the Lord, it would take
more than the movements of a beetle to make you disturb oral
supplication at His footstool. Beware! for God is a jealous God
and He consumes them in wrath who make a noise like a dog.'

My Father took at all times a singular pleasure in repeating that 'our God is a jealous God'. He liked the word, which I suppose he used in an antiquated sense. He was accustomed to tell the 'saints' at the room, – in a very genial manner, and smiling at them as he said it, – 'I am jealous over you, my beloved brothers and sisters, with a godly jealousy ' I know that this was interpreted by some of the saints, – for I heard Mary Grace say so to Miss Marks – as meaning that my Father was resentful because some of them attended the service at the Wesleyan chapel on Thursday evenings. But my Father was utterly incapable of such littleness as this, and when he talked of 'jealousy' he meant a lofty solicitude, a careful watchfulness. He meant that their spiritual honour was a matter of anxiety to him. No doubt when he used to tell me to remember that our God is a jealous God, he meant that my sins and shortcomings were not matters of indifference to the Divine Being. But I think, looking back, that it was very extraordinary for a man, so instructed and so intelligent as he, to dwell so much on the possible anger of the Lord, rather than on his pity and love The theory of extreme Puritanism can surely offer no quainter example of its fallacy than this idea that the omnipotent Jehovah could be seriously offended, and could stoop to revenge, because a little, nervous child of nine had disturbed a prayer by being frightened at a beetle.

The fact that the word 'Carmine' appeared as the goal of my visionary pursuits is not so inexplicable as it may seem My Father was at this time producing numerous water-colour drawings of minute and even of microscopic forms of life. These he executed in the manner of miniature, with an amazing fidelity of form and with a brilliancy of colour which remains unfaded after fifty years. By far the most costly of his pigments was the intense crimson which is manufactured out of the very spirit and essence of cochineal. I had lately become a fervent imitator of his works of art, and I was allowed to use all of his colours, except one; I was strictly forbidden to let a hair of my paint-brush touch the little broken mass of carmine which was all that he possessed. We believed, but I do not know whether this could be the fact, that carmine of this superlative quality was sold at a guinea a cake. 'Carmine', therefore, became my shibboleth of self-indulgence; it was a symbol of all that taste and art and wealth could combine to produce. I imagined, for instance, that at Belshazzar's feast, the loftiest epergne of gold, surrounded by flowers and jewels, carried the monarch's proudest possession, a cake of carmine. I knew of no object in the world of luxury more desirable than this, and its obsession in my waking hours is quite enough, I think, to account for 'carmine' having been the torment of my dreams.

The little incident of the beetle displays my Father's mood at this period in its worst light. His severity was not very creditable, perhaps, to his good sense, but without a word of explanation it may seem even more unreasonable than it was. My Father might have been less stern to my lapses from high conduct, and my own mind at the same time less armoured against his arrows, if our relations had been those which exist in an ordinary religious family. He would have been more indulgent, and my own affections might nevertheless have been more easily alienated, if I had been treated by him as a commonplace child, standing as yet outside the pale of conscious Christianity. But he had formed the idea, and cultivated it assiduously, that I was an *âme d'élite*,[4] a being to whom the mysteries of salvation had been divinely revealed and by whom they had been accepted. I was, to his partial fancy, one in whom the Holy Ghost had already performed a real and peranent work. Hence, I was inside the pale; I had attained that inner position which divided, as we used to say, the Sheep from the Goats. Another little boy might be very well-behaved, but if he had not consciously 'laid hold on Christ', his good deeds, so far, were absolutely useless. Whereas I might be a very naughty boy, and require much chastisement from God and man, but nothing – so my Father thought – could invalidate my election, and sooner or later, perhaps even after many stripes, I must inevitably be brought back to a state of grace.

The paradox between this unquestionable sanctification by faith and my equally unquestionable naughtiness, occupied my Father greatly at this time. He made it a frequent subject of intercession at family prayers, not caring to hide from the servants misdemeanours of mine, which he spread out with a melancholy unction before the Lord. He cultivated the belief that all my little ailments, all my aches and pains, were sent to correct my faults. He carried this persuasion very far, even putting this exhortation before, instead of after, an instant relief of my sufferings. If I burned my finger with a sulphur match, or pinched the end of my nose in the door (to mention but two sorrows that recur to my memory), my Father would solemnly ejaculate: 'O may these afflictions be much sanctified to him!' before offering any remedy for my pain. So that I almost longed, under the pressure of these pangs, to be a godless child, who had never known the privileges of saving grace, since I argued that such a child would be subjected to none of the sufferings which seemed to assail my path.

What the ideas or conduct of 'another child' might be I had, however, at this time no idea, for, strange as it may sound, I had not, until my tenth year was far advanced, made acquaintance with any such creature. The 'saints' had children, but I was not called upon to cultivate their company, and I had not the slightest wish to do so. But early in 1859 I was allowed, at last, to associate with a child of my own age. I do not recall that this permission gave me any rapture; I accepted it philosophically but without that delighted eagerness which I might have been expected to show, My earliest companion, then, was a little boy of almost exactly my own age. His name was Benny, which no doubt was short for Benjamin. His surname was Jeffries; his mother – I think he had no father – was a solemn and shadowy lady of means who lived in a villa, which was older and much larger than ours, on the opposite side of the road. Going to 'play with Benny' involved a small public excursion, and this I was now allowed to make by myself – an immense source of self-respect.

Everything in my little memories seems to run askew; obviously I ought to have been extremely stirred and broadened by this earliest association with a boy of my own age! Yet I cannot truly say that it was so. Benny's mother possessed what seemed to me a vast domain, with lawns winding among broad shrubberies, and a kitchen-garden, with aged fruit-trees in it. The ripeness of this place, mossed and leafy, was gratifying to my senses, on which the rawness of our own bald garden jarred. There was an old brick wall between the two divisions, upon which it was possible for us to climb up, and from this we gained Pisgah-views [5] which were a prodigious pleasure. But I had not the faintest idea how to 'play'; I had never learned, had never heard of any 'games'. I think Benny must have lacked initiative almost as much as I did. We walked about, and shook the bushes, and climbed along the wall; I think that was almost all we did do. And, sadly enough, I cannot recover a phrase from Benny's lips, nor an action, nor a gesture, although I remember quite clearly how some grown-up people of that time looked, and the very words they said.

For example, I recollect Miss Wilkes very distinctly, since I studied her with great deliberation and with a suspicious watchfulness that was above my years. In Miss Wilkes a type that had hitherto been absolutely unfamiliar to us obtruded upon our experience. In our Eveless Eden, Woman, if not exactly *hirsuta et horrida*, [6] had always been 'of a certain age'. But Miss Wilkes was a comparatively young thing, and she advanced not by any means unconscious of her charms. All was feminine, all was impulsive, about Miss Wilkes; every gesture seemed eloquent with girlish innocence and the playful dawn of life. In actual years I fancy she was not so extremely youthful, since she was the responsible and trusted headmistress of a large boarding-school for girls, but in her heart the joy of life ran high. Miss Wilkes had a small, round face, with melting eyes, and when she lifted her head, her ringlets seemed to vibrate and shiver like the bells of a pagoda. She had a charming way of clasping her hands, and holding them against her bodice, while she said, 'O, but – really now?' in a manner inexpressibly engaging. She was very earnest, and she had a pleading way of calling out: 'O, but aren't you teasing me?' which would have brought a tiger fawning to her crinoline.

After we had spent a full year without any social distractions, it seems that our circle of acquaintances had now begun to extend, in spite of my Father's unwillingness to visit his neighbours. He was a fortress that required to be stormed, but there was considerable local curiosity about him, so that by-and-by escalading parties were formed, some of which were partly successful. In the first place, Charles Kingsley had never hesitated to come, from the beginning, ever since our arrival. He had reason to visit our neighbouring town rather frequently, and on such occasions he always marched up and attacked us. It was extraordinary how persistent he was, for my Father must have been a very trying friend. I vividly recollect that a sort of cross-examination of would-be communicants was going on in our half-furnished drawing-room one week-day morning, when Mr Kingsley was announced; my Father, in stentorian tones, replied: 'Tell Mr Kingsley that I am engaged in examining Scripture with certain of the Lord's children.' And I, a little later, kneeling at the window, while the candidates were being dismissed with prayer, watched the author of *Hypatia*[7] nervously careering about the garden, very restless and impatient, yet preferring this ignominy to the chance of losing my Father's company altogether. Kingsley, a daring spirit, used sometimes to drag us out trawling with him in Torbay, and although his hawk's beak and rattling voice frightened me a little, his was always a jolly presence that brought some refreshment to our seriousness.

But the other visitors who came in Kingsley's wake and without his excuse, how they disturbed us! We used to be seated, my Father at his microscope, I with my map or book, in the down-stairs room we called the study. There would be a hush around us in which you could hear a sea-anemone sigh. Then, abruptly, would come a ring at the front door my

Father would bend at me a corrugated brow, and murmur, under his breath, 'What's that?' and then, at the sound of footsteps, would bolt into the verandah, and round the garden into the potting-shed. If it was no visitor more serious than the postman or the tax-gatherer, I used to go forth and coax the timid wanderer home. If it was a caller, above all a female caller, it was my privilege to prevaricate, remarking innocently that 'Papa is out!'

Into a paradise so carefully guarded, I know not how that serpent Miss Wilkes could penetrate, but there she was. She 'broke bread' with the Brethren at the adjacent town, from which she carried on strategical movements, which were, up to a certain point, highly successful. She professed herself deeply interested in microscopy, and desired that some of her young ladies should study it also. She came attended by an unimport-ant mamma, and by pupils to whom I had sometimes, very unwillingly, to show our 'natural objects'. They would invade us, and all our quietness, with chattering noise; I could bear none of them, and I was singularly drawn to Miss Marks by finding that she disliked them too.

By whatever arts she worked, Miss Wilkes certainly achieved a certain ascendancy. When the knocks came at the front door, I was now instructed to see whether the visitor were not she, before my Father bolted to the potting-shed. She was an untir-ing listener, and my Father had a genius for instruction. Miss Wilkes was never weary of expressing what a revelation of the wonderful works of God in creation her acquaintance with us had been. She would gaze through the microscope at awful forms, and would persevere until the silver rim which marked the confines of the drop of water under inspection would ripple inwards with a flash of light and vanish, because the drop itself had evaporated. 'Well, I can only say, how marvellous are Thy doings!' was a frequent ejaculation of Miss Wilkes, and one that was very well received. She learned the Latin names of many of the species, and it seems quite pathetic to me, looking back, to realize how much trouble the poor woman took. She 'hung', as the expression is, upon my Father's every word, and one instance of this led to a certain revelation.

My Father, who had an extraordinary way of saying anything that came up into his mind, stated one day, – the fashions, I must suppose, being under discussion, – that he thought white the only becoming colour for a lady's stockings. The stockings of Miss Wilkes had up to that hour been of a deep violet, but she wore white ones in future whenever she came to our house. This delicacy would have been beyond my unaided infant observation, but I heard Miss Marks mention the matter, in terms which they supposed to be secret, to her confidante, and I verified it at the ankles of the lady. Miss Marks continued by saying, in confidence, and 'quite as between you and me, dear Mary Grace', that Miss Wilkes was a 'minx' I had the greatest curiosity about words, and as this was a new one, I looked it up in our large English Dictionary. But there the definition of the term was this: – 'Minx: the female of minnock, a pert wanton.' I was as much in the dark as ever.

Whether she was the female of a minnock (whatever that may be) or whether she was only a very well-meaning schoolmistress desirous of enlivening a monotonous existence, Miss Wilkes certainly took us out of ourselves a good deal. Did my Father know what danger he ran? It was the opinion of Miss Marks and of Mary Grace that he did not, and in the back-kitchen, a room which served those ladies as a private oratory in the summer-time, much prayer was offered up that his eyes might be opened ere it was too late. But I am inclined to think that they were open all the time, that, at all events, they were what the French call *entr' ouvert*,[8] that enough light for practical purposes came sifted in through his eyelashes. At a later time, being reminded of Miss Wilkes, he said with a certain complaisance, 'Ah, yes! she proffered much entertainment during my widowed years!' He used to go down to her boarding-school, the garden of which had been the scene of a murder, and was romantically situated on the edge of a quarried cliff, he always took me with him, and kept me at his side all

through these visits, notwithstanding Miss Wilkes' solicitude
that the fatigue and excitement would be too much for the
dear child's strength, unless I rested a little on the parlour sofa.

About this time, the question of my education came up for
discussion in the household, as indeed it well might. Miss Marks
had long proved practically inadequate in this respect, her slender acquirements evaporating, I suppose, like the drops of water
under the microscope, while the field of her general duties
became wider. The subjects in which I took pleasure, and upon
which I possessed books, I sedulously taught myself; the other
subjects, which formed the vast majority, I did not learn at all.
Like Aurora Leigh,[9]

> I brushed with extreme flounce
> The circle of the universe,

especially zoology, botany and astronomy, but with the explicit
exception of geology, which my Father regarded as tending
directly to the encouragement of infidelity. I copied a great
quantity of maps, and read all the books of travels that I could
find. But I acquired no mathematics, no languages, no history,
so that I was in danger of gross illiteracy in these important
departments.

My Father grudged the time, but he felt it a duty to do
something to fill up these deficiencies, and we now started
Latin, in a little eighteenth-century reading-book, out of which
my Grandfather had been taught. It consisted of strings of
words, and of grim arrangements of conjunction and declen-
sion, presented in a manner appallingly unattractive. I used
to be set down in the study, under my Father's eye, to learn
a solid page of this compilation, while he wrote or painted.
The window would be open in summer, and my seat was close
to it. Outside, a bee was shaking the clematis-blossom, or a
red-admiral butterfly was opening and shutting his wings on
the hot concrete of the verandah, or a blackbird was racing
across the lawn. It was almost more than human nature could
bear to have to sit holding up to my face the dreary little

Latin book, with its sheepskin cover that smelt of mildewed paste.

But out of this strength there came an unexpected sudden sweetness. The exercise of hearing me repeat my strings of nouns and verbs had revived in my Father his memories of the classics. In the old solitary years, a long time ago, by the shores of Canadian rapids, on the edge of West Indian swamps, his Virgil had been an inestimable solace to him. To extremely devout persons, there is something objectionable in most of the great writers of antiquity. Horace, Lucretius, Terence, Catullus, Juvenal, – in each there is one quality or another definitely repulsive to a reader who is determined to know nothing but Christ and him crucified. From time immemorial, however, it has been recognized in the Christian church that this objection does not apply to Virgil. He is the most evangelical of the classics; he is the one who can be enjoyed with least to explain away and least to excuse. One evening my Father took down his Virgil from an upper shelf, and his thoughts wandered away from surrounding things; he travelled in the past again. The book was a Delphin edition of 1798, which had followed him in all his wanderings; there was a great scratch on the sheepskin cover that a thorn had made in a forest of Alabama. And then, in the twilight, as he shut the volume at last, oblivious of my presence, he began to murmur and to chant the adorable verses by memory.

Tityre, tu patulae recubans sub tegmine fagi,[10]

he warbled; and I stopped my play, and listened as if to a nightingale, till he reached

tu, Tityre, lentus in umbra
Formosam resonare doces Amaryllida silvas.

'O Papa, what is that?' I could not prevent myself from asking. He translated the verses, he explained their meaning, but his exposition gave me little interest. What to me was beautiful Amaryllis? She and her love-sick Tityrus awakened no image whatever in my mind.

But a miracle had been revealed to me, the incalculable, the amazing beauty which could exist in the sound of verses. My prosodical instinct was awakened, quite suddenly that dim evening, as my Father and I sat alone in the breakfast-room after tea, serenely accepting the hour, for once, with no idea of exhortation or profit. Verse, 'a breeze mid blossoms playing', as Coleridge says, descended from the roses as a moth might have done, and the magic of it took hold of my heart for ever. I persuaded my Father, who was a little astonished at my insistence, to repeat the lines over and over again. At last my brain caught them, and as I walked in Benny's garden, or as I hung over the tidal pools at the edge of the sea, all my inner being used to ring out with the sound of

Formosam resonare doces Amaryllida silvas.

CHAPTER VIII

In the previous chapter I have dwelt on some of the lighter conditions of our life at this time; I must now turn to it in a less frivolous aspect. As my tenth year advanced, the development of my character gave my Father, I will not say anxiety, but matter for serious reflection. My intelligence was now perceived to be taking a sudden start; visitors drew my Father's attention to the fact that I was 'coming out so much'. I grew rapidly in stature, having been a little shrimp of a thing up to that time, and I no longer appeared much younger than my years. Looking back, I do not think that there was any sudden mental development, but that the change was mainly a social one. I had been reserved, timid and taciturn; I had disliked the company of strangers. But with my tenth year, I certainly unfolded, so far as to become sociable and talkative, and perhaps I struck those around me as grown 'clever', because I said the things which I had previously only thought. There was a change, no doubt, yet I believe that it was mainly physical, rather than mental. My excessive fragility – or apparent fragility, for I must have been always wiry – decreased; I slept better, and therefore grew less nervous; I ate better, and therefore put on flesh. If I preserved a delicate look – people still used to say in my presence, 'That dear child is not long for this world!' – it was in consequence of a sort of habit into which my body had grown; it was a transparency which did not speak of what was in store for me, but of what I had already passed through.

The increased activity of my intellectual system now showed itself in what I believe to be a very healthy form, direct imitation. The rage for what is called 'originality' is pushed to such a length in these days that even children are not considered promising, unless they attempt things preposterous and unparalleled. From his earliest hour, the ambitious person is told that to make a road where none has walked before, to do easily what it is impossible for others to do at all, to create new forms of thought and expression, are the only recipes for genius; and in trying to escape on all sides from every resemblance to his predecessors, he adopts at once an air of eccentricity and pretentiousness. This continues to be the accepted view of originality; but, in spite of this conventional opinion, I hold that the healthy sign of an activity of mind in early youth is not to be striving after unheard-of miracles, but to imitate closely and carefully what is being said and done in the vicinity. The child of a great sculptor will hang about the studio, and will try to hammer a head out of a waste piece of marble with a nail; it does not follow that he too will be a sculptor. The child of a politician will sit in committee with a row of empty chairs, and will harangue an imaginary senate from behind the curtains. I, the son of a man who looked through a microscope and painted what he saw there, would fain observe for myself, and paint my observations. It did not follow, alas! that I was built to be a miniature-painter or a savant, but the activity of a childish intelligence was shown by my desire to copy the results of such energy as I saw nearest at hand.

In the secular direction, this now took the form of my preparing little monographs on seaside creatures. which were arranged, tabulated and divided as exactly as possible on the pattern of those which my Father was composing for his *Actinologia Britannica*. I wrote these out upon sheets of paper of the same size as his printed page. and I adorned them with watercolour plates, meant to emulate his precise and exquisite illustrations. One or two of these ludicrous pastiches are still preserved, and in glancing at them now I wonder, not at any skill that they possess, but at the perseverance and the patience, the evidence of close and persistent labour. I was not set to these tasks by my Father, who, in fact, did not much approve of them. He was touched, too, with the 'originality' heresy, and exhorted me not to copy him, but to go out into the garden or the shore and describe something new, in a new way. That was quite impossible; I possessed no initiative. But I can now well understand why my Father, very indulgently and good-temperedly, deprecated these exercises of mine. They took up, and, as he might well think, wasted, an enormous quantity of time; and they were, moreover, parodies, rather than imitations, of his writings, for I invented new species, with sapphire spots and crimson tentacles and amber bands, which were close enough to his real species to be disconcerting. He came from conscientiously shepherding the flocks of ocean, and I do not wonder that my ring-straked, speckled and spotted varieties put him out of countenance. If I had not been so innocent and solemn, he might have fancied I was mocking him.

These extraordinary excursions into science, falsely so called, occupied a large part of my time. There was a little spare room at the back of our house, dedicated to lumber and to empty portmanteaux. There was a table in it already, and I added a stool; this cheerless apartment now became my study. I spent so many hours here, in solitude and without making a sound, that my Father's curiosity, if not his suspicion, was occasionally roused, and he would make a sudden raid on me. I was always discovered, doubled up over the table, with my pen and ink, or else my box of colours and tumbler of turbid water by my hand, working away like a Chinese student shut up in his matriculating box.

It might have been done for a wager, if anything so simple had ever been dreamed of in our pious household. The apparatus was slow and laboured. In order to keep my uncouth handwriting in bounds, I was obliged to rule not lines only, but borders to my pages. The subject did not lend itself to any flow of language, and I was obliged incessantly to borrow sentences, word for word, from my Father's published books. Discouraged by everyone around me, daunted by the laborious effort needful to carry out the scheme, it seems odd to me now that I persisted in so strange and wearisome an employment, but it became an absorbing passion, and was indulged in to the neglect of other lessons and other pleasures.

My Father, as the spring advanced, used to come up to the Box-room, as my retreat was called, and hunt me out into the sunshine. But I soon crept back to my mania. It gave him much trouble, and Miss Marks, who thought it sheer idleness, was vociferous in objection. She would gladly have torn up all my writings and paintings, and have set me to a useful task. My Father, with his strong natural individualism, could not take this view. He was interested in this strange freak of mine, and he could not wholly condemn it. But he must have thought it a little crazy, and it is evident to me now that it led to the revolution in domestic policy by which he began to encourage my acquaintance with other young people as much as he had previously discouraged it. He saw that I could not be allowed to spend my whole time in a little stuffy room making solemn and ridiculous imitations of Papers read before the Linnaean Society.[1] He was grieved, moreover, at the badness of my pictures, for I had no native skill; and he tried to teach me his own system of miniature-painting as applied to natural history. I was forced, in deep depression of spirits, to turn from my grotesque monographs, and paint under my Father's eye, and from a finished drawing of his, a gorgeous tropic bird in flight. Aided by my habit of imitation, I did at length produce something which might have shown promise, if it had not been wrung from me, touch by touch, pigment by pigment, under the orders of a task-master.

All this had its absurd side, but I seem to perceive that it had also its value. It is, surely, a mistake to look too near at hand for the benefits of education. What is actually taught in early childhood is often that part of training which makes least impression on the character, and is of the least permanent importance. My labours failed to make me a zoologist, and the multitude of my designs and my descriptions have left me helplessly ignorant of the anatomy of a sea-anemone. Yet I cannot look upon the mental discipline as useless. It taught me to concentrate my attention, to define the nature of distinctions, to see accurately, and to name what I saw. Moreover, it gave me the habit of going on with any piece of work I had in hand, not flagging because the interest or picturesqueness of the theme had declined, but pushing forth towards a definite goal, well foreseen and limited beforehand. For almost any intellectual employment in later life, it seems to me that this discipline was valuable. I am, however, not the less conscious how ludicrous was the mode in which, in my tenth year, I obtained it.

My spiritual condition occupied my Father's thoughts very insistently at this time. Closing, as he did, most of the doors of worldly pleasure and energy upon his conscience, he had con-tinued to pursue his scientific investigations without any sense of sin. Most fortunate it was, that the collecting of marine animals in the tidal pools, and the description of them in pages which were addressed to the wide scientific public, at no time occurred to him as in any way inconsistent with his holy calling. His conscience was so delicate, and often so morbid in its delicacy, that if that had occurred to him, he would certainly have abandoned his investigations, and have been left without an employment. But happily he justified his investigation by regarding it as a glorification of God's created works. In the introduction of his *Actinologia Britannica*, written at the time which I have now reached in this narrative, he sent forth his labours with a phrase which I should think unparalleled in connection with a learned and technical biological treatise. He stated concerning that book, that he published it 'as one more tribute humbly offered to the glory of the Triune God, who is wonderful in counsel, and excellent in working'. Scientific investigation sincerely carried out in that spirit became a kind of week-day interpretation of the current creed of Sundays.

The development of my faculties, of which I have spoken, extended to the religious sphere no less than to the secular. Here, also, as I look back, I see that I was extremely imitative. I expanded in the warmth of my Father's fervour, and, on the whole, in a manner that was satisfactory to him. He observed the richer hold that I was now taking on life; he saw my faculties branching in many directions, and he became very anxious to secure my maintenance in grace. In earlier years, certain sides of my character had offered a sort of passive resistance to his ideas. I had let what I did not care to welcome pass over my mind in the curious density that children adopt in order to avoid receiving impressions – blankly, dumbly, achieving by stupidity what they cannot achieve by argument. I think that I had frequently done this; that he had been brought up against a dead wall; although on other sides of my nature I had been responsive and docile. But now, in my tenth year, the imitative faculty got the upper hand, and nothing seemed so attractive as to be what I was expected to be. If there was a doubt now, it lay in the other direction; it seemed hardly normal that so young a child should appear so receptive and so apt.

My Father believed himself justified, at this juncture, in making a tremendous effort. He wished to secure me finally, exhaustively, before the age of puberty could dawn, before my soul was fettered with the love of carnal things. He thought that if I could now be identified with the 'saints', and could stand on exactly their footing, a habit of conformity would be secured. I should meet the paganizing tendencies of advancing years with security if I could be forearmed with all the weapons of a sanctified life. He wished me, in short, to be received into the community of the Brethren on the terms of an adult. There were difficulties in the way of carrying out this scheme, and they were urged upon him, more or less courageously, by the elders of the church. But he overbore them. What the difficulties were, and what were the arguments which he used to sweep those difficulties away, I must now explain, for in this lay the centre of our future relations as father and son.

In dealing with the peasants around him, among whom he was engaged in an active propaganda, my Father always insisted on the necessity of conversion. There must be a new birth and being, a fresh creation in God. This crisis he was accustomed to regard as manifesting itself in a sudden and definite upheaval. There might have been prolonged practical piety, deep and true contrition for sin, but these, although the natural and suitable prologue to conversion, were not conversion itself. People hung on at the confines of regeneration, often for a very long time; my Father dealt earnestly with them, the elders ministered to them, with explanation, exhortation and prayer. Such persons were in a gracious state, but they were not in a state of grace. If they should suddenly die, they would pass away in an unconverted condition, and all that could be said in their favour was a vague expression of hope that they would benefit from God's uncovenanted mercies.

But on some day, at some hour and minute, if life was spared to them, the way of salvation would be revealed to these persons in such an aspect that they would be enabled instantaneously to accept it. They would take it consciously, as one takes a gift from the hand that offers it. This act of taking was the process of conversion, and the person who so accepted was a child of God now, although a single minute ago he had been a child of wrath. The very root of human nature had to be changed, and, in the majority of cases, this change was sudden, patent, palpable.

I have just said, 'in the majority of cases', because my Father admitted the possibility of exceptions. The formula was, 'If any man hath not the Spirit of Christ, he is none of his.' As a rule, no one could possess the Spirit of Christ, without a conscious and full abandonment of the soul, and this, however carefully led up to, and prepared for with tears and renunciations, was not, could not, be made, except at a set moment of time. Faith, in an esoteric and almost symbolic sense, was necessary, and could not be a result of argument, but was a state of heart. In these opinions my Father departed in no wise from the strict evangelical doctrine of the Protestant churches, but he held it in a mode and with a severity peculiar to himself.

Now, it is plain that this state of heart, this voluntary deed of acceptance, presupposed a full and rational consciousness of the relations of things. It might be clearly achieved by a person of humble cultivation, but only by one who was fully capable of independent thought, in other words by a more or less adult person. The man or woman claiming the privileges of conversion must be able to understand and to grasp what his religious education was aiming at.

It is extraordinary what trouble it often gave my Father to know whether he was justified in admitting to the communion people of very limited powers of expression. A harmless, humble labouring man would come with a request to be allowed to 'break bread'. It was only by the use of strong leading questions that he could be induced to mention Christ as the ground of his trust at all. I recollect an elderly agricultural labourer being closeted for a long time with my Father, who came out at last, in a sort of dazed condition, and replied to our inquiries, – with a shrug of his shoulders as he said, – 'I was obliged to put the Name and Blood and Work of Jesus into his very mouth. It is true that he assented cordially at last, but I confess I was grievously daunted by the poor intelligence!'

But there was, or there might be, another class of persons, whom early training, separation from the world, and the care of godly parents had so early familiarized with the acceptable calling of Christ that their conversion had occurred, unperceived and therefore unrecorded, at an extraordinarily early age. It would be in vain to look for a repetition of the phenomenon in those cases. The heavenly fire must not be expected to descend a second time; the lips are touched with the burning coal once, and once only. If, accordingly, these precociously selected spirits are to be excluded because no new birth is observed in them at a mature age, they must continue outside in the cold, since the phenomenon cannot be repeated. When, therefore, there is not possible any further doubt of their being in possession of salvation, longer delay is useless, and worse than useless. The fact of conversion, though not recorded nor even recollected, must be accepted on the evidence of confession of faith, and as soon as the intelligence is evidently developed, the person not merely may, but should be accepted into communion, although still immature in body, although in years still even a child. This my Father believed to be my case, and in this rare class did he fondly persuade himself to station me.

As I have said, the congregation, – although docile and timid, and little able, as units, to hold their own against their minister, – behind his back were faintly hostile to his plan. None of their own children had ever been so much as suggested for membership, and each of themselves, in ripe years, had been subjected to severe cross-examination. I think it was rather a bitter pill for some of them to swallow that a pert little boy of ten should be admitted, as a grown-up person, to all the hard-won privileges of their order. Mary Grace Burmington came back from her visits to the cottagers, reporting disaffection here and there, grumblings in the rank and file. But quite as many, especially of the women, enthusiastically supported my Father's wish, gloried aloud in the manifestations of my early piety, and professed to see in it something of miraculous promise. The expression 'another Infant Samuel' [2] was widely used. I became quite a subject of contention. A war of the sexes threatened to break out over me; I was a disturbing element at cottage breakfasts. I was mentioned at public prayer-meetings, not indeed by name but, in the extraordinary allusive way customary in our devotions, as 'one amongst us of tender years' or as 'a sapling in the Lord's vineyard'

To all this my Father put a stop in his own high-handed fashion. After the morning meeting, one Sunday in the autumn of 1859, he desired the attention of the Saints to a personal matter which was, perhaps, not unfamiliar to them by rumour That was, he explained, the question of the admission of his beloved little son to the communion of saints in the breaking of bread. He allowed – and I sat there in evidence, palely smiling at the audience, my feet scarcely touching the ground – that I was not what is styled adult; I was not, he frankly admitted, a grown-up person. But I was adult in a knowledge of the Lord; I possessed an insight into the plan of salvation which many a hoary head might envy for its fullness, its clearness, its conformity with Scripture doctrine. This was a palpable hit at more than one stumbler and fumbler after the truth, and several hoary heads were bowed.

My Father then went on to explain very fully the position which I have already attempted to define. He admitted the absence in my case of a sudden, apparent act of conversion resulting upon conviction of sin. But he stated the grounds of his belief that I had, in still earlier infancy, been converted, and he declared that if so, I ought no longer to be excluded from the privileges of communion. He said, moreover, that he was willing on this occasion to waive his own privilege as a minister, and that he would rather call on Brother Fawkes and Brother Bere, the leading elders, to examine the candidate in his stead. This was a master-stroke, for Brothers Fawkes and Bere had been suspected of leading the disaffection, and this threw all the burden of responsibility on them. The meeting broke up in great amiability, and my Father and I went home together in the very highest of spirits. I, indeed, in my pride, crossed the verge of indiscretion by saying: 'When I have been admitted to fellowship, Papa, shall I be allowed to call you "beloved Brother"?' My Father was too well pleased with the morning's work to be critical. He laughed, and answered: 'That, my Love, though strictly correct, would hardly, I fear, be thought judicious!'

It was suggested that my tenth birthday, which followed this public announcement by a few days, would be a capital occasion for me to go through the ordeal. Accordingly, after dark (for our new lamp was lighted for the first time in honour of the event), I withdrew alone into our drawing-room, which had just, at length, been furnished, and which looked, I thought, very smart. Hither came to me, first Brother Fawkes, by himself; then Brother Bere, by himself; and then both to-gether, so that you may say, if you are pedantically inclined, that I underwent three successive interviews. My Father, out of sight somewhere, was, of course, playing the part of stage manager.

I felt not at all shy, but so highly strung that my whole nature seemed to throb with excitement. My first examiner, on the other hand, was extremely confused. Fawkes, who was a builder in a small business of his own, was short and fat; his complexion, which wore a deeper and more uniform rose-colour than usual, I observed to be starred with dew-drops of nervous emotion, which he wiped away at intervals with a large bandana handkerchief. He was so long in coming to the point, that I was obliged to lead him to it myself, and I sat up on the sofa in the full lamplight, and testified my faith in the atonement with a fluency that surprised myself. Before I had done, Fawkes, a middle-aged man with the reputation of being a very stiff employer of labour, was weeping like a child.

Bere, the carpenter, a long, thin and dry man, with a curi-ously immobile eye, did not fall so easily a prey to my fascina-tions. He put me through my paces very sharply, for he had something of the temper of an attorney mingled with his re-ligiousness. However, I was equal to him, and he, too, though he held his own head higher, was not less impressed than Fawkes had been, by the surroundings of the occasion. Neither of them had ever been in our drawing-room since it was fur-nished, and I thought that each of them noticed how smart the wallpaper was. Indeed, I believe I drew their attention to it. After the two solitary examinations were over, the elders came in again, as I have said, and they prayed for a long time. We all three knelt at the sofa, I between them. But by this time, to my great exaltation of spirits there had succeeded an equally dismal depression. It was my turn now to weep, and I dimly remember my Father coming into the room, and my being carried up to bed, in a state of collapse and fatigue, by the silent and kindly Miss Marks.

On the following Sunday morning, I was the principal subject which occupied an unusually crowded meeting. My Father, looking whiter and yet darker than usual, called upon Brother Fawkes and Brother Bere to state to the assembled saints what their experiences had been in connection with their visits to 'one' who desired to be admitted to the breaking of bread. It was tremendously exciting to me to hear myself spoken of with this impersonal publicity, and I had no fear of the result.

Events showed that I had no need of fear. Fawkes and Bere were sometimes accused of a rivalry, which indeed broke out a few years later, and gave my Father much anxiety and pain. But on this occasion their unanimity was wonderful. Each strove to exceed the other in the tributes which they paid to my piety. My answers had been so full and clear, my humility (save the mark!) had been so sweet, my acquaintance with Scripture so amazing, my testimony to all the leading principles of salvation so distinct and exhaustive, that they could only say that they had felt confounded, and yet deeply cheered and led far along their own heavenly path, by hearing such accents fall from the lips of a babe and a suckling. I did not like being described as a suckling, but every lot has its crumpled rose-leaf, and in all other respects the report of the elders was a triumph. My Father then clenched the whole matter by rising and announcing that I had expressed an independent desire to confess the Lord by the act of public baptism, immediately after which I should be admitted to communion 'as an adult'. Emotion ran so high at this, that a large portion of the congregation insisted on walking with us back to our garden-gate, to the stupefaction of the rest of the villagers.

My public baptism was the central event of my whole childhood. Everything, since the earliest dawn of consciousness, seemed to have been leading up to it. Everything, afterwards, seemed to be leading down and away from it. The practice of immersing communicants on the sea-beach at Oddicombe had now been completely abandoned, but we possessed as yet no tank for a baptismal purpose in our own Room. The Room in the adjoining town, however, was really quite a large chapel, and it was amply provided with the needful conveniences. It was our practice, therefore, at this time, to claim the hospitality of our neighbours. Baptisms were made an occasion for friendly relations between the two congregations, and led to pleasant social intercourse. I believe that the ministers and elders of the two meetings arranged to combine their forces at these times, and to baptize communicants from both congregations.

The minister of the town meetings was Mr S., a very hand-some old gentleman, of venerable and powerful appearance. He had snowy hair and a long white beard, but from under shaggy eyebrows there blazed out great black eyes which warned the beholder that the snow was an ornament and not a sign of decrepitude. The eve of my baptism at length drew near; it was fixed for October 12, almost exactly three weeks after my tenth birthday. I was dressed in old clothes, and a suit of smarter things was packed up in a carpet-bag. After night-fall, this carpet-bag, accompanied by my Father, myself, Miss Marks and Mary Grace, was put in a four-wheeled cab, and driven, a long way in the dark, to the chapel of our friends. There we were received, in a blaze of lights, with a pressure of hands, with a murmur of voices, with ejaculations and even with tears, and were conducted, amid unspeakable emotion, to places of honour in the front row of the congregation.

The scene was one which would have been impressive, not merely to such hermits as we were, but even to worldly persons accustomed to life and to its curious and variegated experiences. To me it was dazzling beyond words, inexpressibly exciting, an initiation to every kind of publicity and glory. There were many candidates, but the rest of them, – mere grown-up men and women, – gave thanks aloud that it was their privilege to follow where I led. I was the acknowledged hero of the hour. Those were days when newspaper enterprise was scarcely in its infancy, and the event owed nothing to journalistic effort. In spite of that, the news of this remarkable ceremony, the im-mersion of a little boy of ten years old 'as an adult', had spread far and wide through the county in the course of three weeks. The chapel of our hosts was, as I have said, very large; it was commonly too large for their needs, but on this night it was crowded to the ceiling, and the crowd had come – as every soft murmur assured me – to see *me*.

There were people there who had travelled from Exeter, from Dartmouth, from Totnes, to witness so extraordinary a ceremony. There was one old woman of eighty-five who had come, my neighbours whispered to me, all the way from Moreton-Hampstead, on purpose to see me baptized. I looked at her crumpled countenance with amazement, for there was no curiosity, no interest visible in it. She sat there perfectly listless, looking at nothing, but chewing between her toothless gums what appeared to be a jujube.

In the centre of the chapel-floor a number of planks had been taken up, and revealed a pool which might have been supposed to be a small swimming-bath. We gazed down into this dark square of mysterious waters, from the tepid surface of which faint swirls of vapour rose. The whole congregation was arranged, tier above tier, about the four straight sides of this pool; every person was able to see what happened in it without any unseemly struggling or standing on forms. Mr S. now rose, an impressive hieratic figure, commanding attention and imploring perfect silence. He held a small book in his hand, and he was preparing to give out the number of a hymn, when an astounding incident took place.

There was a great splash, and a tall young woman was perceived to be in the baptismal pool, her arms waving above her head, and her figure held upright in the water by the inflation of the air underneath her crinoline which was blown out like a bladder, as in some extravagant old fashion-plate. Whether her feet touched the bottom of the font I cannot say, but I suppose they did so. An indescribable turmoil of shrieks and cries followed on this extraordinary apparition. A great many people excitedly called upon other people to be calm, and an instance was given of the remark of James Smith[3] that

He who, in quest of quiet, 'Silence!' hoots
Is apt to make the hubbub he imputes.

The young woman, in a more or less fainting condition, was
presently removed from the water, and taken into the sort of
tent which was prepared for candidates. It was found that she
herself had wished to be a candidate and had earnestly desired
to be baptized, but that this had been forbidden by her parents.
On the supposition that she fell in by accident, a pious coincidence was detected in this affair; the Lord had pre-ordained
that she should be baptized in spite of all opposition. But my
Father, in his shrewd way, doubted. He pointed out to us, next
morning, that, in the first place, she had not, in any sense, been
baptized, as her head had not been immersed; and that, in the
second place, she must have deliberately jumped in, since, had
she stumbled and fallen forward, her hands and face would
have struck the water, whereas they remained quite dry. She
belonged, however, to the neighbour congregation, and we
had no responsibility to pursue the inquiry any further.

Decorum being again secured, Mr S., with unimpaired dignity, proposed to the congregation a hymn, which was long
enough to occupy them during the preparations for the actual
baptism. He then retired to the vestry, and I (for I was to be the
first to testify) was led by Miss Marks and Mary Grace into the
species of tent of which I have just spoken. Its pale sides seemed
to shake with the jubilant singing of the saints outside, while
part of my clothing was removed and I was prepared for
immersion. A sudden cessation of the hymn warned us that the
Minister was now ready, and we emerged into the glare of
lights and faces to find Mr S. already standing in the water up
to his knees. Feeling as small as one of our microscopical specimens, almost infinitesimally tiny as I descended into his Titanic
arms, I was handed down the steps to him. He was dressed in a
kind of long surplice, underneath which – as I could not, even
in that moment, help observing – the air gathered in long
bubbles which he strove to flatten out. The end of his noble

159

beard he had tucked away; his shirt-sleeves were turned up at the wrist.

The entire congregation was now silent, so silent that the uncertain splashing of my feet as I descended seemed to deafen me. Mr S., a little embarrassed by my short stature, succeeded at length in securing me with one palm on my chest and the other between my shoulders. He said, slowly, in a loud, sonorous voice that seemed to enter my brain and empty it, 'I baptize thee, my Brother, in the name of the Father and of the Son and of the Holy Ghost!' Having intoned this formula, he then gently flung me backwards until I was wholly under the water, and then – as he brought me up again, and tenderly steadied my feet on the steps of the font, and delivered me, dripping and spluttering, into the anxious hands of the women, who hurried me to the tent – the whole assembly broke forth in a thunder of song, a paean of praise to God for this manifestation of his marvellous goodness and mercy. So great was the enthusiasm, that it could hardly be restrained so as to allow the other candidates, the humdrum adults who followed in my wet and glorious footsteps, to undergo a ritual about which, in their case, no one in the congregation pretended to be able to take even the most languid interest.

My Father's happiness during the next few weeks it is now pathetic to me to look back upon. His sternness melted into a universal complaisance. He laughed and smiled, he paid to my opinions the tribute of the gravest considerations, he indulged – utterly unlike his wont – in shy and furtive caresses. I could express no wish that he did not attempt to fulfil, and the only warning which he cared to give me was one, very gently expressed, against spiritual pride.

This was certainly required, for I was puffed out with a sense of my own holiness. I was religiously confidential with my Father, condescending with Miss Marks (who I think had given up trying to make it all out), haughty with the servants, and insufferably patronizing with those young companions of my own age with whom I was now beginning to associate.

I would fain close this remarkable episode on a key of solemnity, but alas! if I am to be loyal to the truth, I must record that some of the other little boys presently complained to Mary Grace that I put out my tongue at them in mockery, during the service in the Room, to remind them that I now broke bread as one of the Saints and that they did not.

CHAPTER IX

The result of my being admitted into the communion of the 'Saints' was that, as soon as the nine days' wonder of the thing passed by, my position became, if anything, more harassing and pressed than ever. It is true that freedom was permitted to me in certain directions; I was allowed to act a little more on my own responsibility, and was not so incessantly informed what 'the Lord's will' might be in this matter and in that, because it was now conceived that, in such dilemmas, I could command private intelligence of my own. But there was no relaxation of our rigid manner of life, and I think I now began, by comparing it with the habits of others, to perceive how very strict it was.

The main difference in my lot as a communicant from that of a mere dweller in the tents of righteousness was that I was expected to respond with instant fervour to every appeal of conscience. When I did not do this, my position was almost worse than it had been before, because of the livelier nature of the responsibility which weighed upon me. My little faults of conduct, too, assumed shapes of terrible importance, since they proceeded from one so signally enlightened. My Father was never tired of reminding me that, now that I was a professing Christian, I must remember, in everything I did, that I was an example to others. He used to draw dreadful pictures of suppositious little boys who were secretly watching me from afar, and whose whole career, in time and in eternity, might be disastrously affected if I did not keep my lamp burning.

The year which followed upon my baptism did not open very happily at the Room. Considerable changes had now taken place in the community. My Father's impressive services, a certain prestige in his preaching, the mere fact that so vigorous a person was at the head of affairs, had induced a large increase in the attendance. By this time, if my memory does not fail me as to dates, we had left the dismal loft over the stables, and had built ourselves a perfectly plain, but commodious and well-arranged chapel in the centre of the village. This greatly added to the prosperity of the meeting. Everything had combined to make our services popular, and had attracted to us a new element of younger people. Numbers of youthful masons and carpenters, shop-girls and domestic servants, found the Room a pleasant trysting-place, and were more or less superficially induced to accept salvation as it was offered to them in my Father's searching addresses. My Father was very shrewd in dealing with mere curiosity or idle motive, and sharply packed off any youths who simply came to make eyes at the girls, or any 'maids' whose only object was to display their new bonnet-strings. But he was powerless against a temporary sincerity, the simulacrum of a true change of heart. I have often heard him say, – of some young fellow who had attended our services with fervour for a little while, and then had turned cold and left us, – 'and I thought that the Holy Ghost had wrought in him!' Such disappointments grievously depress an evangelist.

Religious bodies are liable to strange and unaccountable fluctuations. At the beginning of the third year since our arrival, the congregation seemed to be in a very prosperous state, as regards attendance, conversions and other outward signs of activity. Yet it was quite soon after this that my Father began to be harassed by all sorts of troubles, and the spring of 1860 was a critical moment in the history of the community. Although he loved to take a very high tone about the Saints, and involved them sometimes in a cloud of laudatory metaphysics, the truth was that they were nothing more than peasants of a somewhat primitive type, not well instructed in the rules of conduct and liable to exactly the same weaknesses as invade the rural character in every country and latitude. That they were

exhorted to behave as 'children of light', and that the majority
of them sincerely desired to do credit to their high calling,
could not prevent their being beset by the sins which had
affected their forebears for generations past.

The addition of so many young persons of each sex to the
communion led to an entirely new class of embarrassment.
Now there arose endless difficulties about 'engagements', about
youthful brethren who 'went out walking' with even more
youthful sisters. Glancing over my Father's notes, I observe the
ceaseless repetition of cases in which So-and-So is 'courting'
Such-an-one, followed by the melancholy record that he has
deserted' her. In my Father's stern language, 'desertion' would
very often mean no more than that the amatory pair had
blamelessly changed their minds; but in some cases it meant
more and worse than this. It was a very great distress to him
that sometimes the young men and women who showed the
most lively interest in Scripture, and who had apparently
accepted the way of salvation with the fullest intelligence, were
precisely those who seemed to struggle with least success against
a temptation to unchastity. He put this down to the concentrated malignity of Satan, who directed his most poisoned
darts against the fairest of the flock.

In addition to these troubles, there came recriminations,
mutual charges of drunkenness in private, all sorts of petty
jealousy and scandal. There were frequent definite acts of 'back-
sliding' on the part of members, who had in consequence to be
'put away' No one of these cases might be in itself extremely
serious, but when many of them came together they seemed to
indicate that the church was in an unhealthy condition. The
particulars of many of these scandals were concealed from me,
but I was an adroit little pitcher, and had cultivated the art of
seeming to be interested in something else, a book or a flower,
while my elders were talking confidentially. As a rule, while I
would fain have acquired more details, I was fairly well-
informed about the errors of the Saints, although I was often
quaintly ignorant of the real nature of those errors.

Not infrequently, persons who had fallen into sin repented of it under my Father's penetrating ministrations. They were apt in their penitence to use strange symbolic expressions. I remember Mrs Pewings, our washerwoman, who had been accused of intemperance and had been suspended from communion, reappearing with a face that shone with soap and sanctification, and saying to me, 'Oh! blessed Child, you're wonderin' to zee old Pewings here again, but He have rolled away my mountain!' For once, I was absolutely at a loss, but she meant that the Lord had removed the load of her sins, and restored her to a state of grace.

It was in consequence of these backslidings, which had become alarmingly frequent, that early in 1860 my Father determined on proclaiming a solemn fast. He delivered one Sunday what seemed to me an awe-inspiring address, calling upon us all closely to examine our consciences, and reminding us of the appalling fate of the church of Laodicea.[1] He said that it was not enough to have made a satisfactory confession of faith, nor even to have sealed that confession in baptism, if we did not live up to our protestations. Salvation, he told us, must indeed precede holiness of life, yet both are essential. It was a dark and rainy winter morning when he made this terrible address, which frightened the congregation extremely. When the marrow was congealed within our bones, and when the bowed heads before him, and the faintly audible sobs of the women in the background, told him that his lesson had gone home, he pronounced the keeping of a day in the following week as a fast of contrition. 'Those of you who have to pursue your daily occupations will pursue them, but sustained only by the bread of affliction and by the water of affliction.'

His influence over these gentle peasant people was certainly remarkable, for no effort was made to resist his exhortation. It was his customary plan to stay a little while, after the morning meeting was over, and in a very affable fashion to shake hands with the Saints. But on this occasion he stalked forth without a word, holding my hand tight until we had swept out into the street.

How the rest of the congregation kept this fast I do not know. But it was a dreadful day for us. I was awakened in the pitchy night to go off with my Father to the Room, where a scanty gathering held a penitential prayer-meeting. We came home, as dawn was breaking, and in the process of time sat down to breakfast, which consisted – at that dismal hour – of slices of dry bread and a tumbler of cold water each. During the morning, I was not allowed to paint, or write, or withdraw to my study in the box-room. We sat, in a state of depression not to be described, in the breakfast-room, reading books of a devotional character, with occasional wailing of some very doleful hymn. Our midday dinner came at last; the meal was strictly confined, as before, to dry slices of the loaf and a tumbler of water.

The afternoon would have been spent as the morning was, and so my Father spent it. But Miss Marks, seeing my white cheeks and the dark rings round my eyes, besought leave to take me for a walk. This was permitted, with a pledge that I should be given no species of refreshment. Although I told Miss Marks, in the course of the walk, that I was feeling 'so leer' (our Devonshire phrase for hungry), she dared not break her word. Our last meal was of the former character, and the day ended by our trapesing through the wet to another prayer-meeting, whence I returned in a state bordering on collapse and was put to bed without further nourishment. There was no great hardship in all this, I daresay, but it was certainly rigorous. My Father took pains to see that what he had said about the bread and water of affliction was carried out in the bosom of his own family, and by no one more unflinchingly than by himself.

My attitude to other people's souls when I was out of my Father's sight was now a constant anxiety to me. In our tattling world of small things he had extraordinary opportunities of learning how I behaved when I was away from home; I did not realize this, and I used to think his acquaintance with my deeds and words savoured almost of wizardry. He was accustomed to urge upon me the necessity of 'speaking for Jesus in season and out of season', and he so worked upon my feelings that I would start forth like St Teresa, wild for the Moors and martyrdom. But any actual impact with persons marvellously cooled my zeal, and I should hardly ever have 'spoken' at all if it had not been for that unfortunate phrase 'out of season'. It really seemed that one must talk of nothing else, since if an occasion was not in season it was out of season; there was no alternative, no close time for souls.[2]

My Father was very generous. He used to magnify any little effort that I made, with stammering tongue, to sanctify a visit; and people, I now see, were accustomed to give me a friendly lead in this direction, so that they might please him by reporting that I had 'testified' in the Lord's service. The whole thing, however, was artificial, and was part of my Father's restless inability to let well alone. It was not in harshness or in ill-nature that he worried me so much; on the contrary, it was all part of his too-anxious love. He was in a hurry to see me become a shining light, everything that he had himself desired to be, yet with none of his shortcomings.

It was about this time that he harrowed my whole soul into painful agitation by a phrase that he let fall, without, I believe, attaching any particular importance to it at the time. He was occupied, as he so often was, in polishing and burnishing my faith, and he was led to speak of the day when I should ascend the pulpit to preach my first sermon. 'Oh! if I may be there, out of sight, and hear the gospel message proclaimed from your lips, then I shall say, "My poor work is done. Oh! Lord Jesus, receive my spirit".' I cannot express the dismay which this aspiration gave me, the horror with which I anticipated such a *nunc dimittis*.[3] I felt like a small and solitary bird, caught and hung out hopelessly and endlessly in a glittering cage. The clearness of the personal image affected me as all the texts and prayers and predictions had failed to do. I saw myself

167

imprisoned for ever in the religious system which had caught me and would whirl my helpless spirit as in the concentric wheels of my nightly vision. I did not struggle against it, because I believed that it was inevitable, and that there was no other way of making peace with the terrible and ever-watchful 'God who is a jealous God'. But I looked forward to my fate without zeal and without exhilaration, and the fear of the Lord altogether swallowed up and cancelled any notion of the love of Him.

I should do myself an injustice, however, if I described my attitude to faith at this time as wanting in candour. I did very earnestly desire to follow where my Father led. That passion for imitation, which I have already discussed, was strongly developed at this time, and it induced me to repeat the language of pious books in godly ejaculations which greatly edified my grown-up companions, and were, so far as I can judge, perfectly sincere. I wished extremely to be good and holy, and I had no doubt in my mind of the absolute infallibility of my Father as a guide in heavenly things. But I am perfectly sure that there never was a moment in which my heart truly responded, with native ardour, to the words which flowed so readily, in such a stream of unction, from my anointed lips. I cannot recall anything but an intellectual surrender; there was never joy in the act of resignation, never the mystic's rapture at feeling his phantom self, his own threadbare soul, suffused, thrilled through, robed again in glory by a fire which burns up everything personal and individual about him.

Through thick and thin I clung to a hard nut of individuality, deep down in my childish nature. To the pressure from without I resigned everything else, my thoughts, my words, my anticipations, my assurances, but there was something which I never resigned, my innate and persistent self. Meek as I seemed, and gently respondent, I was always conscious of that innermost quality which I had learned to recognize in my earlier days in Islington, that existence of two in the depths who could speak to one another in inviolable secrecy.

This a natural man may discourse of, and that very knowingly, and give a kind of natural credit to it, as to a history that may be true; but firmly to believe that there is divine truth in all these things, and to have a persuasion of it stronger than of the very thing we see with our eyes; such an assent as this is the peculiar work of the Spirit of God, and is certainly saving faith.

This passage is not to be found in the writings of any extravagant Plymouth Brother, but in one of the most solid classics of the Church, in Archbishop Leighton's [4] *Commentary on the First Epistle of Peter*. I quote it because it defines, more exactly than words of my own could hope to do, the difference which already existed and in secrecy began forthwith to be more and more acutely accentuated, between my Father and myself. He did indeed possess this saving faith, which could move mountains of evidence and suffer no diminution under the action of failure or disappointment. I, on the other hand – as I began to feel dimly then, and see luminously now – had only acquired the habit of giving what the Archbishop means by 'a kind of natural credit' to the doctrine so persistently impressed upon my conscience. From its very nature this could not but be molten in the dews and exhaled in the sunshine of life and thought and experience.

My Father, by an indulgent act for the caprice of which I cannot wholly account, presently let in a flood of imaginative light which was certainly hostile to my heavenly calling. My instinctive interest in geography has already been mentioned. This was the one branch of knowledge in which I needed no instruction, geographical information seeming to soak into the cells of my brain without an effort. At the age of eleven, I knew a great deal more of maps, and of the mutual relation of localities all over the globe, than most grown-up people do. It was almost a mechanical acquirement. I was now greatly taken with the geography of the West Indies, of every part of which I had made MS. maps. There was something powerfully attractive to my fancy in the great chain of the Antilles, lying on the sea like an open bracelet, with its big jewels and little jewels

strung on an invisible thread. I liked to shut my eyes and see it
all, in a mental panorama, stretched from Cape Sant' Antonio
to the Serpent's Mouth. Several of these lovely islands, these
emeralds and amethysts set in the Caribbean Sea, my Father
had known well in his youth, and I was importunate in ques-
tioning him about them. One day, as I multiplied inquiries, he
rose in his impetuous way, and climbing to the top of a book-
case, brought down a thick volume and presented it to me.
'You'll find all about the Antilles there,' he said, and left me
with *Tom Cringle's Log*[5] in my possession.

The embargo laid upon every species of fiction by my
Mother's powerful scruple had never been raised, although she
had been dead four years. As I have said in an earlier chapter,
this was a point on which I believe that my Father had never
entirely agreed with her. He had, however, yielded to her
prejudice; and no work of romance, no fictitious story, had
ever come in my way. It is remarkable that among our books,
which amounted to many hundreds, I had never discovered a
single work of fiction until my Father himself revealed the
existence of Michael Scott's wild masterpiece. So little did I
understand what was allowable in the way of literary invention
that I began the story without a doubt that it was true, and I
think it was my Father himself who, in answer to an inquiry,
explained to me that it was 'all made up'. He advised me to
read the descriptions of the sea, and of the mountains of Jamaica,
and 'skip' the pages which gave imaginary adventures and
conversations. But I did not take his counsel; these latter were
the flower of the book to me. I had never read, never dreamed
of anything like them, and they filled my whole horizon with
glory and with joy.

I suppose that when my Father was a younger man, and less
pietistic, he had read *Tom Cringle's Log* with pleasure, because
it recalled familiar scenes to him. Much was explained by the
fact that the frontispiece of this edition was a delicate line-
engraving of Blewfields, the great lonely house in a garden of
Jamaican all-spice where for eighteen months he had worked

as a naturalist. He could not look at this print without recalling exquisite memories and airs that blew from a terrestrial paradise. But Michael Scott's noisy amorous novel of adventure was an extraordinary book to put in the hands of a child who had never been allowed to glance at the mildest and most febrifugal story-book.[6]

It was like giving a glass of brandy neat to some one who had never been weaned from a milk diet. I have not read *Tom Cringle's Log* from that day to this, and I think that I should be unwilling now to break the charm of memory, which may be largely illusion. But I remember a great deal of the plot and not a little of the language, and, while I am sure it is enchantingly spirited, I am quite as sure that the persons it describes were far from being unspotted by the world. The scenes at night in the streets of Spanish Town surpassed not merely my experience, but, thank goodness, my imagination. The nautical personages used, in their conversations, what is called 'a class of language', and there ran, if I am not mistaken, a glow and gust of life through the romance from beginning to end which was nothing if it was not resolutely pagan.

There were certain scenes and images in *Tom Cringle's Log* which made not merely a lasting impression upon my mind, but tinged my outlook upon life. The long adventures, fightings and escapes, sudden storms without, and mutinies within, drawn forth as they were, surely with great skill, upon the fiery blue of the boundless tropical ocean, produced on my inner mind a sort of glimmering hope, very vaguely felt at first, slowly developing, long stationary and faint, but always tending towards a belief that I should escape at last from the narrowness of the life we led at home, from this bondage to the Law and the Prophets.

I must not define too clearly, nor endeavour too formally to insist on the blind movements of a childish mind. But of this I am quite sure, that the reading and re-reading of *Tom Cringle's Log* did more than anything else, in this critical eleventh year of my life, to give fortitude to my individuality, which was in great danger – as I now see – of succumbing to the pressure my Father brought to bear upon it from all sides. My soul was shut up, like Fatima, in a tower[7] to which no external influences could come, and it might really have been starved to death, or have lost the power of recovery and rebound, if my captor, by some freak not yet perfectly accounted for, had not gratuitously opened a little window in it and added a powerful telescope. The daring chapters of Michael Scott's picaresque romance of the tropics were that telescope and that window.

In the spring of this year, I began to walk about the village and even proceed for considerable distances into the country by myself, and after reading *Tom Cringle's Log* those expeditions were accompanied by a constant hope of meeting with some adventures. I did not court events, however, except in fancy, for I was very shy of real people, and would break off some gallant dream of prowess on the high seas to bolt into a field and hide behind the hedge, while a couple of labouring men went by. Sometimes, however, the wave of a great purpose would bear me on, as when once, but certainly at an earlier date than I have now reached, hearing the dangers of a persistent drought much dwelt upon, I carried my small red watering pot, full of water, up to the top of the village, and then all the way down Petittor Lane, and discharged its contents in a cornfield, hoping by this act to improve the prospects of the harvest. A more eventful excursion must be described, because of the moral impression it left indelibly upon me.

I have described the sequestered and beautiful hamlet of Barton, to which I was so often taken visiting by Mary Grace Burmington. At Barton there lived a couple who were objects of peculiar interest to me, because of the rather odd fact that having come, out of pure curiosity, to see me baptized, they had been then and there deeply convinced of their spiritual danger. These were John Brooks, an Irish quarryman, and his wife, Ann Brooks. These people had not merely been hitherto unconverted, but they had openly treated the Brethren with anger and contempt. They came, indeed, to my baptism to mock, but they went away impressed.

Next morning, when Mrs Brooks was at the wash tub as she told us, Hell opened at her feet, and the Devil came out holding a long scroll on which the list of her sins was written. She was so much excited, that the motion brought about a miscarriage and she was seriously ill. Meanwhile, her husband, who had been equally moved at the baptism, was also converted, and as soon as she was well enough, they were baptized together, and then 'broke bread' with us. The case of the Brookses was much talked about, and was attributed, in a distant sense, to me; that is to say, if I had not been an object of public curiosity, the Brookses might have remained in the bond of iniquity. I, therefore, took a very particular interest in them, and as I presently heard that they were extremely poor, I was filled with a fervent longing to minister to their necessities.

Somebody had lately given me a present of money, and I begged little sums here and there until I reached the very considerable figure of seven shillings and sixpence. With these coins safe in a little linen bag, I started one Sunday afternoon, without saying anything to any one, and I arrived at the Brookses' cottage in Barton. John Brooks was a heavy dirty man, with a pock-marked face and two left legs; his broad and red face carried small side-whiskers in the manner of that day, but was otherwise shaved. When I reached the cottage, husband and wife were at home, doing nothing at all in the approved Sunday style. I was received by them with some surprise, but I quickly explained my mission, and produced my linen bag. To my disgust, all John Brooks said was, 'I know'd the Lord would provide,' and after emptying my little bag into the palm of an enormous hand, he swept the contents into his trousers pocket, and slapped his leg. He said not one single word of thanks or appreciation, and I was absolutely cut to the heart.

I think that in the course of a long life I have never experienced a bitterer disappointment. The woman, who was quicker, and more sensitive, doubtless saw my embarrassment, but the form of comfort which she chose was even more wounding to my pride. 'Never mind, little master,' she said, 'you shall come and see me feed the pigs.' But there is a limit to endurance, and with a sense of having been cruelly torn by the tooth of ingratitude, I fled from the threshold of the Brookses, never to return.

At tea that afternoon, I was very much downcast, and under cross-examination from Miss Marks, all my little story came out. My Father, who had been floating away in a meditation, as he very often did, caught a word that interested him and descended to consciousness. I had to tell my tale over again, this time very sadly, and with a fear that I should be reprimanded. But on the contrary, both my Father and Miss Marks were attentive and most sympathetic, and I was much comforted. 'We must remember they are the Lord's children,' said my Father. 'Even the Lord can't make a silk purse out of a sow's ear,' said Miss Marks, who was considerably ruffled. 'Alas! alas!' replied my Father, waving his hand with a deprecating gesture. 'The dear child!' said Miss Marks, bristling with indignation, and patting my hand across the tea-table. 'The Lord will reward your zealous loving care of his poor, even if they have neither the grace nor the knowledge to thank you,' said my Father, and rested his brown eyes meltingly upon me. 'Brutes!' said Miss Marks, thinking of John and Ann Brooks. 'Oh no! no!' replied my Father, 'but hewers of wood and drawers of water! We must bear with the limited intelligence.' All this was an emollient to my wounds, and I became consoled. But the springs of benevolence were dried up within me, and to this day I have never entirely recovered from the shock of John Brooks's coarse leer and his 'I know'd the Lord would provide.' The infant plant of philanthropy was burned in my bosom as if by quick-lime.

In the course of the summer, a young schoolmaster called on my Father to announce to him that he had just opened a day-school for the sons of gentlemen in our vicinity, and he begged for the favour of a visit. My Father returned his call; he lived in one of the small white villas, buried in laurels, which gave a discreet animation to our neighbourhood. Mr M. was frank and modest, deferential to my Father's opinions and yet capable of defending his own. His school and he produced an excellent impression, and in August I began to be one of his pupils. The school was very informal; it was held in the two principal dwelling-rooms on the ground-floor of the villa, and I do not remember that Mr M. had any help from an usher.

There were perhaps twenty boys in the school at most, and often fewer. I made the excursion between home and school four times a day; if I walked fast, the transit might take five minutes, and, as there were several objects of interest in the way, it might be spread over an hour. In fine weather the going to and from school was very delightful, and small as the scope of it was, it could be varied almost indefinitely. I would sometimes meet with a schoolfellow proceeding in the same direction, and my Father, observing us over the wall one morning, was amused to notice that I always progressed by dancing along the curbstone sideways, my face turned inwards and my arms beating against my legs, conversing loudly all the time. This was a case of pure heredity, for so he used to go to his school, forty years before, along the streets of Poole.

One day when fortunately I was alone, I was accosted by an old gentleman, dressed as a dissenting minister. He was pleased with my replies, and he presently made it a habit to be taking his constitutional when I was likely to be on the high road. We became great friends, and he took me at last to his house, a very modest place, where to my great amazement, there hung in the dining-room, two large portraits, one of a man, the other of a woman, in extravagant fancy-dress. My old friend told me that the former was a picture of himself as he had appeared, 'long ago, in my unconverted days, on the stage'.

I was so ignorant as not to have the slightest conception of what was meant by the stage, and he explained to me that he had been an actor and a poet, before the Lord had opened his eyes to better things. I knew nothing about actors, but poets were already the objects of my veneration. My friend was the first poet I had ever seen. He was no less a person than James Sheridan Knowles,[8] the famous author of *Virginius* and *The Hunchback*, who had become a Baptist minister in his old age. When, at home, I mentioned this acquaintance, it awakened no interest. I believe that my Father had never heard, or never noticed, the name of one who had been by far the most eminent English playwright of that age.

It was from Sheridan Knowles' lips that I first heard fall the name of Shakespeare. He was surprised, I fancy, to find me so curiously advanced in some branches of knowledge, and so utterly ignorant of others. He could hardly credit that the names of Hamlet and Falstaff and Prospero meant nothing to a little boy who knew so much theology and geography as I did. Mr Knowles suggested that I should ask my schoolmaster to read some of the plays of Shakespeare with the boys, and he proposed *The Merchant of Venice* as particularly well-suited for this purpose. I repeated what my aged friend (Mr Sheridan Knowles must have been nearly eighty at that time) had said, and Mr M. accepted the idea with promptitude. (All my memories of this my earliest schoolmaster present him to me as intelligent, amiable and quick, although I think not very soundly prepared for his profession.)

Accordingly, it was announced that the reading of Shakespeare would be one of our lessons, and on the following afternoon we began *The Merchant of Venice* There was one large volume, and it was handed about the class; I was permitted to read the part of Bassanio, and I set forth, with ecstatic pipe, how

> In Belmont is a lady richly left,
> And she is fair, and fairer than that word!

Mr M. must have had some fondness for the stage himself; his pleasure in the Shakespeare scenes was obvious, and nothing else that he taught me made so much impression on me as what he said about a proper emphasis in reading aloud. I was in the seventh heaven of delight, but alas! we had only reached the second act of the play, when the readings mysteriously stopped. I never knew the cause, but I suspect that it was at my Father's desire. He prided himself on never having read a page of Shakespeare, and on never having entered a theatre but once. I think I must have spoken at home about the readings, and that he must have given the schoolmaster a hint to return to the ordinary school curriculum.

The fact that I was 'a believer', as it was our custom to call one who had been admitted to the arcana of our religion, and that therefore, in all commerce with 'unbelievers', it was my duty to be 'testifying for my Lord, in season and out of season' – this prevented my forming any intimate friendships at my first school. I shrank from the toilsome and embarrassing act of button-holing a schoolfellow as he rushed out of class, and of pressing upon him the probably unintelligible question 'Have you found Jesus?' It was simpler to avoid him, to slip like a lizard through the laurels and emerge into solitude.

The boys had a way of plunging out into the road in front of the school-villa when afternoon school was over; it was a pleasant rural road lined with high hedges and shadowed by elm-trees. Here, especially towards the summer twilight, they used to linger and play vague games, swooping and whirling in the declining sunshine, and I was glad to join these bat-like sports. But my company, though not avoided, was not greatly sought for. I think that something of my curious history was known, and that I was, not unkindly but instinctively, avoided, as an animal of a different species, not allied to the herd. The conventionality of little boys is constant; the colour of their traditions is uniform. At the same time, although I made no friends, I found no enemies. In class, except in my extraordinary aptitude for geography, which was looked upon as incomprehensible and almost uncanny, I was rather behind than in front of the others. I, therefore, awakened no jealousies, and, intent on my own dreams, I think my little shadowy presence escaped the notice of most of my schoolfellows.

By the side of the road I have mentioned, between the school and my home, there was a large horse-pond. The hedge folded round three sides of it, while ancient pollard elms bent over it, and chequered with their foliage in it the reflection of the sky. The roadside edge of this pond was my favourite station; it consisted of a hard clay which could be moulded into fairly tenacious forms. Here I created a maritime empire – islands, a seaboard with harbours, light-houses, fortifications. My geographical imitativeness had its full swing. Sometimes, while I was creating, a cart would be driven roughly into the pond, and a horse would drink deep of my ocean, his hooves trampling my archipelagoes and shattering my ports with what was worse than a typhoon. But I immediately set to work, as soon as the cart was gone and the mud had settled, to tidy up my coastline again and to scoop out anew my harbours.

My pleasure in this sport was endless, and what I was able to see, in my mind's eye, was not the edge of a morass of mud, but a splendid line of coast, and gulfs of the type of Tor Bay. I do not recollect a sharper double humiliation than when Old Sam Lamble, the blacksmith, who was one of the 'saints', being asked by my Father whether he had met me, replied 'Yes, I zeed 'un up-long, making mud pies in the ro-ad!' What a position for one who had been received into communion 'as an adult'! What a blot on the scutcheon of a would-be Columbus! 'Mud-pies', indeed!

Yet I had an appreciator. One afternoon, as I was busy on my geographical operations, a good-looking middle-aged lady, with a soft pink cheek and a sparkling hazel eye, paused and asked me if my name was not what it was. I had seen her before; a stranger to our parts, with a voice without a trace in it of the Devonshire drawl. I knew, dimly, that she came sometimes to the meeting, that she was lodging at Upton with some friends of ours who accepted paying guests in an old house that was simply a basket of roses. She was

Miss Brightwen, and I now conversed with her for the first time.

Her interest in my harbours and islands was marked; she did not smile; she asked questions about my peninsulas which were intelligent and pertinent. I was even persuaded at last to leave my creations and walk with her towards the village. I was pleased with her voice, her refinements, her dress, which was more delicate, and her manners, which were more easy, than what I was accustomed to. We had some very pleasant conversation, and when we parted I had the satisfaction of feeling that our intercourse had been both agreeable to me and instructive to her. I told her that I should be glad to tell her more on a future occasion; she thanked me very gravely, and then she laughed a little. I confess I did not see that there was anything to laugh at. We parted on warm terms of mutual esteem, but I little thought that this sympathetic Quakerish lady was to become my mother.

CHAPTER X

I slept in a little bed in a corner of the room, and my Father in the ancestral four-poster nearer to the door. Very early one bright September morning at the close of my eleventh year, my Father called me over to him. I climbed up, and was snugly wrapped in the coverlid; and then we held a momentous conversation. It began abruptly by his asking me whether I should like a new mamma. I was never a sentimentalist, and I therefore answered, cannily, that that would depend on who she was. He parried this, and announced that, anyway, a new mamma was coming; I was sure to like her. Still in a non-committal mood, I asked: 'Will she go with me to the back of the lime-kiln?' This question caused my Father a great bewilderment. I had to explain that the ambition of my life was to go up behind the lime-kiln on the top of the hill that hung over Barton, a spot which was forbidden ground, being locally held one of extreme danger. 'Oh! I daresay she will,' my Father then said, 'but you must guess who she is.' I guessed one or two of the less comely of the female 'saints', and, this embarrassing my Father, – since the second I mentioned was a married woman who kept a sweet-shop in the village, – he cut my inquiries short by saying, 'It is Miss Brightwen.'

So far so good, and I was well pleased. But unfortunately I remembered that it was my duty to testify 'in season and out of season'. I therefore asked, with much earnestness, 'But, Papa, is she one of the Lord's children?' He replied, with gravity, that she was. 'Has she taken up her cross in baptism?' I went on, for this was my own strong point as a believer. My Father looked a little shame-faced, and replied: 'Well, she has not as yet seen the necessity of that, but we must pray that the Lord may make her way clear before her. You see, she has been brought up, hitherto, in the so-called Church of England.'

Our positions were now curiously changed. It seemed as if it were I who were the jealous monitor, and my Father the deprecating penitent. I sat up in the coverlid, and I shook a finger at him. 'Papa,' I said, 'don't tell me that she's a pedo-baptist?' [1] I had lately acquired that valuable word, and I seized this remarkable opportunity of using it. It affected my Father painfully, but he repeated his assurance that if we united our prayers, and set the Scripture plan plainly before Miss Brightwen, there could be no doubt that she would see her way to accepting the doctrine of adult baptism. And he said we must judge not, lest we ourselves be judged. I had just enough tact to let that pass, but I was quite aware that our whole system was one of judging, and that we had no intention whatever of being judged ourselves. Yet even at the age of eleven one sees that on certain occasions to press home the truth is not convenient.

Just before Christmas, on a piercing night of frost, my Father brought to us his bride. The smartening up of the house, the new furniture, the removal of my own possessions to a private bedroom, the wedding-gifts of the 'saints', all these things paled in interest before the fact that Miss Marks had made a 'scene', in the course of the afternoon. I was dancing about the drawing-room, and was saying: 'Oh! I am so glad my new Mamma is coming,' when Miss Marks called out, in an un-natural voice, 'Oh! you cruel child.' I stopped in amazement and stared at her, whereupon she threw prudence to the winds, and moaned: 'I once thought I should be your dear mamma.' I was simply stupefied, and I expressed my horror in terms that were clear and strong. Thereupon Miss Marks had a wild fit of hysterics, while I looked on, wholly unsympathetic and still deeply affronted. She was right; I was cruel, alas! but then, what a silly woman she had been! The consequence was that she withdrew in a moist and quivering condition to her boudoir, where she had locked herself in when I, all smiles and caresses, was welcoming the bride and bridegroom on the doorstep as politely as if I had been a valued old family retainer.

My stepmother immediately became a great ally of mine. She was never a tower of strength to me, but at least she was always a lodge in my garden of cucumbers.[2] She was a very well-meaning pious lady, but she was not a fanatic, and her mind did not naturally revel in spiritual aspirations. Almost her only social fault was that she was sometimes a little fretful; this was the way in which her bruised individuality asserted itself. But she was affectionate, serene, and above all refined. Her refinement was extraordinarily pleasant to my nerves, on which much else in our surroundings jarred.

How life may have jarred, poor insulated lady, on her during her first experience of our life at the Room, I know not, but I think she was a philosopher. She had, with surprising rashness, and in opposition to the wishes of every member of her own family, taken her cake, and now she recognized that she must eat it, to the last crumb. Over her wishes and prejudices my Father exercised a constant, cheerful and quiet pressure. He was never unkind or abrupt, but he went on adding avoirdupois until her will gave way under the sheer weight. Even to public immersion, which, as was natural in a shy and sensitive lady of advancing years, she regarded with a horror which was long insurmountable, – even to baptism she yielded, and my Father had the joy to announce to the Saints one Sunday morning at the breaking of bread that 'my beloved wife has been able at length to see the Lord's Will in the matter of baptism, and will testify to the faith which is in her on Thursday evening next.' No wonder my stepmother was sometimes fretful.

On the physical side, I owe her an endless debt of gratitude. Her relations, who objected strongly to her marriage, had told her, among other pleasant prophecies, that 'the first thing you will have to do will be to bury that poor child'. Under the old-world sway of Miss Marks, I had slept beneath a load of blankets, had never gone out save weighted with great coat and comforter, and had been protected from fresh air as if from a pestilence. With real courage my stepmother reversed all this. My bedroom window stood wide open all night long, wraps were done away with, or exchanged for flannel garments next the skin, and I was urged to be out and about as much as possible.

All the quidnuncs[3] among the 'saints' shook their heads; Mary Grace Burmington, a little embittered by the downfall of her Marks, made a solemn remonstrance to my Father, who, however, allowed my stepmother to carry out her excellent plan. My health responded rapidly to this change of regime, but increase of health did not bring increase of spirituality. My Father, fully occupied with moulding the will and inflaming the piety of my stepmother, left me now, to a degree not precedented, in undisturbed possession of my own devices. I did not lose my faith, but many other things took a prominent place in my mind.

It will, I suppose, be admitted that there is no greater proof of complete religious sincerity than fervour in private prayer. If an individual, alone by the side of his bed, prolongs his intercessions, lingers wrestling with his divine Companion, and will not leave off until he has what he believes to be evidence of a reply to his entreaties – then, no matter what the character of his public protestations, or what the frailty of his actions, it is absolutely certain that he believes in what he professes.

My Father prayed in private in what I may almost call a spirit of violence. He entreated for spiritual guidance with nothing less than importunity. It might be said that he stormed the citadels of God's grace, refusing to be baffled, urging his intercessions without mercy upon a Deity who sometimes struck me as inattentive to his prayers or wearied by them. My Father's acts of supplication, as I used to witness them at night, when I was supposed to be asleep, were accompanied by stretchings out of the hands, by cracking of the joints of the fingers, by deep breathings, by murmurous sounds which seemed just breaking out of silence, like Virgil's bees out of the hive, 'magnis clamoribus'. My Father fortified his religious life by prayer as an athlete does his physical life by lung-gymnastics and vigorous rubbings.

It was a trouble to my conscience that I could not emulate this fervour. The poverty of my prayers had now long been a source of distress to me, but I could not discover how to enrich them. My Father used to warn us very solemnly against 'lip-service', by which he meant singing hymns of experience and joining in ministrations in which our hearts took no vital or personal part. This was an outward act, the tendency of which I could well appreciate, but there was a 'lip-service' even more deadly than that, against which it never occurred to him to warn me. It assailed me when I had come alone by my bedside, and blown out the candle, and had sunken on my knees in my night-gown. Then it was that my deadness made itself felt, in the mechanical address I put up, the emptiness of my language, the absence of all real unction.

I never could contrive to ask God for spiritual gifts in the same voice and spirit in which I could ask a human being for objects which I knew he could give me and which I earnestly desired to possess. That sense of the reality of intercession was for ever denied me, and it was, I now see, the stigma of my want of faith. But at the time, of course, I suspected nothing of the kind, and I tried to keep up my zeal by a desperate mental flogging, as if my soul had been a peg-top.

In nothing did I gain from the advent of my stepmother more than in the encouragement she gave to my friendships with a group of boys of my own age, of whom I had now lately formed the acquaintance. These friendships she not merely tolerated, but fostered; it was even due to her kind arrangements that they took a certain set form, that our excursions started from this house or from that on regular days. I hardly know by what stages I ceased to be a lonely little creature of mock-monographs and mud-pies, and became a member of a sort of club of eight or ten active boys. The long summer holidays of 1861 were set in an enchanting brightness.

Looking back, I cannot see a cloud on the terrestrial horizon – I see nothing but a blaze of sunshine; descents of slippery grass to moons of snow-white shingle, cold to the bare flesh; red promontories running out into a sea that was like sapphire; and our happy clan climbing, bathing, boating, lounging, chattering, all the hot day through. Once more I have to record the fact, which I think is not without interest, that precisely as my life ceases to be solitary, it ceases to be distinct. I have no difficulty in recalling, with the minuteness of a photograph, scenes in which my Father and I were the sole actors within the four walls of a room, but of the glorious life among wild boys on the margin of the sea I have nothing but vague and broken impressions, delicious and illusive.

It was a remarkable proof of my Father's temporary lapse into indulgence that he made no effort to thwart my intimacy with these my new companions. He was in an unusually humane mood himself. His marriage was one proof of it; another was the composition at this time of the most picturesque, easy and graceful of all his writings, *The Romance of Natural History*,[4] even now a sort of classic. Everything combined to make him believe that the blessing of the Lord was upon him, and to clothe the darkness of the world with at least a mist of rose-colour. I do not recollect that ever at this time he bethought him, when I started in the morning for a long day with my friends on the edge of the sea, to remind me that I must speak to them, in season and out of season, of the Blood of Jesus. And I, young coward that I was, let sleeping dogmas lie.

My companions were not all of them the sons of saints in our communion; their parents belonged to that professional class which we were only now beginning to attract to our services. They were brought up in religious, but not in fanatical, families, and I was the only 'converted' one among them. Mrs Paget, of whom I shall have presently to speak, characteristically said that it grieved her to see 'one lamb among so many kids'. 'But 'kid' is a word of varied significance and the symbol did not seem to us effectively applied. As a matter of fact, we made what I still feel was an excellent tacit compromise. My young companions never jeered at me for being 'in communion with the saints', and I, on my part, never urged the Atonement upon them. I began, in fact, more and more to keep my own religion for use on Sundays.

It will, I hope, have been observed that among the very curious grown-up people into whose company I was thrown, although many were frail and some were foolish, none, so far as I can discern, were hypocritical. I am not one of those who believe that hypocrisy is a vice that grows on every bush. Of course, in religious more than in any other matters, there is a perpetual contradiction between our thoughts and our deeds which is inevitable to our social order, and is bound to lead to *cette tromperie mutuelle*[5] of which Pascal[6] speaks. But I have often wondered, while admiring the splendid portrait of Tartuffe,[7] whether such a monster ever, or at least often, has walked the stage of life; whether Molière observed, or only invented him.

To adopt a scheme of religious pretension, with no belief whatever in its being true, merely for sensuous advantage, openly acknowledging to one's inner self the brazen system of deceit, – such a course may, and doubtless has been, trodden, yet surely much less frequently than cynics love to suggest. But at the juncture which I have now reached in my narrative, I had the advantage of knowing a person who was branded before the whole world, and punished by the law of his country, as a felonious hypocrite. My Father himself could only sigh and admit the charge. And yet – I doubt.

About half-way between our village and the town there lay a comfortable villa inhabited by a retired solicitor, or perhaps attorney, whom I shall name Mr Dormant. We often called at his half-way house, and, although he was a member of the town-meeting, he not unfrequently came up to us for 'the breaking of bread'. Mr Dormant was a solid, pink man, of a cosy habit. He had beautiful white hair, a very soft voice, and a welcoming, wheedling manner; he was extremely fluent and zealous in using the pious phraseology of the sect. My Father had never been very much attracted to him, but the man professed, and I think felt, an overwhelming admiration for my Father. Mr Dormant was not very well off, and in the previous year he had persuaded an aged gentleman of wealth to come and board with him. When, in the course of the winter, this gentleman died, much surprise was felt at the report that he had left almost his entire fortune, which was not inconsiderable, to Mr Dormant.

Much surprise – for the old gentleman had a son to whom he had always been warmly attached, who was far away, I think in South America, practising a perfectly respectable profession of which his father entirely approved. My own Father always preserved a delicacy and a sense of honour about money which could not have been more sensitive if he had been an ungodly man, and I am very much pleased to remember that when the legacy was first spoken of, he regretted that Mr Dormant should have allowed the old gentleman to make this will. If he knew the intention, my Father said, it would have shown a more proper sense of his responsibility if he had dissuaded the testator from so unbecoming a disposition. That was long before any legal question arose; and now Mr Dormant came into his fortune, and began to make handsome gifts to missionary societies, and to his own meeting in the town. If I do not mistake, he gave, unsolicited, a sum to our building fund, which my Father afterwards returned. But in process of time we heard that the son had come back from the Antipodes, and was making investigations. Before we knew where we were, the news burst upon us, like a bomb-shell, that Mr Dormant had been arrested on a criminal charge and was now in gaol at Exeter.

Sympathy was at first much extended amongst us to the prisoner. But it was lessened when we understood that the old gentleman had been 'converted' while under Dormant's roof, and had given the fact that his son was 'an unbeliever' as a reason for disinheriting him. All doubt was set aside when it was divulged, under pressure, by the nurse who attended on the old gentleman, herself one of the 'saints', that Dormant had traced the signature to the will by drawing the fingers of the testator over the document when he was already and finally comatose.

My Father, setting aside by a strong effort of will the repugnance which he felt, visited the prisoner in gaol before this final evidence had been extracted. When he returned he said that Dormant appeared to be enjoying a perfect confidence of heart, and had expressed a sense of his joy and peace in the Lord; my Father regretted that he had not been able to persuade him to admit any error, even of judgement. But the prisoner's attitude in the dock, when the facts were proved, and not by him denied, was still more extraordinary. He could be induced to exhibit no species of remorse, and, to the obvious anger of the judge himself, stated that he had only done his duty as a Christian, in preventing this wealth from coming into the hands of an ungodly man, who would have spent it in the service of the flesh and of the devil. Sternly reprimanded by the judge, he made the final statement that at that very moment he was conscious of his Lord's presence, in the dock at his side, whispering to him 'Well done, thou good and faithful servant!' In this frame of conscience, and with a glowing countenance, he was hurried away to penal servitude.

This was a very painful incident, and it is easy to see how compromising, how cruel, it was in its effect upon our communion; what occasion it gave to our enemies to blaspheme. No one, in either meeting, could or would raise a voice to defend Mr Dormant. We had to bow our heads when we met our enemies in the gate. The blow fell more heavily on the meeting of which he had been a prominent and communicating member, but it fell on us too, and my Father felt it severely. For many years he would never mention the man's name, and he refused all discussion of the incident.

Yet I was never sure, and I am not sure now, that the wretched being was a hypocrite. There are as many vulgar fanatics as there are distinguished ones, and I am not convinced that Dormant, coarse and narrow as he was, may not have sincerely believed that it was better for the money to be used in religious propaganda than in the pleasures of the world, of which he doubtless formed a very vague idea. On this affair I meditated much, and it awakened in my mind, for the first time, a doubt whether our exclusive system of ethics was an entirely salutary one, if it could lead the conscience of a believer to tolerate such acts as these, acts which my Father himself had denounced as dishonourable and disgraceful.

My stepmother brought with her a little library of such books as we had not previously seen, but which yet were known to all the world except us. Prominent among these was a set of the poems of Walter Scott, and in his unwonted geniality and provisional spirit of compromise, my Father must do no less than read these works aloud to my stepmother in the quiet spring evenings. This was a sort of aftermath of courtship, a tribute of song to his bride, very sentimental and pretty. She would sit, sedately, at her workbox, while, he, facing her, poured forth the verses at her like a blackbird. I was not considered in this arrangement, which was wholly matrimonial, but I was present, and the exercise made more impression upon me than it did upon either of the principal agents.

My Father read the verse admirably, with a full, – some people (but not I) might say with a too full – perception of the metre as well as of the rhythm, rolling out the rhymes, and glorying in the proper names. He began, and it was a happy choice, with 'The Lady of the Lake'.[8] It gave me a singular pleasure to hear his large voice do justice to 'Duncrannon' and 'Cambus-Kenneth', and wake the echoes with 'Rhoderigh Vich Alphine dhu, ho! ieroe!' I almost gasped with excitement, while a shudder floated down my backbone, when we came to:

> A sharp and shrieking echo gave,
> Coir-Uriskin, thy goblin cave!
> And the grey pass where birches wave,
> On Beala-nam-bo,

a passage which seemed to me to achieve the ideal of sublime romance. My thoughts were occupied all day long with the adventures of Fitzjames and the denizens of Ellen's Isle. It became an obsession, and when I was asked whether I remembered the name of the cottage where the minister of the Bible Christians lodged, I answered, dreamily, 'Yes, – Beala-nam-bo.'

Seeing me so much fascinated, thrown indeed into a temporary frenzy, by the epic poetry of Sir Walter Scott, my stepmother asked my Father whether I might not start reading the Waverley Novels. But he refused to permit this, on the ground that those tales gave false and disturbing pictures of life, and would lead away my attention from heavenly things. I do not fully apprehend what distinction he drew between the poems, which he permitted, and the novels, which he refused. But I suppose he regarded a work in verse as more artificial, and therefore less likely to make a realistic impression, than one in prose. There is something quaint in the conscientious scruple which allows *The Lord of the Isles*[9] and excludes *Rob Roy*.[10]

But stranger still, and amounting almost to a whim, was his sudden decision that, although I might not touch the novels of Scott, I was free to read those of Dickens. I recollect that my stepmother showed some surprise at this, and that my Father explained to her that Dickens 'exposes the passion of love in a ridiculous light'. She did not seem to follow this recommendation, which indeed tends to the ultra-subtle, but she procured for me a copy of *Pickwick*,[11] by which I was instantly and gloriously enslaved. My shouts of laughing at the richer passages were almost scandalous, and led to my being reproved for disturbing my Father while engaged, in an upper room, in the study of God's Word. I must have expended months on the perusal of *Pickwick*, for I used to rush through a chapter, and then read it over again very slowly, word for word, and then shut my eyes to realize the figures and the action.

I suppose no child will ever again enjoy that rapture of unresisting humorous appreciation of 'Pickwick'. I felt myself to be in the company of a gentleman so extremely funny that I began to laugh before he began to speak; no sooner did he remark 'the sky was dark and gloomy, the air was damp and raw', than I was in fits of hilarity. My retirement in our sequestered corner of life made me, perhaps, even in this matter, somewhat old-fashioned, and possibly I was the latest of the generation who accepted Mr Pickwick with an unquestioning and hysterical abandonment. Certainly few young people now seem sensitive, as I was, and as thousands before me had been, to the quality of his fascination.

It was curious that living in a household where a certain delicate art of painting was diligently cultivated, I had yet never seen a real picture, and was scarcely familiar with the design of one in engraving. My stepmother, however, brought a flavour of the fine arts with her; a kind of aesthetic odour, like that of lavender, clung to her as she moved. She had known authentic artists in her youth; she had watched Old Crome [12] painting, and had taken a course of drawing-lessons from no less a person than Cotman. [13] She painted small water-colour landscapes herself, with a delicate economy of means and a graceful Norwich convention; her sketch-books were filled with abbeys gently washed in, river-banks in sepia by which the elect might be dimly reminded of *Liber Studiorum*, [14] and woodland scenes over which the ghost of Creswick had faintly breathed. It was not exciting art, but it was, so far as it went, in its lady-like reserve, the real thing. Our sea-anemones, our tropic birds, our bits of spongy rock frilled and sprayed with corallines, had been very conscientious and skilful, but, essentially, so far as art was concerned, the wrong thing.

Thus I began to acquire, without understanding the value of

it, some conception of the elegant phases of early English water-colour painting, and there was one singular piece of a marble well brimming with water, and a greyish-blue sky over it, and dark-green poplars, shaped like wet brooms, menacing the middle distance, which Cotman himself had painted; and this seemed beautiful and curious to me in its dim, flat frame, when it was hoisted to a place on our drawing-room wall.

But still I had never seen a subject-picture, although my stepmother used to talk of the joys of the Royal Academy, and it was therefore with a considerable sense of excitement that I went, with my Father, to examine Mr Holman Hunt's 'Finding of Christ in the Temple'[15] which at this time was announced to be on public show at our neighbouring town. We paid our shillings and ascended with others to an upper room, bare of every disturbing object, in which a strong toplight raked the large and uncompromising picture. We looked at it for some time in silence, and then my Father pointed out to me various details, such as the phylacteries[16] and the mitres, and the robes which distinguished the high priest.

Some of the other visitors, as I recollect, expressed astonishment and dislike of what they called the 'Preraphaelite' treatment,[17] but we were not affected by that. Indeed, if anything, the exact, minute and hard execution of Mr Hunt was in sympathy with the methods we ourselves were in the habit of using when we painted butterflies and seaweeds, placing perfectly pure pigments side by side, without any nonsense about chiaroscuro.[18] This large, bright, comprehensive picture made a very deep impression upon me, not exactly as a work of art, but as a brilliant natural specimen. I was pleased to have seen it, as I was pleased to have seen the comet, and the whale which was brought to our front door on a truck. It was a prominent addition to my experience.

The slender expansions of my interest which were now budding hither and thither do not seem to have alarmed my Father at all. His views were short; if I appeared to be contented and obedient, if I responded pleasantly when he appealed to me, he was not concerned to discover the source of my cheerfulness. He put it down to my happy sense of joy in Christ, a reflection of the sunshine of grace beaming upon me through no intervening clouds of sin or doubt. The 'saints' were, as a rule, very easy to comprehend; their emotions lay upon the surface. If they were gay, it was because they had no burden on their consciences, while, if they were depressed, the symptom might be depended upon as showing that their consciences were troubling them, and if they were indifferent and cold, it was certain that they were losing their faith and becoming hostile to godliness. It was almost a mechanical matter with these simple souls. But, although I was so much younger, I was more complex and more crafty than the peasant 'saints'. My Father, not a very subtle psychologist, applied to me the same formulas which served him well at the chapel, but in my case the results were less uniformly successful.

The excitement of school-life and the enlargement of my circle of interests, combined to make Sunday, by contrast, a very tedious occasion. The absence of every species of recreation on the Lord's Day grew to be a burden which might scarcely be borne. I have said that my freedom during the week had now become considerable; if I was at home punctually at meal times, the rest of my leisure was not challenged. But this liberty, which in the summer holidays came to surpass that of 'fishes that tipple in the deep', was put into more and more painful contrast with the unbroken servitude of Sunday.

My Father objected very strongly to the expression Sabbath-day, as it is commonly used by Presbyterians and others. He said, quite justly, that it was an inaccurate modern innovation, that Sabbath was a Saturday, the Seventh day of the week, not the first, a Jewish festival and not a Christian commemoration. Yet his exaggerated view with regard to the observance of the First Day, namely, that it must be exclusively occupied with public and private exercises of divine worship, was based much more upon a Jewish than upon a Christian law. In fact, I do not remember that my Father ever produced a definite argument from the New Testament in support of his excessive passivity on the Lord's Day. He followed the early Puritan practice, except that he did not extend his observance, as I believe the old Puritans did, from sunset on Saturday to sunset on Sunday.

The observance of the Lord's Day has already become universally so lax that I think there may be some value in preserving an accurate record of how our Sundays were spent five and forty years ago. We came down to breakfast at the usual time. My Father prayed briefly before we began the meal; after it, the bell was rung, and, before the breakfast was cleared away, we had a lengthy service of exposition and prayer with the servants. If the weather was fine, we then walked about the garden doing nothing, for about half an hour. We then sat, each in a separate room, with our Bibles open and some commentary on the text beside us, and prepared our minds for the morning service. A little before 11 a.m. we sallied forth, carrying our Bibles and hymn-books, and went through the morning-service of two hours at the Room; this was the central event of Sunday.

We then came back to dinner, – curiously enough to a hot dinner, always, with a joint, vegetables and puddings, so that the cook at least must have been busily at work, – and after it my Father and my stepmother took a nap, each in a different room, while I slipped out into the garden for a little while, but never venturing farther afield. In the middle of the afternoon, my stepmother and I proceeded up the village to Sunday School, where I was early promoted to the tuition of a few very little boys. We returned in time for tea, immediately after which we all marched forth, again armed as in the morning, with Bibles and hymn-books, and we went through the evening-service, at which my Father preached. The hour was now already past my week-day bedtime, but we had another service to attend, the Believers' Prayer Meeting, which commonly occupied forty minutes more. Then we used to creep home, I often so tired that the weariness was like physical pain, and I was permitted, without further 'worship', to slip upstairs to bed.

What made these Sundays, the observance of which was absolutely uniform, so peculiarly trying was that I was not permitted the indulgence of any secular respite. I might not open a scientific book, nor make a drawing, nor examine a specimen. I was not allowed to go into the road, except to proceed with my parents to the Room, nor to discuss worldly subjects at meals, nor to enter the little chamber where I kept my treasures. I was hotly and tightly dressed in black, all day long, as though ready at any moment to attend a funeral with decorum. Sometimes, towards evening, I used to feel the monotony and weariness of my position to be almost unendurable, but at this time I was meek, and I bowed to what I supposed to be the order of the universe.

CHAPTER XI

As my mental horizon widened, my Father followed the direction of my spiritual eyes with some bewilderment, and knew not at what I gazed. Nor could I have put into words, nor can I even now define, the visions which held my vague and timid attention. As a child develops, those who regard it with tenderness or impatience are seldom even approximately correct in their analysis of its intellectual movements, largely because, if there is anything to record, it defies adult definition. One curious freak of mentality I must now mention, because it took a considerable part in the enfranchisement of my mind, or rather in the formation of my thinking habits. But neither my Father nor my stepmother knew what to make of it, and to tell the truth I hardly know what to make of it myself.

Among the books which my new mother had brought with her were certain editions of the poets, an odd assortment. Campbell was there, and Burns, and Keats, and the 'Tales' of Byron.[1] Each of these might have been expected to appeal to me; but my emotion was too young, and I did not listen to them yet. Their imperative voices called me later. By the side of these romantic classics stood a small, thick volume, bound in black morocco, and comprising four reprinted works of the eighteenth century, gloomy, funereal poems[2] of an order as wholly out of date as are the crossbones and ruffled cherubim on the gravestones in a country churchyard. The four – and in this order, as I never shall forget – were 'The Last Day' of Dr Young, Blair's 'Grave', 'Death' by Bishop Beilby Porteus, and 'The Deity' of Samuel Boyse. These lugubrious effusions, all in blank verse or in the heroic couplet, represented, in its most redundant form, the artistic theology of the middle of the eighteenth century. They were steeped in such vengeful and hortatory sentiments as passed for elegant piety in the reign of George II.

How I came to open this solemn volume is explained by the oppressive exclusiveness of our Sundays. On the afternoon of the Lord's Day, as I have already explained, I might neither walk, nor talk, nor explore our scientific library, nor indulge in furious feats of water-colour painting. The Plymouth-Brother theology which alone was open to me produced, at length, and particularly on hot afternoons, a faint physical nausea, a kind of secret headache. But, hitting one day upon the doleful book of verses, and observing its religious character, I asked 'May I read that?' and after a brief, astonished glance at the contents, I received 'O certainly – if you can!'

The lawn sloped directly from a verandah at our drawing-room window, and it contained two immense elm trees, which had originally formed part of the hedge of a meadow. In our trim and polished garden they then remained – they were soon afterwards cut down – rude and obtuse, with something primeval about them, something autochthonous; [3] they were like two peasant ancestors surviving in a family that had advanced to gentility. They rose each out of a steep turfed hillock, and the root of one of them was long my favourite summer reading-desk; for I could lie stretched on the lawn, with my head and shoulders supported by the elm-tree hillock, and the book in a fissure of the rough turf. Thither then I escaped with my graveyard poets, and who shall explain the rapture with which I followed their austere morality?

Whether I really read consecutively in my black-bound volume I can no longer be sure, but it became a companion whose society I valued, and at worst it was a thousand times more congenial to me than Jukes' *On the Pentateuch* [4] or than a perfectly excruciating work ambiguously styled *The Javelin of Phineas*, [5] which lay smouldering in a dull red cover on the drawing-room table. I dipped my bucket here and there into my poets, and I brought up strange things. I brought up out of the depths of 'The Last Day'[6] the following ejaculation of a soul roused by the trump of resurrection:

> Father of mercies! Why from silent earth
> Didst thou awake, and curse me into birth?
> Tear me from quiet, ravish me from night,
> And make a thankless present of thy light?
> Push into being a reverse of thee,
> And animate a clod with misery?

I read these lines with a shiver of excitement, and in a sense I suppose little intended by the sanctimonious rector of Welwyn.[7] I also read in the same piece the surprising description of how

> Now charnels rattle, scattered limbs, and all
> The various bones, obsequious to the call,
> Self-mov'd, advance – the neck perhaps to meet
> The distant head, the distant legs the feet,

but rejected it as not wholly supported by the testimony of Scripture. I think that the rhetoric and vigorous advance of Young's verse were pleasant to me. Beilby Porteus[8] I discarded from the first as impenetrable. In 'The Deity', – I knew nothing then of the life of its extravagant and preposterous author,[9] – I took a kind of persistent, penitential pleasure, but it was Blair's 'Grave'[10] that really delighted me, and I frightened myself with its melodious doleful images in earnest.

About this time there was a great flow of tea-table hospitality in the village, and my friends and their friends used to be asked out, by respective parents and by more than one amiable spinster, to faint little entertainments where those sang who were ambitious to sing, and where all played post and forfeits after a rich tea. My Father was constantly exercised in mind as to whether I should or should not accept these glittering invitations. There hovered before him a painful sense of danger in resigning the soul to pleasures which savoured of 'the world'.

198

These, though apparently innocent in themselves, might give an appetite for yet more subversive dissipations.

I remember, on one occasion, – when the Browns, a family of Baptists who kept a large haberdashery shop in the neighbouring town, asked for the pleasure of my company 'to tea and games', and carried complacency so far as to offer to send that local vehicle, 'the midge', to fetch me and bring me back, – my Father's conscience was so painfully perplexed, that he desired me to come up with him to the now-deserted 'boudoir' of the departed Marks, that we might 'lay the matter before the Lord'. We did so, kneeling side by side, with our backs to the window and our foreheads pressed upon the horsehair cover of the small, coffin-like sofa. My Father prayed aloud, with great fervour, that it might be revealed to me, by the voice of God, whether it was or was not the Lord's will that I should attend the Browns' party. My Father's attitude seemed to me to be hardly fair, since he did not scruple to remind the Deity of various objections to a life of pleasure and of the snakes that lie hidden in the grass of evening parties. It would have been more scrupulous, I thought, to give no sort of hint of the kind of answer he desired and expected.

It will be justly said that my life was made up of very trifling things, since I have to confess that this incident of the Browns' invitation was one of its landmarks. As I knelt, feeling very small, by the immense bulk of my Father, there gushed through my veins like a wine the determination to rebel. Never before, in all these years of my vocation, had I felt my resistance take precisely this definite form. We rose presently from the sofa, my forehead and the backs of my hands still chafed by the texture of the horsehair, and we faced one another in the dreary light. My Father, perfectly confident in the success of what had really been a sort of incantation, asked me in a loud wheedling voice, 'Well, and what is the answer which our Lord vouchsafes?' I said nothing, and so my Father, more sharply, continued, 'We have asked Him to direct you to a true knowledge of His will. We have desired Him to let you know whether it is, or is not, in accordance with His wishes that you should accept this invitation from the Browns.' He positively beamed down at me; he had no doubt of the reply. He was already, I believe, planning some little treat to make up to me for the material deprivation. But my answer came, in the high-piping accents of despair: 'The Lord says I may go to the Browns.' My Father gazed at me in speechless horror. He was caught in his own trap, and though he was certain that the Lord had said nothing of the kind, there was no road open for him but just sheer retreat. Yet surely it was an error in tactics to slam the door.

It was at this party at the Browns – to which I duly went, although in sore disgrace – that my charnel poets played me a mean trick. It was proposed that 'our young friends' should give their elders the treat of repeating any pretty pieces that they knew by heart. Accordingly a little girl recited 'Casabianca',[11] and another little girl 'We are Seven',[12] and various children were induced to repeat hymns, 'some rather long', as Calverley[13] says, but all very mild and innocuously evangelical. I was then asked by Mrs Brown's maiden sister, a gushing lady in cork-screw curls, who led the revels, whether I also would not indulge them 'by repeating some sweet stanzas'. No one more ready than I. Without a moment's hesitation, I stood forth, and in a loud voice I began one of my favourite passages from Blair's 'Grave':

> If death were nothing, and nought after death –
> If when men died at once they ceased to be, –
> Returning to the barren Womb of Nothing
> Whence first they sprung, then might the debauchee . . .

'Thank you, dear, that will do nicely!' interrupted the lady with the curls. 'But that's only the beginning of it,' I cried. 'Yes, dear, but that will quite do! We won't ask you to repeat any more of it,' and I withdrew to the borders of the company in bewilderment. Nor did the Browns or their visitors ever learn what it was the debauchee might have said or done in more favourable circumstances.

The growing eagerness which I displayed for the society of selected schoolfellows and for such gentle dissipations as were within my reach exercised my Father greatly. His fancy rushed forward with the pace of a steam-engine, and he saw me the life and soul of a gambling club, or flaunting it at the Mabille. He had no confidence in the action of moderating powers, and he was fond of repeating that the downward path is easy. If one fretted to be bathing with one's companions on the shingle, and preferred this exercise to the study of God's Word, it was a symbol of a terrible decline, the angle of which would grow steeper and steeper, till one plunged into perdition. He was, himself, timid and reclusive, and he shrank from all avoidable companionship with others, except on the footing of a master and teacher. My stepmother and I, who neither taught nor ruled, yearned for a looser chain and lighter relationships. With regard to myself, my Father about this time hit on a plan from which he hoped much, but from which little resulted. He looked to George to supply what my temperament seemed to require of congenial juvenile companionship.

If I have not mentioned 'George' until now, it is not that he was a new acquaintance. When we first came down into the country, our sympathy had been called forth by an accident to a little boy, who was knocked over by a horse, and whose thigh was broken. Somebody (I suppose Mary Grace, since my Father could rarely bring himself to pay these public visits) went to see the child in the infirmary, and accidentally discovered that he was exactly the same age that I was. This, and the fact that he was a meditative and sober little boy, attracted us all still further to George, who became converted under one of my Father's sermons. He attended my public baptism, and was so much moved by this ceremony that he passionately desired to be baptized also, and was in fact so immersed, a few months later, slightly to my chagrin, since I thereupon ceased to be the only infant prodigy in communion. When we were both in our thirteenth year, George became an outdoor servant to us, and did odd jobs under the gardener. My Father, finding him, as he said, 'docile, obedient and engaging', petted George a good deal, and taught him a little botany. He called George, by a curious contortion of thought, my 'spiritual foster-brother', and anticipated for him, I think, a career, like mine, in the Ministry.

Our garden suffered from an incursion of slugs, which laid the verbenas in the dust, and shore off the carnations as if with pairs of scissors. To cope with this plague we invested in a drake and a duck, who were christened Philemon and Baucis. Every night large cabbage-leaves, containing the lees of beer, were spread about the flower-beds as traps, and at dawn these had become green parlours crammed with intoxicated slugs. One of George's earliest morning duties was to free Philemon and Baucis from their coop, and, armed with a small wand, to guide their footsteps to the feast of one cabbage-leaf after another. My Father used to watch this performance from an upper window, and, in moments of high facetiousness, he was wont to parody the poet Gray:[14]

How jocund doth George drive his team afield!

This is all, or almost all, that I remember about George's occupations, but he was singularly blameless.

My Father's plan now was that I should form a close intimacy with George, as a boy of my own age, of my own faith, of my own future. My stepmother, still in bondage to the social conventions, was passionately troubled at this, and urged the barrier of class–differences. My Father replied that such an intimacy would keep me 'lowly', and that from so good a boy as George I could learn nothing undesirable. 'He will encourage him not to wipe his boots when he comes into the house,' said my stepmother, and my Father sighed to think how narrow is the horizon of Woman's view of heavenly things.

In this caprice, if I may call it so, I think that my Father had before him the fine republican example of 'Sandford and Merton',[15] some parts of which book he admired extremely. Accordingly George and I were sent out to take walks together, and as we started, my Father, with an air of great benevolence, would suggest some passage of Scripture, or 'some aspect of God's bountiful scheme in creation, on which you may profitably meditate together.' George and I never pursued the discussion of the text with which my Father started us for more than a minute or two; then we fell into silence, or investigated current scenes and rustic topics.

As is natural among the children of the poor, George was precocious where I was infantile, and undeveloped where I was elaborate. Our minds could hardly find a point at which to touch. He gave me, however, under cross-examination, interesting hints about rural matters, and I liked him, although I felt his company to be insipid. Sometimes he carried my books by my side to the larger and more distant school which I now attended, but I was always in a fever of dread lest my schoolfellows should see him, and should accuse me of having to be 'brought' to school. To explain to them that the companionship of this wholesome and rather blunt young peasant was part of my spiritual discipline would have been all beyond my powers.

It was soon after this that my stepmother made her one vain effort to break through the stillness of our lives. My Father's energy seemed to decline, to become more fitful, to take unseasonable directions. My mother instinctively felt that his peculiarities were growing upon him; he would scarcely stir from his microscope, except to go to the chapel, and he was visible to fewer and fewer visitors. She had taken a pleasure in his literary eminence, and she was aware that this, too, would slip from him; that, so persistently kept out of sight, he must soon be out of mind. I know not how she gathered courage for her tremendous effort, but she took me, I recollect, into her counsels. We were to unite to oblige my Father to start to his feet and face the world. Alas! we might as well have attempted to rouse the summit of Yes Tor into volcanic action. To my mother's arguments, my Father – with that baffling smile of his – replied: 'I esteem the reproach of Christ greater riches

203

than the treasures of Egypt!' and that this answer was indirect made it none the less conclusive. My mother wished him to give lectures, to go to London, to read papers before the Royal Society, to enter into controversy with foreign *savants*,[16] to conduct classes of outdoor zoology at fashionable watering-places. I held my breath with admiration as she poured forth her scheme, so daring, so brilliant, so sure to cover our great man with glory. He listened to her with an ambiguous smile, and shook his head at us, and resumed the reading of his Bible.

At the date of which I write these pages, the arts of illustration are so universally diffused that it is difficult to realize the darkness in which a remote English village was plunged half a century ago. No opportunity was offered to us dwellers in remote places of realizing the outward appearances of unfamiliar persons, scenes or things. Although ours was perhaps the most cultivated household in the parish, I had never seen so much as a representation of a work of sculpture till I was thirteen. My mother then received from her earlier home certain volumes, among which was a gaudy gift-book of some kind, containing a few steel engravings of statues.

These attracted me violently, and here for the first time I gazed on Apollo with his proud gesture, Venus in her undulations, the kirtled shape of Diana, and Jupiter voluminously bearded. Very little information, and that to me not intelligible, was given in the text, but these were said to be figures of the old Greek gods. I asked my Father to tell me about these 'old Greek gods'. His answer was direct and disconcerting. He said – how I recollect the place and time, early in the morning, as I stood beside the window in our garish breakfast-room – he said that the so–called gods of the Greeks were the shadows cast by the vices of the heathen, and reflected their infamous lives; 'it was for such things as these that God poured down brimstone and fire on the Cities of the Plain, and there is nothing in the legends of these gods, or rather devils, that it is not better for a Christian not to know'. His face blazed white with Puritan fury as he said this – I see him now in my mind's eye, in his violent emotion. You might have thought that he had himself escaped with horror from some Hellenic hippodrome.

My Father's prestige was by this time considerably lessened in my mind, and though I loved and admired him, I had now long ceased to hold him infallible. I did not accept his condemnation of the Greeks, although I bowed to it. In private I returned to examine my steel engravings of the statues, and I reflected that they were too beautiful to be so wicked as my Father thought they were. The dangerous and pagan notion that beauty palliates evil budded in my mind, without any external suggestion, and by this reflection alone I was still further sundered from the faith in which I had been trained. I gathered very diligently all I could pick up about the Greek gods and their statues; it was not much, it was indeed ludicrously little and false, but it was a germ. And at this aesthetic juncture I was drawn into what was really rather an extraordinary circle of incidents.

Among the 'Saints' in our village there lived a shoemaker and his wife, who had one daughter, Susan Flood. She was a flighty, excited young creature, and lately, during the passage of some itinerary revivalists, she had been 'converted' in the noisiest way, with sobs, gasps and gurglings. When this crisis passed, she came with her parents to our meetings, and was received quietly enough to the breaking of bread. But about the time I speak of, Susan Flood went up to London to pay a visit to an unconverted uncle and aunt. It was first whispered amongst us, and then openly stated, that these relatives had taken her to the Crystal Palace, where, in passing through the Sculpture Gallery, Susan's sense of decency had been so grievously affronted, that she had smashed the naked figures with the handle of her parasol, before her horrified companions could stop her. She had, in fact, run amok among the statuary, and had, to the intense chagrin of her uncle and aunt, very worthy persons, been arrested and brought before a magistrate, who dismissed her with a warning to her relations that she had better be sent home to Devonshire and 'looked after'. Susan

Flood's return to us, however, was a triumph; she had no sense of having acted injudiciously or unbecomingly; she was ready to recount to every one, in vague and veiled language, how she had been able to testify for the Lord 'in the very temple of Belial', for so she poetically described the Crystal Palace. She was, of course, in a state of unbridled hysteria, but such physical explanations were not encouraged amongst us, and the case of Susan Flood awakened a great deal of sympathy.

There was held a meeting of the elders in our drawing-room to discuss it, and I contrived to be present, though out of observation. My Father, while he recognized the purity of Susan Flood's zeal, questioned its wisdom. He noted that the statuary was not her property, but that of the Crystal Palace. Of the other communicants, none, I think, had the very slightest notion what the objects were that Susan had smashed, or tried to smash, and frankly maintained that they thought her conduct magnificent. As for me, I had gathered by persistent inquiry enough information to know that what her sacrilegious parasol had attacked were bodies of my mysterious friends, the Greek gods, and if all the rest of the village applauded iconoclastic Susan, I at least would be ardent on the other side.

But I was conscious that there was nobody in the world to whom I could go for sympathy. If I had ever read 'Hellas' [17] I should have murmured

> Apollo, Pan and Love,
> And even Olympian Jove,
> Grew weak, when killing Susan glared on them.

On the day in question, I was unable to endure the drawing-room meeting to its close, but, clutching my volume of the Funereal Poets, I made a dash for the garden. In the midst of a mass of laurels, a clearing had been hollowed out, where ferns were grown and a garden-seat was placed. There was no regular path to this asylum; one dived under the snake-like boughs of the laurel and came up again in absolute seclusion.

Into this haunt I now fled to meditate about the savage godliness of that vandal, Susan Flood. So extremely ignorant was I that I supposed her to have destroyed the originals of the statues, marble and unique. I knew nothing about plaster casts, and I thought the damage (it is possible that there had really been no damage whatever) was of an irreparable character. I sank into the seat, with the great wall of laurels whispering around me, and I burst into tears. There was something, surely, quaint and pathetic in the figure of a little Plymouth Brother sitting in that advanced year of grace, weeping bitterly for indignities done to Hermes and to Aphrodite. Then I opened my book for consolation, and I read a great block of pompous verse out of 'The Deity', in the midst of which exercise, yielding to the softness of the hot and aromatic air, I fell fast asleep.

Among those who applauded the zeal of Susan Flood's parasol, the Pagets were prominent. These were a retired Baptist minister and his wife, from Exmouth, who had lately settled amongst us, and joined in the breaking of bread. Mr Paget was a fat old man, whose round pale face was clean-shaven, and who carried a full crop of loose white hair above it; his large lips were always moving, whether he spoke or not. He resembled, as I now perceive, the portraits of S. T. Coleridge[18] in age, but with all the intellect left out of them. He lived in a sort of trance of solemn religious despondency. He had thrown up his cure of souls, because he became convinced that he had committed the Sin against the Holy Ghost. His wife was younger than he, very small, very tight, very active, with black eyes like pin-pricks at the base of an extremely high and narrow forehead, bordered with glossy ringlets. He was very cross to her, and it was murmured that 'dear Mrs Paget had often had to pass through the waters of affliction'. They were very poor, but rigidly genteel, and she was careful, so far as she could, to conceal from the world the caprices of her poor lunatic husband.

In our circle, it was never for a moment admitted that Mr Paget was a lunatic. It was said that he had gravely sinned, and was under the Lord's displeasure; prayers were abundantly offered up that he might be led back into the pathway of light, and that the Smiling Face might be drawn forth for him from behind the Frowning Providence. When the man had an epileptic seizure in the High Street, he was not taken to a hospital, but we repeated to one another, with shaken heads, that Satan, that crooked Serpent, had been unloosed for a season. Mr Paget was fond of talking, in private and in public, of his dreadful spiritual condition and he would drop his voice while he spoke of having committed the Unpardonable Sin, with a sort of shuddering exultation, such as people sometimes feel in the possession of a very unusual disease.

It might be thought that the position held in any community by persons so afflicted and eccentric as the Pagets would be very precarious. But it was not so with us; on the contrary, they took a prominent place at once. Mr Paget, in spite of his spiritual bankruptcy, was only too anxious to help my Father in his ministrations, and used to beg to be allowed to pray and exhort. In the latter case he took the tone of a wounded veteran, who, though fallen on the bloody field himself, could still encourage younger warriors to march forward to victory. Everybody longed to know what the exact nature had been of that sin against the Holy Ghost which had deprived Mr Paget of every glimmer of hope for time or for eternity. It was whispered that even my Father himself was not precisely acquainted with the character of it.

This mysterious disability clothed Mr Paget for us with a kind of romance. We watched him as the women watched Dante in Verona, whispering:

> Behold him how Hell's reek
> Has crisped his hair and singed his cheek![19]

His person lacked, it is true, something of the dignity of Dante's, for it was his caprice to walk up and down the High Street at noonday with one of those cascades of coloured paper which were known as 'ornaments for your fireplace' slung over the back and another over the front of his body. These he manufactured for sale, and he adopted the quaint practice of wearing the exuberant objects as a means for their advertisement.

Mrs Paget had been accustomed to rule in the little ministry from which Mr Paget's celebrated Sin had banished them, and she was inclined to clutch at the sceptre now. She was the only person I ever met with who was not afraid of the displeasure of my Father. She would fix her viper-coloured eyes on his, and say with a kind of gimlet firmness, 'I hardly think that is the true interpretation, Brother G.', or, 'But let us turn to Colossians, and see what the Holy Ghost says there upon this matter.' She fascinated my Father, who was not accustomed to this kind of interruption, and as she was not to be softened by any flattery (such as: – 'Marvellous indeed, Sister, is your acquaintance with the means of grace!') she became almost a terror to him.

She abused her powers by taking great liberties, which culminated in her drawing his attention to the fact that my poor stepmother displayed 'an overweening love of dress'. The accusation was perfectly false; my stepmother was, if rather richly, always plainly dressed, in the sober Quaker mode; almost her only ornament was a large carnelian brooch, set in flowered flat gold. To this the envenomed Paget drew my Father's attention as 'likely to lead "the little ones of the flock" into temptation'. My poor Father felt it his duty, thus directly admonished, to speak to my mother. 'Do you not think, my Love, that you should, as one who sets an example to others, discard the wearing of that gaudy brooch?' 'One must fasten one's collar with something, I suppose?' 'Well, but how does Sister Paget fasten her collar?' 'Sister Paget,' replied my Mother, stung at last into rejoinder, 'fastens her collar with a pin, – and that is a thing which I would rather die than do!'

Nor did I escape the attentions of this zealous reformer. Mrs Paget was good enough to take a great interest in me, and she was not satisfied with the way in which I was being brought up. Her presence seemed to pervade the village, and I could neither come in nor go out without seeing her hard bonnet and her pursed-up lips. She would hasten to report to my Father that she saw me laughing and talking 'with a lot of unconverted boys', these being the companions with whom I had full permission to bathe and boat. She urged my Father to complete my holy vocation by some definite step, by which he would dedicate me completely to the Lord's service. Further schooling she thought needless, and merely likely to foster intellectual pride. Mr Paget, she remarked, had troubled very little in his youth about worldly knowledge, and yet how blessed he had been in the conversion of souls until he had incurred the displeasure of the Holy Ghost!

I do not know exactly what she wanted my Father to do with me; perhaps she did not know herself; she was meddlesome, ignorant and fanatical, and she liked to fancy that she was exercising influence. But the wonderful, the inexplicable thing is that my Father, – who, with all his limitations, was so distinguished and high-minded, – should listen to her for a moment, and still more wonderful is it that he really allowed her, grim vixen that she was, to disturb his plans and retard his purposes. I think the explanation lay in the perfectly logical position she took up. My Father found himself brought face to face at last, not with a disciple, but with a trained expert in his own peculiar scheme of religion. At every point she was armed with arguments the source of which he knew and the validity of which he recognized. He trembled before Mrs Paget as a man in a dream may tremble before a parody of his own central self, and he could not blame her without laying himself open somewhere to censure.

But my stepmother's instincts were more primitive and her actions less wire-drawn than my Father's. She disliked Mrs Paget as much as one earnest believer can bring herself to dislike a sister in the Lord. My stepmother had quietly devoted herself to what she thought the best way of bringing me up, and she did not propose now to be thwarted by the wife of a lunatic Baptist. At this time I was a mixture of childishness and priggishness, of curious knowledge and dense ignorance. Certain portions of my intellect were growing with unwholesome activity, while others were stunted, or had never stirred at all. I was like a plant on which a pot has been placed, with the effect that the centre is crushed and arrested, while shoots are straggling up to the light on all sides. My Father himself was aware of this, and in a spasmodic way he wished to regulate my thoughts. But all he did was to try to straighten the shoots without removing the pot which kept them resolutely down.

It was my stepmother who decided that I was now old enough to go to boarding-school, and my Father, having discovered that an elderly couple of Plymouth Brethren kept an 'academy for young gentlemen' in a neighbouring seaport town,[20] – in the prospectus of which the knowledge and love of the Lord were mentioned as occupying the attention of the headmaster and his assistants far more closely than any mere considerations of worldly tuition, – was persuaded to entrust me to its care. He stipulated, however, that I should always come home from Saturday night to Monday morning, not, as he said, that I might receive any carnal indulgence, but that there might be no cessation of my communion as a believer with the Saints in our village on Sundays. To this school, therefore, I presently departed, gawky and homesick, and the rift between my soul and that of my Father widened a little more.

CHAPTER XII

Little boys from quiet, pious households, commonly found, in those days, a chasm yawning at the feet of their inexperience when they arrived at Boarding-school. But the fact that I still slept at home on Saturday and Sunday nights preserved me, I fancy, from many surprises. There was a crisis, but it was broad and slow for me. On the other hand, for my Father I am inclined to think that it was definite and sharp. Permission for me to desert the parental hearth, even for five days in certain weeks, was tantamount, in his mind, to admitting that the great scheme, so long caressed, so passionately fostered, must in its primitive bigness be now dropped.

The Great Scheme (I cannot resist giving it the mortuary of capital letters) had been, as my readers know, that I should be exclusively and consecutively dedicated through the whole of my life, to the manifest and uninterrupted and uncompromised 'service of the Lord'. That had been the aspiration of my Mother, and at her death she had bequeathed that desire to my Father, like a dream of the Promised Land. In their ecstasy, my parents had taken me, as Elkanah and Hannah had long ago taken Samuel,[1] from their mountain-home of Ramathaim-Zophim down to sacrifice to the Lord of Hosts in Shiloh. They had girt me about with a linen ephod, and had hoped to leave me there; 'as long as he liveth,' they had said, 'he shall be lent unto the Lord.'

Doubtless in the course of these fourteen years it had occasionally flashed upon my Father, as he overheard some speech of mine, or detected some idiosyncrasy, that I was not one of those whose temperament points them out as ultimately fitted for an austere life of religion. What he hoped, however, was that when the little roughnesses of childhood were rubbed away, there would pass a deep mellowness over my soul. He had a touching way of condoning my faults of conduct, directly after reproving them, and he would softly deprecate my frailty, saying, in a tone of harrowing tenderness, 'Are you not the child of many prayers?' He continued to think that prayer, such passionate importunate prayer as his, must prevail. Faith could move mountains; should it not be able to mould the little ductile heart of a child, since he was sure that his own faith was unfaltering? He had yearned and waited for a son who should be totally without human audacities, who should be humble, pure, not troubled by worldly agitations, a son whose life should be cleansed and straightened from above, *in custodiendo sermones Dei*;[2] in whom everything should be sacrificed except the one thing needful to salvation.

How such a marvel of lowly piety was to earn a living had never, I think, occurred to him. My Father was singularly indifferent about money. Perhaps his notion was that, totally devoid of ambitions as I was to be, I should quietly become adult, and continue his ministrations among the poor of the Christian flock. He had some dim dream, I think, of there being just enough for us all without my having to take up any business or trade. I believe it was immediately after my first term at boarding-school, that I was a silent but indignant witness of a conversation between my Father and Mr Thomas Brightwen, my stepmother's brother, who was a banker in one of the Eastern Counties.

This question, 'What is he to be?' in a worldly sense, was being discussed, and I am sure that it was for the first time, at all events in my presence. Mr Brightwen, I fancy, had been worked upon by my stepmother, whose affection for me was always on the increase, to suggest, or faintly to stir the air in the neighbourhood of suggesting, a query about my future. He was childless and so was she, and I think a kind impulse led them to 'feel the way', as it is called. I believe he said that the banking business, wisely and honourably conducted, sometimes led, as we know that it is apt to lead, to affluence. To my horror, my Father, with rising emphasis, replied that 'if there were offered to his beloved child what is called "an opening" that would lead to an income of £10,000 a year, and that would divert his thoughts and interest from the Lord's work he would reject it on his child's behalf'. Mr Brightwen, a precise and polished gentleman who evidently never made an exaggerated statement in his life, was, I think, faintly scandalized; he soon left us, and I do not recollect his paying us a second visit.

For my silent part, I felt very much like Gehazi,[3] and I would fain have followed after the banker if I had dared to do so, into the night. I would have excused to him the ardour of my Elisha, and I would have reminded him of the sons of the prophets – 'Give me, I pray thee,' I would have said, 'a talent of silver and two changes of garments.' It seemed to me very hard that my Father should dispose of my possibilities of wealth in so summary a fashion, but the fact that I did resent it, and regretted what I supposed to be my 'chance', shows how far apart we had already swung. My Father, I am convinced, thought that he gave words to my inward instincts when he repudiated the very mild and inconclusive benevolence of his brother-in-law. But he certainly did not do so. I was conscious of a sharp and instinctive disappointment at having had, as I fancied, wealth so near my grasp, and at seeing it all cast violently into the sea of my Father's scruples.

Not one of my village friends attended the boarding-school to which I was now attached, and I arrived there without an acquaintance. I should soon, however, have found a corner of my own if my Father had not unluckily stipulated that I was not to sleep in the dormitory with the boys of my own age, but in the room occupied by the two elder sons of a prominent Plymouth Brother whom he knew. From a social point of view this was an unfortunate arrangement, since these youths were some years older and many years riper than I; the eldest, in fact, was soon to leave; they had enjoyed their independence, and they now greatly resented being saddled with the presence of an unknown urchin. The supposition had been that they would protect and foster my religious practices; would encourage me, indeed, as my Father put it, to approach the Throne of Grace with them at morning and evening prayer. They made no pretence, however, to be considered godly; they looked upon me as an intruder; and after a while the younger, and ruder, of them openly let me know that they believed I had been put into their room to 'spy upon' them; it had been a plot, they knew, between their father and mine; and he darkly warned me that I should suffer if 'anything got out'. I had, however, no wish to trouble them, nor any faint interest in their affairs. I soon discovered that they were absorbed in a silly kind of amorous correspondence with the girls of a neighbouring academy, but 'what were all such toys to me?'

These young fellows, who ought long before to have left the school, did nothing overtly unkind to me, but they condemned me to silence. They ceased to address me except with an occasional command. By reason of my youth, I was in bed and asleep before my companions arrived upstairs, and in the morning I was always routed up and packed about my business while they still were drowsing. But the fact that I had been cut off from my coevals by night, cut me off from them also by day – so that I was nothing to them, neither a boarder nor a day-scholar, neither flesh, fish nor fowl. The loneliness of my life was extreme, and that I always went home on Saturday afternoon and returned on Monday morning still further checked my companionships at school. For a long time, round the outskirts of that busy throng of opening lives, I 'wandered lonely as a cloud', and sometimes I was more unhappy than I had ever been before. No one, however, bullied me, and though I was dimly and indefinably witness to acts of uncleanness and cruelty, I was the victim of no such acts and the recipient of no dangerous confidences. I suppose that my queer reputation for sanctity, half dreadful, half ridiculous, sur-rounded me with a non-conducting atmosphere.

We are the victims of hallowed proverbs, and one of the most classic of these tells us that 'the child is father of the man'. But in my case I cannot think that this was true. In mature years I have always been gregarious, a lover of my kind, de-pendent upon the company of friends for the very pulse of moral life. To be marooned, to be shut up in a solitary cell, to inhabit a lighthouse, or to camp alone in a forest, these have always seemed to me afflictions too heavy to be borne, even in imagination. A state in which conversation exists not, is for me an air too empty of oxygen for my lungs to breathe it.

Yet when I look back upon my days at boarding-school, I see myself unattracted by any of the human beings around me. My grown-up years are made luminous to me in memory by the ardent faces of my friends, but I can scarce recall so much as the names of more than two or three of my schoolfellows. There is not one of them whose mind or whose character made any lasting impression upon me. In later life, I have been im-patient of solitude, and afraid of it; at school, I asked for no more than to slip out of the hurly-burly and be alone with my reflections and my fancies. That magnetism of humanity which has been the agony of mature years, of this I had not a trace when I was a boy. Of those fragile loves to which most men look back with tenderness and passion, emotions to be ex-plained only as Montaigne[4] explained them, *parceque c'était lui, parceque c'était moi*,[5] I knew nothing. I, to whom friendship has since been like sunlight and like sleep, left school unbrightened and unrefreshed by commerce with a single friend.

If I had been clever, I should doubtless have attracted the jealousy of my fellows, but I was spared this by the mediocrity of my success in the classes. One little fact I may mention, because it exemplifies the advance in observation which has been made in forty years. I was extremely nearsighted, and in consequence was placed at a gross disadvantage, by being unable to see the slate or the black-board on which our tasks were explained. It seems almost incredible, when one reflects upon it, but during the whole of my school life, this fact was never commented upon or taken into account by a single person, until the Polish lady who taught us the elements of German and French drew someone's attention to it in my sixteenth year. I was not quick, but I passed for being denser than I was because of the myopic haze that enveloped me. But this is not an autobiography, and with the cold and shrouded details of my uninteresting school-life I will not fatigue the reader.

I was not content, however, to be the cipher that I found myself, and when I had been at school for about a year, I 'broke out', greatly, I think, to my own surprise, in a popular act. We had a young usher whom we disliked. I suppose, poor half-starved phthisic lad,[6] that he was the most miserable of us all. He was, I think, unfitted for the task which had been forced upon him; he was fretful, unsympathetic, agitated. The school-house, an old rambling place, possessed a long cellar-like room that opened from our general corridor and was lighted by deep windows, carefully barred, which looked into an inner garden. This vault was devoted to us and to our play-boxes: by a tacit law, no master entered it. One evening, just at dusk, a great number of us were here when the bell for night-school rang, and many of us dawdled at the summons. Mr B., tactless in his anger, bustled in among us, scolding in a shrill voice, and proceeded to drive us forth. I was the latest to emerge, and as he turned away to see if any other truant might not be hiding, I determined upon action. With a quick movement, I drew the door behind me and bolted it, just in time to hear the imprisoned usher scream with vexation. We boys all trooped upstairs and it is characteristic of my isolation that I had not one 'chum' to whom I could confide my feat.

That Mr B. had been shut in became, however, almost instantly known, and the night-class, usually so unruly, was awed by the event into exemplary decorum. There, with no master near us, in a silence rarely broken by a giggle or a cat-call, we sat diligently working, or pretending to work. Through my brain, as I hung over my book a thousand new thoughts began to surge. I was the liberator, the tyrannicide; I had freed all my fellows from the odious oppressor. Surely, when they learned that it was I, they would cluster round me; surely, now, I should be somebody in the school-life, no longer a mere trotting shadow or invisible presence. The interval seemed long; at length Mr B. was released by a servant, and he came up into the school-room to find us in that ominous condition of suspense.

At first he said nothing. He sank upon a chair in a half-fainting attitude, while he pressed his hand to his side; his distress and silence redoubled the boys' surprise, and filled me with something like remorse. For the first time, I reflected that he was human, that perhaps he suffered. He rose presently and took a slate, upon which he wrote two questions: 'Did you do it?' 'Do you know who did?' and these he propounded to each boy in rotation. The prompt, redoubled 'No' in every case seemed to pile up his despair.

One of the last to whom he held, in silence, the trembling slate was the perpetrator. As I saw the moment approach, an unspeakable timidity swept over me. I reflected that no one had seen me, that no one could accuse me. Nothing could be easier or safer than to deny, nothing more perplexing to the enemy, nothing less perilous for the culprit. A flood of plausible reasons invaded my brain; I seemed to see this to be a case in which to tell the truth would be not merely foolish, it would be wrong. Yet when the usher stood before me, holding the slate out in his white and shaking hand, I seized the pencil, and, ignoring the first question, I wrote 'Yes' firmly against the second. I suppose that the ambiguity of this action puzzled Mr B. He pressed me to answer: 'Did *you* do it?' but to that I was obstinately dumb; and away I was hurried to an empty bed-room, where for the whole of that night and the next day I was held a prisoner, visited at intervals by the headmaster and other inquisitorial persons, until I was gradually persuaded to make a full confession and apology.

This absurd little incident had one effect, it revealed me to my schoolfellows as an existence. From that time forth I lay no longer under the stigma of invisibility; I had produced my material shape and had thrown my shadow for a moment into a legend. But, in other respects, things went on much as before: curiously uninfluenced by my surroundings, I in my turn failed to exercise influence, and my practical isolation was no less than it had been before. It was thus that it came about that my social memories of my boarding-school life are monotonous and vague. It was a period during which, as it appears to me now on looking back, the stream of my spiritual nature spread out into a shallow pool which was almost stagnant. I was labouring to gain those elements of conventional knowledge, which had, in many cases, up to that time been singularly lacking. But my brain was starved, and my intellectual perceptions were veiled. Elder persons who in later years would speak to me frankly of my school-days assured me that, while I had often struck them as a smart and quaint and even interesting child, all promise seemed to fade out of me as a school-boy, and that those who were most inclined to be indulgent gave up the hope that I should prove a man in any way remarkable. This was particularly the case with the most indulgent of my protectors, my refined and gentle stepmother.

As this record can, however, have no value that is not based on its rigorous adhesion to the truth, I am bound to say that the dreariness and sterility of my school-life were more apparent than real. I was pursuing certain lines of moral and mental development all the time, and since my schoolmasters and my school-fellows combined in thinking me so dull, I will display a tardy touch of 'proper spirit' and ask whether it may not partly have been because they were themselves so commonplace. I think that if some drops of sympathy, that magic dew of Paradise, had fallen upon my desert, it might have blossomed like the rose, or, at all events, like that chimerical flower, the Rose of Jericho.[7] As it was, the conventionality around me, the intellectual drought, gave me no opportunity of outward growth. They did not destroy, but they cooped up, and rendered slow and inefficient, that internal life which continued, as I have said, to live on unseen. This took the form of dreams and speculations, in the course of which I went through many tortuous processes of the mind, the actual aims of which were futile, although the movements themselves were useful. If I may more minutely define my meaning, I would say that in my school-days, without possessing thoughts, I yet prepared my mind for thinking, and learned how to think.

The great subject of my curiosity at this time was words, as instruments of expression. I was incessant in adding to my vocabulary, and in finding accurate and individual terms for things. Here, too, the exercise preceded the employment, since I was busy providing myself with words before I had any ideas to express with them. When I read Shakespeare and came upon the passage in which Prospero tells Caliban that he had no thoughts till his master taught him words, I remember starting with amazement at the poet's intuition, for such a Caliban had I been:

> I pitied thee,
> Took pains to make thee speak, taught thee each hour
> One thing or other, when thou didst not, savage,
> Know thine own meaning, but wouldst gabble, like
> A thing most brutish; I endow'd thy purposes
> With words that made them know.

For my Prosperos I sought vaguely in such books as I had access to, and I was conscious that as the inevitable word seized hold of me, with it out of the darkness into strong light came the image and the idea.

My Father possessed a copy of Bailey's *Etymological Dictionary*, a book published early in the eighteenth century. Over this I would pore for hours, playing with the words in a fashion which I can no longer reconstruct, and delighting in the savour of the rich, old-fashioned country phrases. My Father finding me thus employed, fell to wondering at the nature of my pursuit, and I could offer him, indeed, no very intelligible explanation of it. He urged me to give up such idleness, and to make practical use of language. For this purpose he conceived an exercise which he obliged me to adopt, although it was hateful to me. He sent me forth, it might be, up the lane to Warbury Hill and round home by the copses; or else down one chine to the sea and along the shingle to the next cutting in the cliff, and so back by way of the village; and he desired me to put down, in language as full as I could, all that I had seen in each excursion. As I have said, this practice was detestable and irksome to me, but, as I look back, I am inclined to believe it to have been the most salutary, the most practical piece of training which my Father ever gave me. It forced me to observe sharply and clearly, to form visual impressions, to retain them in the brain, and to clothe them in punctilious and accurate language.

It was in my fifteenth year that I became again, this time intelligently, acquainted with Shakespeare. I got hold of a single play, *The Tempest*, in a school edition, prepared, I suppose, for one of the university examinations which were then being instituted in the provinces. This I read through and through, not disdaining the help of the notes, and revelling in the glossary. I studied *The Tempest* as I had hitherto studied no classic work, and it filled my whole being with music and romance. This book was my own hoarded possession; the rest of Shakespeare's works were beyond my hopes. But gradually I contrived to borrow a volume here and a volume there. I completed *The Merchant of Venice*, read *Cymbeline*, *Julius Caesar* and *Much Ado*; most of the others, I think, remained closed to me for a long time. But these were enough to steep my horizon with all the colours of sunrise. It was due, no doubt, to my bringing up, that the plays never appealed to me as bounded by the exigencies of a stage or played by actors. The images they raised in my mind were of real people moving in the open air, and uttering, in the natural play of life, sentiments that were clothed in the most lovely, and yet, as it seemed to me, the most obvious and the most inevitable language.

It was while I was thus under the full spell of the Shakespearean necromancy that a significant event occurred. My Father took me up to London for the first time since my infancy. Our visit was one of a few days only, and its purpose was that we might take part in some enormous Evangelical conference. We stayed in a dark hotel off the Strand, where I found the noise by day and night very afflicting. When we were not at the conference, I spent long hours, among crumbs and bluebottle flies, in the coffee-room of this hotel, my Father being busy at the British Museum and the Royal Society. The conference was held in an immense hall, somewhere in the north of London. I remember my short-sighted sense of the terrible vastness of the crowd, with rings on rings of dim white faces fading in the fog. My Father, as a privileged visitor, was obliged with seats on the platform, and we were in the heart of the first really large assemblage of persons that I had ever seen.

The interminable ritual of prayers, hymns and addresses left no impression on my memory, but my attention was suddenly stung into life by a remark. An elderly man, fat and greasy, with a voice like a bassoon, and an imperturbable assurance, was denouncing the spread of infidelity, and the lukewarmness of professing Christians, who refrained from battling with the wickedness at their doors. They were like the Laodiceans, whom the angel of the Apocalypse spewed out of his mouth. For instance, who, the orator asked, is now rising to check the outburst of idolatry in our midst? 'At this very moment,' he went on, 'there is proceeding, unreproved, a blasphemous celebration of the birth of Shakespeare, a lost soul now suffering for his sins in hell!' My sensation was that of one who has suddenly been struck on the head; stars and sparks beat around me. If some person I loved had been grossly insulted in my presence, I could not have felt more powerless in anguish. No one in that vast audience raised a word of protest, and my spirits fell to their nadir. This, be it remarked, was the earliest intimation that had reached me of the tercentenary of the Birth at Stratford, and I had not the least idea what could have provoked the outburst of outraged godliness.

But Shakespeare was certainly in the air. When we returned to the hotel that noon, my Father of his own accord reverted to the subject. I held my breath, prepared to endure fresh torment. What he said, however, surprised and relieved me. 'Brother So and So,' he remarked, 'was not, in my judgement, justified in saying what he did. The uncovenanted mercies of God are not revealed to us. Before so rashly speaking of Shakespeare as "a lost soul in hell", he should have remembered how little we know of the poet's history. The light of salvation was widely disseminated in the land during the reign of Queen Elizabeth, and we cannot know that Shakespeare did not accept the atonement of Christ in simple faith before he came to die.' The concession will today seem meagre to gay and worldly spirits, but words cannot express how comfortable it was to me. I gazed at my Father with loving eyes across the cheese and celery, and if the waiter had not been present I believe I might have hugged him in my arms.

This anecdote may serve to illustrate the attitude of my conscience, at this time, with regard to theology. I was not consciously in any revolt against the strict faith in which I had been brought up, but I could not fail to be aware of the fact that literature tempted me to stray up innumerable paths which meandered in directions at right angles to that direct strait way which leadeth to salvation. I fancied, if I may pursue the image, that I was still safe up these pleasant lanes if I did not stray far enough to lose sight of the main road. If, for instance, it had been quite certain that Shakespeare had been irrecoverably damnable and damned, it would scarcely have been possible for me to have justified myself in going on reading *Cymbeline*. One who broke bread with the Saints every Sunday morning, who 'took a class' at Sunday school, who made, as my Father loved to remind me, a public weekly confession of his willingness to bear the Cross of Christ, such an one could hardly, however bewildering and torturing the thought, continue to admire a lost soul. But that happy possibility of an ultimate repentance, how it eased me! I could always console myself with the belief that when Shakespeare wrote any passage of intoxicating beauty, it was just then that he was beginning to breathe the rapture that faith in Christ brings to the anointed soul. And it was with a like casuistry that I condoned my other intellectual and personal pleasures.

My Father continued to be under the impression that my boarding-school, which he never again visited after originally leaving me there, was conducted upon the same principles as his own household. I was frequently tempted to enlighten him, but I never found the courage to do so. As a matter of fact the piety of the establishment, which collected to it the sons of a large number of evangelically minded parents throughout that part of the country, resided mainly in the prospectus. It proceeded no further than the practice of reading the Bible aloud, each boy in successive order one verse, in the early morning before breakfast. There was no selection and no exposition; where the last boy sat, there the day's reading ended, even if it were in the middle of a sentence, and there it began next morning.

Such reading of 'the chapter' was followed by a long dry prayer. I do not know that this morning service would appear more perfunctory than usual to other boys, but it astounded and disgusted me, accustomed as I was to the ministrations at home, where my Father read 'the word of God' in a loud passionate voice, with dramatic emphasis, pausing for commentary and paraphrase, and treating every phrase as if it were part of a personal message or of thrilling family history. At school, 'morning prayer' was a dreary, unintelligible exercise, and with this piece of mumbo-jumbo, religion for the day began and ended. The discretion of little boys is extraordinary. I am quite certain no one of us ever revealed this fact to our godly parents at home.

If any one was to do this, it was of course I who should first of all have 'testified'. But I had grown cautious about making confidences. One never knew how awkwardly they might develop or to what disturbing excesses of zeal they might precipitously lead. I was on my guard against my Father, who was, all the time, only too openly yearning that I should approach him for help, for comfort, for ghostly counsel. Still 'delicate', though steadily gaining in solidity of constitution, I was liable to severe chills and to fugitive neuralgic pangs. My Father was, almost maddeningly, desirous that these afflictions should be sanctified to me, and it was in my bed, often when I was much bowed in spirit by indisposition, that he used to triumph over me most pitilessly. He retained the singular superstition, amazing in a man of scientific knowledge and long human experience, that all pains and ailments were directly sent by the Lord in chastisement for some definite fault, and not in relation to any physical cause. The result was sometimes quite startling, and in particular I recollect that my stepmother and I exchanged impressions of astonishment at my Father's action when Mrs Goodyer, who was one of the 'Saints' and the wife of a young journeyman cobbler, broke her leg. My Father, puzzled for an instant as to the meaning of this accident, since Mrs Goodyer was the gentlest and most inoffensive of our church members, decided that it must be because she had made an idol of her husband, and he reduced the poor thing to tears by standing at her bed-side and imploring the Holy Spirit to bring this sin home to her conscience.

When, therefore, I was ill at home with one of my trifling disorders, the problem of my spiritual state always pressed violently upon my Father, and this caused me no little mental uneasiness. He would appear at my bed-side, with solemn solicitude, and sinking on his knees would earnestly pray aloud that the purpose of the Lord in sending me this affliction might graciously be made plain to me; and then, rising, and standing by my pillow, he would put me through a searching spiritual inquiry as to the fault which was thus divinely indicated to me as observed and reprobated on high.

It was not on points of moral behaviour that he thus cross-examined me; I think he disdained such ignoble game as that. But uncertainties of doctrine, relinquishment of faith in the purity of this dogma or of that, lukewarm zeal in 'taking up the cross of Christ', growth of intellectual pride, – such were the insidious offences in consequence of which, as he supposed, the cold in the head or the toothache had been sent as heavenly messengers to recall my straggling conscience to its plain path of duty.

What made me very uncomfortable on these occasions was my consciousness that confinement to bed was hardly an affliction at all. It kept me from the boredom of school, in a fire-lit bedroom at home, with my pretty, smiling stepmother lavishing luxurious attendance upon me, and it gave me long, unbroken days for reading. I was awkwardly aware that I simply had not the effrontery to 'approach the Throne of Grace' with a request to know for what sin I was condemned to such a very pleasant disposition of my hours.

The current of my life ran, during my school-days, most merrily and fully in the holidays, when I resumed my outdoor exercises with those friends in the village of whom I have spoken earlier. I think they were more refined and better bred than any of my schoolfellows, at all events it was among these homely companions alone that I continued to form congenial and sympathetic relations. In one of these boys, – one of whom I have heard or seen nothing now for nearly a generation, – I found tastes singularly parallel to my own, and we scoured the horizon in search of books in prose and verse, but particularly in verse.

As I grew stronger in muscle, I was capable of adding considerably to my income by an exercise of my legs. I was allowed money for the railway ticket between the town where the school lay and the station nearest to my home. But, if I chose to walk six or seven miles along the coast, thus more than halving the distance by rail from school-house to home, I might spend as pocket money the railway fare I thus saved.

Such considerable sums I fostered in order to buy with them editions of the poets. These were not in those days, as they are now, at the beck and call of every purse, and the attainment of each little masterpiece was a separate triumph. In particular I shall never forget the excitement of reaching at length the exorbitant price the bookseller asked for the only, although imperfect, edition of the poems of S. T. Coleridge. At last I could meet his demand, and my friend and I went down to consummate the solemn purchase. Coming away with our treasure, we read aloud from the orange-coloured volume, in turns, as we strolled along, until at last we sat down on the bulging root of an elm tree in a secluded lane. Here we stayed, in a sort of poetical *nirvana*, reading, reading, forgetting the passage of time, until the hour of our neglected mid-day meal was a long while past, and we had to hurry home to bread and cheese and a scolding.

There was occasionally some trouble about my reading, but now not much nor often I was rather adroit, and careful not to bring prominently into sight anything of a literary kind which could become a stone of stumbling. But, when I was nearly sixteen, I made a purchase which brought me into sad trouble, and was the cause of a permanent wound to my self-respect. I had long coveted in the book-shop window a volume in which the poetical works of Ben Jonson and Christopher Marlowe[8] were said to be combined. This I bought at length, and I carried it with me to devour as I trod the desolate road that brought me along the edge of the cliff on Saturday afternoons. Of Ben Jonson I could make nothing, but when I turned to 'Hero and Leander',[9] I was lifted to a heaven of passion and music. It was a marvellous revelation of romantic beauty to me, and as I paced along that lonely and exquisite highway, with its immense command of the sea, and its peeps every now and then, through slanting thickets, far down to the snow-white shingle, I lifted up my voice, singing the verses, as I strolled along:

Buskins of shells, all silver'd, used she,
And branch'd with blushing coral to the knee,
Where sparrows perched, of hollow pearl and gold,
Such as the world would wonder to behold, –

so it went on, and I thought I had never read anything so lovely, –

Amorous Leander, beautiful and young,
Whose tragedy divine Musaeus sung, –

it all seemed to my fancy intoxicating beyond anything I had ever even dreamed of, since I had not yet become acquainted with any of the modern romanticists.

When I reached home, tired out with enthusiasm and exercise, I must needs, so soon as I had eaten, search out my stepmother that she might be a partner in my joys. It is remarkable to me now, and a disconcerting proof of my still almost infantile innocence, that, having induced her to settle to her knitting, I began, without hesitation, to read Marlowe's voluptuous poem aloud to that blameless Christian gentlewoman. We got on very well in the opening, but at the episode of Cupid's pining, my stepmother's needles began nervously to clash, and when we launched on the description of Leander's person, she interrupted me by saying, rather sharply, 'Give me that book, please, I should like to read the rest to myself.' I resigned the reading in amazement, and was stupefied to see her take the volume, shut it with a snap and hide it under her needlework. Nor could I extract from her another word on the subject.

The matter passed from my mind, and I was therefore extremely alarmed when, soon after my going to bed that night, my Father came into my room with a pale face and burning eyes, the prey of violent perturbation. He set down the candle and stood by the bed, and it was some time before he could resolve on a form of speech. Then he denounced me, in unmeasured terms, for bringing into the house, for possessing at all or reading, so abominable a book. He explained that my stepmother had shown it to him, and that he had looked through it, and had burned it.

The sentence in his tirade which principally affected me was this. He said, 'You will soon be leaving us, and going up to lodgings in London, and if your landlady should come into your room, and find such a book lying about, she would immediately set you down as a profligate.' I did not understand this at all, and it seems to me now that the fact that I had so very simply and childishly volunteered to read the verses to my stepmother should have proved to my Father that I connected it with no ideas of an immoral nature.

I was greatly wounded and offended, but my indignation was smothered up in the alarm and excitement which followed the news that I was to go up to live in lodgings, and, as it was evident, alone, in London. Of this no hint or whisper had previously reached me. On reflection, I can but admit that my Father, who was little accustomed to seventeenth-century literature, must have come across some startling exposures in Ben Jonson, and probably never reached 'Hero and Leander' at all. The artistic effect of such poetry on an innocently pagan mind did not come within the circle of his experience. He judged the outspoken Elizabethan poets, no doubt, very much in the spirit of the problematical landlady.

Of the world outside, of the dim wild whirlpool of London, I was much afraid, but I was now ready to be willing to leave the narrow Devonshire circle, to see the last of the red mud, of the dreary village street, of the plethoric elders,[10] to hear the last of the drawling voices of the 'Saints'. Yet I had a great difficulty in persuading myself that I could ever be happy away from home, and again I compared my lot with that of one of the speckled soldier-crabs that roamed about in my Father's aquarium, dragging after them great whorl-shells. They, if by chance they were turned out of their whelk-habitations, trailed about a pale soft body in search of another house, visibly broken-hearted and the victims of every ignominious accident.

My spirits were divided pathetically between the wish to stay on, a guarded child, and to proceed into the world, a budding man, and, in my utter ignorance, I sought in vain to conjure up what my immediate future would be. My Father threw no light upon the subject, for he had not formed any definite idea of what I could possibly do to earn an honest living. As a matter of fact I was to stay another year at school and home.

This last year of my boyish life passed rapidly and pleasantly. My sluggish brain waked up at last and I was able to study with application. In the public examinations I did pretty well, and may even have been thought something of a credit to the school. Yet I formed no close associations, and I even contrived to avoid, as I had afterwards occasion to regret, such lessons as were distasteful to me, and therefore particularly valuable. But I read with unchecked voracity, and in several curious directions. Shakespeare now passed into my possession entire, in the shape of a reprint more hideous and more offensive to the eyesight than would in these days appear conceivable. I made acquaintance with Keats, who entirely captivated me; with Shelley, whose 'Queen Mab'[11] at first repelled me from the threshold of his edifice; and with Wordsworth, for the exercise of whose magic I was still far too young. My Father presented me with the entire bulk of Southey's stony verse, which I found it impossible to penetrate, but my stepmother lent me *The Golden Treasury*,[12] in which almost everything seemed exquisite.

Upon this extension of my intellectual powers, however, there did not follow any spirit of doubt or hostility to the faith. On the contrary, at first there came a considerable quickening of fervour. My prayers became less frigid and mechanical; I no longer avoided as far as possible the contemplation of religious ideas; I began to search the Scriptures for myself with interest and sympathy, if scarcely with ardour. I began to perceive, without animosity, the strange narrowness of my Father's system, which seemed to take into consideration only a selected circle of persons, a group of disciples peculiarly illuminated, and to have no message whatever for the wider Christian community.

On this subject I had some instructive conversations with my Father, whom I found not reluctant to have his convictions pushed to their logical extremity. He did not wish to judge, he protested; but he could not admit that a single Unitarian (or 'Socinian', as he preferred to say)[13] could possibly be redeemed; and he had no hope of eternal salvation for the inhabitants of Catholic countries. I recollect his speaking of Austria. He questioned whether a single Austrian subject, except, as he said, here and there a pious and extremely ignorant individual, who had not comprehended the errors of the Papacy, but had humbly studied his Bible, could hope to find eternal life. He thought that the ordinary Chinaman or savage native of Fiji had a better chance of salvation than any cardinal in the Vatican. And even in the priesthood of the Church of England he believed that while many were called, few indeed would be found to have been chosen.

I could not sympathize, even in my then state of ignorance, with so rigid a conception of the Divine mercy. Little inclined as I was to be sceptical, I still thought it impossible, that a secret of such stupendous importance should have been entrusted to a little group of Plymouth Brethren, and have been hidden from millions of disinterested and pious theologians. That the leaders of European Christianity were sincere, my Father did not attempt to question. But they were all of them wrong, *incorrect*; and no matter how holy their lives, how self-sacrificing their actions, they would have to suffer for their inexactitude through aeons of undefined torment. He would speak with a solemn complacency of the aged nun, who, after a long life of renunciation and devotion, died at last, 'only to discover her mistake'.

He who was so tender-hearted that he could not bear to witness the pain or distress of any person, however disagreeable or undeserving, was quite acquiescent in believing that God would punish human beings, in millions, for ever, for a purely intellectual error of comprehension. My Father's inconsistencies of perception seem to me to have been the result of a curious

231

irregularity of equipment. Taking for granted, as he did, the absolute integrity of the Scriptures, and applying to them his trained scientific spirit, he contrived to stifle, with a deplorable success, alike the function of the imagination, the sense of moral justice, and his own deep and instinctive tenderness of heart.

There presently came over me a strong desire to know what doctrine indeed it was that the other Churches taught. I expressed a wish to be made aware of the practices of Rome, or at least of Canterbury, and I longed to attend the Anglican and the Roman services. But to do so was impossible. My Father did not, indeed, forbid me to enter the fine parish church of our village, or the stately Puginesque cathedral which Rome had just erected[14] at its side, but I knew that I could not be seen at either service without his immediately knowing it, or without his being deeply wounded. Although I was sixteen years of age, and although I was treated with indulgence and affection, I was still but a bird fluttering in the net-work of my Father's will, and incapable of the smallest independent action. I resigned all thought of attending any other services than those at our 'Room', but I did no longer regard this exclusion as a final one. I bowed, but it was in the house of Rimmon, from which I now knew that I must inevitably escape. All the liberation, however, which I desired or dreamed of was only just so much as would bring me into communion with the outer world of Christianity without divesting me of the pure and simple principles of faith.

Of so much emancipation, indeed, I now became ardently desirous, and in the contemplation of it I rose to a more considerable degree of religious fervour than I had ever reached before or was ever to experience later. Our thoughts were at this time abundantly exercised with the expectation of the immediate coming of the Lord, who, as my Father and those who thought with him believed, would suddenly appear, without the least warning, and would catch up to be with Him in everlasting glory all whom acceptance of the Atonement had sealed for immortality. These were, on the whole, not numerous, and our belief was that the world, after a few days' amazement at the total disappearance of these persons, would revert to its customary habits of life, merely sinking more rapidly into a moral corruption due to the removal of these souls of salt. This event an examination of prophecy had led my Father to regard as absolutely imminent, and sometimes, when we parted for the night, he would say with a sparkling rapture in his eyes, 'Who knows? We may meet next in the air, with all the cohorts of God's saints!'

This conviction I shared, without a doubt; and, indeed, – in perfect innocency, I hope, but perhaps with a touch of slyness too, – I proposed at the end of the summer holidays that I should stay at home. 'What is the use of my going to school? Let me be with you when we rise to meet the Lord in the air!' To this my Father sharply and firmly replied that it was our duty to carry on our usual avocations to the last, for we knew not the moment of His coming, and we should be together in an instant on that day, how far soever we might be parted upon earth. I was ashamed, but his argument was logical, and, as it proved, judicious. My Father lived for nearly a quarter of a century more, never losing the hope of 'not tasting death', and as the last moments of mortality approached, he was bitterly disappointed at what he held to be a scanty reward of his long faith and patience. But if my own life's work had been, as I proposed, shelved in expectation of the Lord's imminent advent, I should have cumbered the ground until this day.

To school, therefore, I returned with a brain full of strange discords, in a huddled mixture of 'Endymion' [15] and the Book of Revelation, John Wesley's hymns and 'Midsummer Night's Dream'. Few boys of my age, I suppose, carried about with them such a confused throng of immature impressions and contradictory hopes. I was at one moment devoutly pious, at the next haunted by visions of material beauty and longing for sensuous impressions. In my hot and silly brain, Jesus and Pan

233

held sway together, as in a wayside chapel discordantly and impishly consecrated to Pagan and to Christian rites. But for the present, as in the great chorus which so marvellously portrays our double nature,[16] 'the folding-star of Bethlehem' was still dominant. I became more and more pietistic. Beginning now to versify, I wrote a tragedy in pale imitation of Shakespeare,[17] but on a Biblical and evangelistic subject; and odes that were parodies of those in 'Prometheus Unbound',[18] but dealt with the approaching advent of our Lord and the rapture of His saints. My unwholesome excitement, bubbling up in this violent way, reached at last a climax and foamed over.

It was a summer afternoon, and, being now left very free in my movements, I had escaped from going out with the rest of my school-fellows in their formal walk in charge of an usher. I had been reading a good deal of poetry, but my heart had translated Apollo and Bacchus into terms of exalted Christian faith. I was alone, and I lay on a sofa, drawn across a large open window at the top of the school-house, in a room which was used as a study by the boys who were 'going up for examination'. I gazed down on a labyrinth of garden sloping to the sea, which twinkled faintly beyond the towers of the town. Each of these gardens held a villa in it, but all the near landscape below me was drowned in foliage. A wonderful warm light of approaching sunset modelled the shadows and set the broad summits of the trees in a rich glow. There was an absolute silence below and around me; a magic of suspense seemed to keep every topmost twig from waving.

Over my soul there swept an immense wave of emotion. Now, surely, now the great final change must be approaching. I gazed up into the tenderly-coloured sky, and I broke irresistibly into speech. 'Come now, Lord Jesus,' I cried, 'come now and take me to be for ever with Thee in Thy Paradise. I am ready to come. My heart is purged from sin, there is nothing that keeps me rooted to this wicked world. Oh, come now, now, and take me before I have known the temptations of life, before I have to go to London and all the dreadful things that happen there!' And I raised myself on the sofa, and leaned upon the window-sill, and waited for the glorious apparition.

This was the highest moment of my religious life, the apex of my striving after holiness. I waited awhile, watching; and then I felt a faint shame at the theatrical attitude I had adopted, although I was alone. Still I gazed and still I hoped. Then a little breeze sprang up and the branches danced. Sounds began to rise from the road beneath me. Presently the colour deepened, the evening came on. From far below there rose to me the chatter of the boys returning home. The tea-bell rang, – last word of prose to shatter my mystical poetry. 'The Lord has not come, the Lord will never come,' I muttered, and in my heart the artificial edifice of extravagant faith began to totter and crumble. From that moment forth my Father and I, though the fact was long successfully concealed from him and even from myself, walked in opposite hemispheres of the soul, with 'the thick o' the world between us'.

EPILOGUE

This narrative, however, must not be allowed to close with the Son in the foreground of the piece. If it has a value, that value consists in what light it may contrive to throw upon the unique and noble figure of the Father. With the advance of years, the characteristics of this figure became more severely outlined, more rigorously confined within settled limits. In relation to the Son – who presently departed, at a very immature age, for the new life in London – the attitude of the Father continued to be one of extreme solicitude, deepening by degrees into disappointment and disenchantment. He abated no jot or tittle of his demands upon human frailty. He kept the spiritual cord drawn tight; the Biblical bearing-rein was incessantly busy, jerking into position the head of the dejected neophyte. That young soul, removed from the Father's personal inspection, began to blossom forth crudely and irregularly enough, into new provinces of thought, through fresh layers of experience. To the painful mentor at home in the West, the centre of anxiety was still the meek and docile heart, dedicated to the Lord's service, which must, at all hazards and with all defiance of the rules of life, be kept unspotted from the world.

The torment of a postal inquisition began directly I was settled in my London lodgings. To my Father – with his ample leisure, his palpitating apprehension; his ready pen – the flow of correspondence offered no trouble at all; it was a grave but gratifying occupation. To me the almost daily letter of exhortation, with its string of questions about conduct, its series of warnings, grew to be a burden which could hardly be borne, particularly because it involved a reply as punctual and if possible as full as itself. At the age of seventeen, the metaphysics of the soul are shadowy, and it is a dreadful thing to be forced to define the exact outline of what is so undulating and so shapeless. To my Father there seemed no reason why I should hesitate to give answers of full metallic ring to his hard and oft-repeated questions; but to me this correspondence was torture. When I feebly expostulated, when I begged to be left a little to myself, these appeals of mine automatically stimulated, and indeed blew up into fierce flames, the ardour of my Father's alarm.

The letter, the only too-confidently expected letter, would lie on the table as I descended to breakfast. It would commonly be, of course, my only letter, unless tempered by a cosy and chatty note from my dear and comfortable stepmother, dealing with such perfectly tranquillizing subjects as the harvest of roses in the garden or the state of health of various neighbours. But the other, the solitary letter, in its threatening whiteness, with its exquisitely penned address – there it would lie awaiting me, destroying the taste of the bacon, reducing the flavour of the tea to insipidity. I might fatuously dally with it, I might pretend not to observe it, but there it lay. Before the morning's exercise began, I knew that it had to be read, and what was worse, that it had to be answered. Useless the effort to conceal from myself what it contained. Like all its precursors, like all its followers, it would insist, with every variety of appeal, on a reiterated declaration that I still fully intended, as in the days of my earliest childhood, 'to be on the Lord's side' in everything.

In my replies, I would sometimes answer precisely as I was desired to answer; sometimes I would evade the queries, and write about other things; sometimes I would turn upon the tormentor, and urge that my tender youth might be let alone. It little mattered what form of weakness I put forth by way of baffling my Father's direct, firm, unflinching strength. To an appeal against the bondage of a correspondence of such unbroken solemnity I would receive – with what a paralysing promptitude! – such a reply as this: –

Let me say that the 'solemnity' you complain of has only been the expression of tender anxiousness of a father's heart, that his only child, just turned out upon the world, and very far out of his sight and hearing, should be walking in God's way. Recollect that it is not now as it was when you were at school, when we had personal communication with you at intervals of five days: – we now know absolutely nothing of you, save from your letters, and if they do not indicate your spiritual prosperity, the deepest solicitudes of our hearts have nothing to feed on. But I will try henceforth to trust you, and lay aside my fears; for you are worthy of my confidence; and your own God and your father's God will hold you with His right hand.

Over such letters as these I am not ashamed to say that I sometimes wept; the old paper I have just been copying shows traces of tears shed upon it more than forty years ago, tears commingled of despair at my own feebleness, distraction, at my want of will, pity for my Father's manifest and pathetic distress. He would 'try henceforth to trust' me, he said. Alas! the effort would be in vain; after a day or two, after a hollow attempt to write of other things, the importunate subject would recur; there would intrude again the inevitable questions about the Atonement and the Means of Grace, the old anxious fears lest I was 'yielding' my intimacy to agreeable companions who were not 'one with me in Christ', fresh passionate entreaties to be assured, in every letter, that I was walking in the clear light of God's presence.

It seems to me now profoundly strange, although I knew too little of the world to remark it at the time, that these incessant exhortations dealt, not with conduct, but with faith. Earlier in this narrative I have noted how disdainfully, with what an austere pride, my Father refused to entertain the subject of personal shortcomings in my behaviour. There were enough of them to blame, Heaven knows, but he was too lofty-minded a gentleman to dwell upon them, and, though by nature deeply suspicious of the possibility of frequent moral lapses, even in the very elect, he refused to stoop to anything like espionage. I owe him a deep debt of gratitude for his beautiful faith in me in this respect, and now that I was alone in London, at this tender time of life, 'exposed', as they say, to all sorts of dangers, as defenceless as a fledgling that has been turned out of its nest, yet my Father did not, in his uplifted Quixotism,[1] allow himself to fancy me guilty of any moral misbehaviour, but concentrated his fears entirely upon my faith.

'Let me know more of your inner light. Does the candle of the Lord shine on your soul?' This would be the ceaseless inquiry. Or, again, 'Do you get any spiritual companionship with young men? You passed over last Sunday without even a word, yet this day is the most interesting to me in your whole week. Do you find the ministry of the Word pleasant, and, above all, profitable? Does it bring your soul into exercise before God? The Coming of Christ draweth nigh. Watch, therefore and pray always, that you may be counted worthy to stand before the Son of Man.'

If I quote such passages as this from my Father's letters to me, it is not that I seek entertainment in a contrast between his earnestness and the casuistical inattention and provoked distractedness of a young man to whom the real world now offered its irritating and stimulating scenes of animal and intellectual life, but to call out sympathy, and perhaps wonder, at the spectacle of so blind a Roman firmness as my Father's spiritual attitude displayed.

His aspirations were individual and metaphysical. At the present hour, so complete is the revolution which has overturned the puritanism of which he was perhaps the latest surviving type, that all class of religious persons combine in placing philanthropic activity, the objective attitude, in the foreground. It is extraordinary how far-reaching the change has been, so that nowadays a religion which does not combine with its subjective faith a strenuous labour for the good of others is hardly held to possess any religious principle worth proclaiming.

This propaganda of beneficence, this constant attention to the moral and physical improvement of persons who have been neglected, is quite recent as a leading feature of religion, though indeed it seems to have formed some part of the Saviour's original design. It was unknown to the great preachers of the seventeenth century, whether Catholic or Protestant, and it offered but a shadowy attraction to my Father, who was the last of their disciples. When Bossuet[2] desired his hearers to listen to the *cri de misère à l'entour de nous, qui devrait nous fondre le coeur*,[3] he started a new thing in the world of theology. We may search the famous 'Rule and Exercises of Holy Living' from cover to cover, and not learn that Jeremy Taylor[4] would have thought that any activity of the district-visitor or the Salvation lassie came within the category of saintliness.

My Father, then, like an old divine, concentrated on thoughts upon the intellectual part of faith. In his obsession about me, he believed that if my brain could be kept unaffected by any of the seductive errors of the age, and my heart centred in the adoring love of God, all would be well with me in perpetuity. He was still convinced that by intensely directing my thoughts, he could compel them to flow in a certain channel, since he had not begun to learn the lesson, so mournful for saintly men of his complexion, that 'virtue would not be virtue, could it be given by one fellow creature to another'. He had recognized, with reluctance, that holiness was not hereditary, but he continued to hope that it might be compulsive. I was still 'the child of many prayers', and it was not to be conceded that these prayers could remain unanswered.

The great panacea was now, as always, the study of the Bible, and this my Father never ceased to urge upon me. He presented to me a copy of Dean Alford's edition of the Greek New Testament, in four great volumes, and these he had had so magnificently bound in full morocco that the work shone on my poor shelf of sixpenny poets like a duchess among dairymaids. He extracted from me a written promise that I would translate and meditate upon a portion of the Greek text every morning before I started for business. This promise I presently failed to keep, my good intentions being undermined by an invincible *ennui*; I concealed the dereliction from him, and the sense that I was deceiving my Father ate into my conscience like a canker. But the dilemma was now before me that I must either deceive my Father in such things or paralyse my own character.

My growing distaste for the Holy Scriptures began to occupy my thoughts, and to surprise as much as it scandalized me. My desire was to continue to delight in those sacred pages, for which I still had an instinctive veneration. Yet I could not but observe the difference between the zeal with which I snatched at a volume of Carlyle or Ruskin [5] – since these magicians were now first revealing themselves to me – and the increasing languor with which I took up Alford for my daily 'passage'. Of course, although I did not know it, and believed my reluctance to be sinful, the real reason why I now found the Bible so difficult to read was my familiarity with its contents. These had the colourless triteness of a story retold a hundred times. I longed for something new, something that would gratify curiosity and excite surprise. Whether the facts and doctrines contained in the Bible were true or false was not the question that appealed to me; it was rather that they had been presented to me so often and had sunken into me so far that, as someone has said, they 'lay bedridden in the dormitory of the soul', and made no impression of any kind upon me.

It often amazed me, and I am still unable to understand the fact, that my Father, through his long life – or till nearly the close of it – continued to take an eager pleasure in the text of the Bible. As I think I have already said, before he reached middle life, he had committed practically the whole of it to memory, and if started anywhere, even in a Minor Prophet, he could go on without a break as long as ever he was inclined for that exercise. He, therefore, at no time can have been assailed by the satiety of which I have spoken, and that it came so soon to me I must take simply as an indication of difference of temperament. It was not possible, even through the dark glass of correspondence, to deceive his eagle eye in this matter, and his suspicions accordingly took another turn. He conceived me to have become, or to be becoming, a victim of 'the infidelity of the age'.

In this new difficulty, he appealed to forms of modern literature by the side of which the least attractive pages of Leviticus or Deuteronomy struck me as even thrilling. In particular, he urged upon me a work, then just published, called *The Continuity of Scripture*[6] by William Page Wood, afterwards Lord Chancellor Hathérley. I do not know why he supposed that the lucubrations of an exemplary lawyer, delivered in a style that was like the trickling of sawdust, would succeed in rousing emotions which the glorious rhetoric of the Orient had failed to awaken; but Page Wood had been a Sunday School teacher for thirty years, and my Father was always unduly impressed by the acumen of pious barristers.

As time went on, and I grew older and more independent in mind, my Father's anxiety about what he called 'the pitfalls and snares which surround on every hand the thoughtless giddy youth of London' became extremely painful to himself. By harping in private upon these 'pitfalls' – which brought to my imagination a funny rough woodcut in an old edition of Bunyan,[7] where a devil was seen capering over a sort of box let neatly into the ground – he worked himself up into a frame of mind which was not a little irritating to his hapless correspondent, who was now 'snared' indeed, limed by the pen like a bird by the feet, and could not by any means escape. To a peck or a flutter from the bird the implacable fowler would reply:

You charge me with being suspicious, and I fear I cannot deny the charge. But I can appeal to your own sensitive and thoughtful mind for a considerable allowance. My deep and tender love for you; your youth and inexperience; the examples of other young men; your distance from parental counsel; our absolute and painful ignorance of all the details of your daily life, except what you yourself tell us: – try to throw yourself into the standing of a parent, and say if my suspiciousness is unreasonable. I rejoicingly acknowledge that from all I see you are pursuing a virtuous, steady, worthy course. One good thing my suspiciousness does: – ever and anon it brings out from you assurances, which greatly refresh and comfort me. And again, it carries me ever to God's Throne of Grace on your behalf. Holy Job *suspected* that his sons might have sinned, and cursed God in their heart. Was not his suspicion much like mine, grounded on the same reasons and productive of the same results? For it drove him to God in intercession. I have adduced the example of this Patriarch before, and he will endure being looked at again.

In fact, Holy Job continued to be frequently looked at, and for this Patriarch I came to experience a hatred which was as venomous as it was undeserved. But what youth of eighteen would willingly be compared with the sons of Job? And indeed, for my part, I felt much more like that justly exasperated character, Elihu the Buzite, of the kindred of Ram.[8]

As time went on, the peculiar strain of inquisition was relaxed, and I endured fewer and fewer of the torments of religious correspondence. Nothing abides in one tense projection, and my Father, resolute as he was, had other preoccupations. His orchids, his microscope, his physiological researches, his interpretations of prophecy, filled up the hours of his active and strenuous life, and, out of his sight, I became not indeed out of his mind, but no longer ceaselessly in the painful foreground of it. Yet, although the reiteration of his anxiety might weary him a little as it had wearied me well nigh to groans of despair, there was not the slightest change in his real attitude towards the subject or towards me.

I have already had occasion to say that he had nothing of the mystic or the visionary about him. At certain times and on certain points, he greatly desired that signs and wonders, such as had astonished and encouraged the infancy of the Christian Church, might again be vouchsafed to it, but he did not pretend to see such miracles himself, nor give the slightest credence to others who asserted that they did. He often congratulated himself on the fact that although his mind dwelt so constantly on

243

spiritual matters it was never betrayed into any suspension of the rational functions.

Cross-examination by letter slackened, but on occasion of my brief and usually summer visits to Devonshire I suffered acutely from my Father's dialectical appetites. He was surrounded by peasants, on whom the teeth of his arguments could find no purchase. To him, in that intellectual Abdera,[9] even an unwilling youth from London offered opportunities of pleasant contest. He would declare himself ready, nay eager, for argument. With his mental sleeves turned up, he would adopt a fighting attitude, and challenge me to a round on any portion of the Scheme of Grace. His alacrity was dreadful to me, his well-aimed blows fell on what was rather a bladder or a pillow than a vivid antagonist.

He was, indeed, most unfairly handicapped, – I was naked, he in a suit of chain armour, – for he had adopted a method which I thought, and must still think, exceedingly unfair. He assumed that he had private knowledge of the Divine Will, and he would meet my temporizing arguments by asseverations, – 'So sure as my God liveth!' or by appeals to a higher authority, – 'But what does *my* Lord tell me in Paul's Letter to the Philippians?' It was the prerogative of his faith to know, and of his character to overpower objection; between these two millstones I was rapidly ground to powder.

These 'discussions', as they were rather ironically called, invariably ended for me in disaster. I was driven out of my *papier-mâché* fastnesses, my canvas walls rocked at the first peal from my Father's clarion, and the foe pursued me across the plains of Jericho until I lay down ignominiously and covered my face. I seemed to be pushed with horns of iron, such as those which Zedekiah the son of Chenaanah prepared for the encouragement of Ahab.[10]

When I acknowledged defeat and cried for quarter, my Father would become radiant, and I still seem to hear the sound of his full voice, so thrilling, so warm, so painful to my overstrained nerves, bursting forth in a sort of benediction at the end of each of these one-sided contentions, with 'I bow my knees unto the Father of our Lord Jesus Christ, that He would grant you, according to the riches of His glory, to be strengthened with might by His Spirit in the inner man; that Christ may dwell in your heart by faith; that you, being rooted and grounded in love, may be able to comprehend with all saints what is the breadth, and length, and depth, and height, and to know the love of Christ which passeth knowledge, that you might be filled with the fullness of God.'

Thus solemn and thus ceremonious was my Father apt to become, without a moment's warning, on plain and domestic occasions; abruptly brimming over with emotion like a basin which an unseen flow of water has filled and over-filled.

I earnestly desire that no trace of that absurd self-pity which is apt to taint recollections of this nature should give falsity to mine. My Father, let me say once more, had other interests than those of his religion. In particular, at this time, he took to painting in water-colours in the open air, and he resumed the assiduous study of botany. He was no fanatical monomaniac. Nevertheless, there was, in everything he did and said, the central purpose present. He acknowledged it plainly; 'with me,' he confessed, 'every question assumes a Divine standpoint and is not adequately answered if the judgement-seat of Christ is not kept in sight.'

This was maintained whether the subject under discussion was poetry, or society, or the Prussian war with Austria, or the stamen of a wild flower. Once, at least, he was himself conscious of the fatiguing effect on my temper of this insistency, for, raising his great brown eyes with a flash of laughter in them, he closed the Bible suddenly after a very lengthy disquisition, and quoted his Virgil to startling effect: –

Claudite jam rivos, pueri: Sat prata biberunt.[11]

The insistency of his religious conversation was, probably, the less incomprehensible to me on account of the evangelical training to which I had been so systematically subjected. It was, however, none the less intolerably irksome, and would have been exasperating, I believe, even to a nature in which a powerful and genuine piety was inherent. To my own, in which a feeble and imitative faith was expiring, it was deeply vexatious. It led, alas! to a great deal of bowing in the house of Rimmon, to much hypocritical ingenuity in drawing my Father's attention away, if possible, as the terrible subject was seen to be looming and approaching. In this my stepmother would aid and abet, sometimes producing incongruous themes, likely to attract my Father aside, with a skill worthy of a parlour conjurer, and much to my admiration. If, however, she was not unwilling to come, in this way, to the support of my feebleness, there was no open collusion between us. She always described my Father, when she was alone with me, admiringly, as one 'whose trumpet gave no uncertain sound'. There was not a tinge of infidelity upon her candid mind, but she was human, and I think that now and then she was extremely bored.

My Father was entirely devoid of the prudence which turns away its eyes and passes as rapidly as possible in the opposite direction. The peculiar kind of drama in which every sort of social discomfort is welcomed rather than that the characters should be happy when guilty of 'acting a lie', was not invented in those days, and there can hardly be imagined a figure more remote from my Father than Ibsen. Yet when I came, at a far later date, to read *The Wild Duck*,[12] memories of the embarrassing household of my infancy helped me to realize Gregers Werle, with his determination to pull the veil of illusion away from every compromise that makes life bearable.

I was docile, I was plausible, I was anything but combative; if my Father could have persuaded himself to let me alone, if he could merely have been willing to leave my subterfuges and my explanations unanalysed, all would have been well. But he refused to see any difference in temperament between a lad of twenty and a sage of sixty. He had no vital sympathy for youth, which in itself had no charm for him. He had no compassion for the weaknesses of immaturity, and his one and only anxiety was to be at the end of his spiritual journey, safe with me in the house where there are many mansions. The incidents of human life upon the road to glory were less than nothing to him.

My Father was very fond of defining what was his own attitude at this time, and he was never tired of urging the same ambition upon me. He regarded himself as the faithful steward of a Master who might return at any moment, and who would require to find everything ready for his convenience. That master was God, with whom my Father seriously believed himself to be in relations much more confidential than those vouchsafed to ordinary pious persons. He awaited, with anxious hope, 'the coming of the Lord', an event which he still frequently believed to be imminent. He would calculate, by reference to prophecies in the Old and New Testament, the exact date of this event; the date would pass, without the expected Advent, and he would be more than disappointed, – he would be incensed. Then he would understand that he must have made some slight error in calculation, and the pleasures of anticipation would recommence.

Me in all this he used as a kind of inferior coadjutor, much as a responsible and upper servant might use a footboy. I, also, must be watching; it was not important that I should be seriously engaged in any affairs of my own. I must be ready for the Master's coming; and my Father's incessant cross-examination was made in the spirit of a responsible servant who fidgets lest some humble but essential piece of household work has been neglected.

My holidays, however, and all my personal relations with my Father were poisoned by this insistency. I was never at my ease in his company; I never knew when I might not be subjected to a series of searching questions which I should not be allowed to evade. Meanwhile, on every other stage of experience I was gaining the reliance upon self and the respect for the opinion of others which come naturally to a young man of sober habits who earns his own living and lives his own life. For this kind of independence my Father had no respect or consideration, when questions of religion were introduced, although he handsomely conceded it on the other points. And now first there occurred to me the reflection, which in years to come I was to repeat over and over, with an ever sadder emphasis, – what a charming companion, what a delightful parent, what a courteous and engaging friend my Father would have been, and would pre-eminently have been to me, if it had not been for this stringent piety which ruined it all.

Let me speak plainly. After my long experience, after my patience and forbearance, I have surely the right to protest against the untruth (would that I could apply to it any other word!) that evangelical religion, or any religion in a violent form, is a wholesome or valuable or desirable adjunct to human life. It divides heart from heart. It sets up a vain, chimerical ideal, in the barren pursuit of which all the tender, indulgent affections, all the genial play of life, all the exquisite pleasures and soft resignations of the body, all that enlarges and calms the soul are exchanged for what is harsh and void and negative. It encourages a stern and ignorant spirit of condemnation; it throws altogether out of gear the healthy movement of the conscience; it invents virtues which are sterile and cruel; it invents sins which are no sins at all, but which darken the heaven of innocent joy with futile clouds of remorse. There is something horrible, if we will bring ourselves to face it, in the fanaticism that can do nothing with this pathetic and fugitive existence of ours but treat it as if it were the uncomfortable ante-chamber to a palace which no one has explored and of the plan of which we know absolutely nothing. My Father, it is true, believed that he was intimately acquainted with the form and furniture of this habitation, and he wished me to think of nothing else but of the advantages of an eternal residence in it.

Then came a moment when my self-sufficiency revolted against the police-inspection to which my 'views' were incessantly subjected. There was a morning, in the hot-house at home, among the gorgeous waxen orchids which reminded my Father of the tropics in his youth, when my forbearance or my timidity gave way. The enervated air, soaked with the intoxicating perfumes of all those voluptuous flowers, may have been partly responsible for my outburst. My Father had once more put to me the customary interrogatory. Was I 'walking closely with God'? Was my sense of the efficacy of the Atonement clear and sound? Had the Holy Scriptures still their full authority with me? My replies on this occasion were violent and hysterical. I have no clear recollection what it was that I said, – I desire not to recall the whimpering sentences in which I begged to be let alone, in which I demanded the right to think for myself, in which I repudiated the idea that my Father was responsible to God for my secret thoughts and my most intimate convictions.

He made no answer; I broke from the odorous furnace of the conservatory, and buried my face in the cold grass upon the lawn. My visit to Devonshire, already near its close, was hurried to an end. I had scarcely arrived in London before the following letter, furiously despatched in the track of the fugitive, buried itself like an arrow in my heart:

When your sainted Mother died, she not only tenderly committed you to God, but left you also as a solemn charge to me, to bring you up in the nurture and admonition of the Lord. That responsibility I have sought constantly to keep before me: I can truly aver that it *has* been ever before me – in my choice of a housekeeper, in my choice of a school, in my ordering of your holidays, in my choice of a second wife, in my choice of an occupation for you, in my choice of a residence for you; and in multitudes of lesser things – I have sought to act for you, not in the light of this present world, but with a view to Eternity.

Before your childhood was past, there seemed God's manifest blessing on our care; for you seemed truly converted to Him; you confessed, in solemn baptism, that you had died and had been raised with Christ; and you were received with joy into the bosom of the Church of God, as one alive from the dead.

All this filled my heart with thankfulness and joy, whenever I thought of you: – how could it do otherwise? And when I left you in London, on that dreary winter evening, my heart, full of sorrowing love, found its refuge and its resource in this thought, – that you were one of the lambs of Christ's flock; sealed with the Holy Spirit as His; renewed in heart to holiness, in the image of God.

For a while, all appeared to go on fairly well: we yearned, indeed, to discover more of heart in your allusions to religious matters, but your expressions towards us were filial and affectionate; your conduct, so far as we could see, was moral and becoming; you mingled with the people of God, spoke of occasional delight and profit in His ordinances; and employed your talents in service to Him.

But of late, and specially during the past year, there has become manifest a rapid progress towards evil. (I must beg you here to pause, and again to look to God for grace to weigh what I am about to say; or else wrath will rise.)

When you came to us in the summer, the heavy blow fell full upon me; and I discovered how very far you had departed from God. It was not that you had yielded to the strong tide of youthful blood, and had fallen a victim to fleshly lusts; in that case, however sad, your enlightened conscience would have spoken loudly, and you would have found your way back to the blood which cleanseth us from all sin, to humble confession and self-abasement, to forgiveness and to recommunion with God. It was not this; it was worse. It was that horrid, insidious infidelity, which had already worked in your mind and heart with terrible energy. Far worse, I say, because this was sapping the very foundations of faith, on which all true godliness, all real religion, must rest.

Nothing seemed left to which I could appeal. We had, I found, no common ground. The Holy Scriptures had no longer any authority: you had taught yourself to evade their inspiration. Any particular Oracle of God which pressed you, you could easily explain away; even the very character of God you weighed in your balance of fallen reason, and fashioned it accordingly. You were thus sailing down the rapid tide of time towards Eternity, without a single authoritative guide (having cast your chart overboard), except what you might fashion and forge on your own anvil, – except what you might *guess*, in fact.

Do not think I am speaking in passion, and using unwarrantable strength of words. If the written Word is not absolutely authoritative, what do we know of God? What more then can we infer, that is, guess, – as the thoughtful heathens guessed, – Plato, Socrates, Cicero, – from dim and mute surrounding phenomena? What do we know of Eternity? Of our relations to God? Especially of the relations of a *sinner* to God? What of reconciliation? What of the capital question – How can a God of perfect spotless rectitude deal with me, a corrupt sinner, who have trampled on those of His laws which were even written on my conscience? . . .

This dreadful conduct of yours I had intended, after much prayer, to pass by in entire silence; but your apparently sincere inquiries after the cause of my sorrow have led me to go to the root of the matter, and I could not stop short of the development contained in this letter. It is with pain, not in anger, that I send it; hoping that you may be induced to review the whole course, of which this is only a stage, before God. If this grace were granted to you, oh! how joyfully should I bury all the past, and again have sweet and tender fellowship with my beloved Son, as of old.

The reader who has done me the favour to follow this record of the clash of two temperaments will not fail to perceive the crowning importance of the letter from which I have just made a long quotation. It sums up, with the closer logic, the whole history of the situation, and I may leave it to form the epigraph of this little book.

All that I need further say is to point out that when such defiance is offered to the intelligence of a thoughtful and honest young man with the normal impulses of his twenty-one years, there are but two alternatives Either he must cease to think for himself; or his individualism must be instantly confirmed, and the necessity of religious independence must be emphasized.

No compromise, it is seen, was offered; no proposal of a truce would have been acceptable. It was a case of 'Everything or Nothing'; and thus desperately challenged, the young man's conscience threw off once for all the yoke of his 'dedication', and, as respectfully as he could, without parade or remonstrance, he took a human being's privilege to fashion his inner life for himself.

NOTES

INTRODUCTION

1 (p. 10). Howard Furness to Edmund Gosse: letter quoted in *Transatlantic Dialogue: Selected American Correspondence of Edmund Gosse*, ed. Paul Mattheisen and Michael Millgate (University of Texas Press, 1965), pp. 260–61.

2 (p. 10). William Howells to Edmund Gosse: letter quoted in *Transatlantic Dialogue*, ibid., p. 267.

3 (p. 10). ibid, p. 270.

4 (p. 10). George Bernard Shaw: letter to Philip Gosse quoted in Evan Charteris *The Life and Letters of Sir Edmund Gosse* (Heinemann, 1931), p. 505.

5 (p. 10). Ezra Pound in review of Edmund Gosse's *Life of Swinburne* in *Nation* (cxi, 22 May 1920), pp. 691–2.

6 (p. 10). Harold Nicolson in *The Development of English Biography* (Hogarth Press, 1927), p. 148.

7 (p. 11). Charteris, op. cit., p. 42.

8 (p. 12). Edmund Gosse in *Some Diversions of a Man of Letters* (Heinemann, 1919), p. 321.

9 (p. 15). Edmund Gosse in a letter to Gide dated 22 August 1926 quoted in *Correspondence of André Gide and Edmund Gosse* (Owen, 1960), p. 183.

10 (p. 15). Edmund Gosse quoted in Charteris, op. cit., p. 323.

11 (p. 15). ibid.

12 (p. 15). ibid, p. 444.

13 (p. 18). Jean-Jacques Rousseau, *Confessions*: this translation given in *Selected Essays of Sainte-Beuve*, translated and edited by Steegmuller and Guterman (Methuen, 1965), pp. 195–6.

14 (p. 19). Phyllis Grosskurth in *Approaches to Victorian Autobiography*, ed. George Landow (Ohio University Press, 1979), p. 28.

15 (p. 19). John Addington Symonds in preface to *The Memoirs of Count Carlo Gozzi* (J. C. Nimmo, 1890), p. 9.

16 (p. 19). Edmund Gosse in *Leaves and Fruit* (Heinemann, 1927), pp. 19–20.

17 (p. 20). Edmund Gosse in *Critical Kit-Kats* (Heinemann, 1896), p. 266.

18 (p. 20). Herbert Spencer, *An Autobiography* (Williams, 1904), p. 7.

19 (p. 20). Anthony Trollope, *An Autobiography* (Blackwell, 1929), p. 1.

20 (p. 20). ibid., p. 53.

21 (p. 20). Virginia Woolf, *Collected Essays*, Vol. IV (Hogarth Press, 1967), p. 84.

22 (p. 21). op. cit., p. 146.

23 (p. 23). Edmund Gosse, *Father and Son* (Penguin Books, 1983), p. 33.

24 (p. 23). *Father and Son* (Oxford University Press, 1974), p. 3.

25 (p. 24). op. cit., p. 7.

26 (p. 24). Edmund Gosse: letter quoted in Charteris, op. cit., p. 478.

27 (p. 24). Sainte-Beuve in *Selected Essays* translated and edited by Steegmuller and Guterman (Methuen, 1965), p. 383.

28 (p. 24). ibid., p. 292.

29 (p. 24). op. cit., p. 102.

30 (p. 24). op. cit., p. 102.

31 (p. 25). op. cit., p. 65.

32 (p. 27). op. cit., pp. 79–80.

33 (p. 27). op. cit., p. 167.

34 (p. 28). David Grylls in *Guardians and Angels*, op. cit., p. 177.

35 (p. 28). op. cit., p. 248.

36 (p. 28). op. cit., p. 236.

37 (p. 29). op. cit., p. 251.

38 (p. 30). op. cit., p. 55.

39 (p. 31). Edmund Gosse: letter quoted in Charteris, p. 311.

40 (p. 31). ibid., p. 313.

CHAPTER I

1 (p. 36). *Rousseau*: Jean-Jacques Rousseau (1712–78), major philo-

sopher and writer. In his influential book *Émile* (1762) he outlined an ideal education based on the principles of self-regulation and indirect enquiry.

2 (p. 37). *Plymouth Brethren*: a Protestant group formed around 1830 in the West of England (hence Plymouth). Gosse himself describes their doctrinal beliefs.

3 (p. 38). *Waverley Novels*: the historical novels of Sir Walter Scott (1771–1832), the first of which was called *Waverley*.

4 (p. 42). *intellectual Thebaïd*: an intellectual Thebes.

5 (p. 43). *more than one biographer*: Emily Gosse's life was described in Anna Shipton's *Tell Jesus* (1863) and in Philip Gosse's *A Memorial of the Last Day on Earth of Emily Gosse* (1857). Edmund Gosse himself wrote the biography of his father *Life of Philip Henry Gosse FRS*, published in 1890.

6 (p. 43). *My serious duty . . . is other*: both quotations are taken from stanza 18 of 'One Word More' by Robert Browning (1812–89).

7 (p. 44). *carefully tended social parterre*: from French *par terre*, a level ornamental garden. Thus, a carefully arranged social life.

CHAPTER II

1 (p. 45). *Miss Edgeworth*: Maria Edgeworth (1757–1849), prolific Irish novelist and friend of Walter Scott.

2 (p. 46). *ultima Thule*: furthest Thule. Thule was the most northerly island known to the Greeks. Hence from a most distant point.

3 (p. 48). *that then popular writer, the Rev. George Croly*: George Croly (1780–1860), author of a number of popular novels including *Salathiel*, published in 1829.

4 (p. 49). *Bulwer Lytton*: Bulwer Lytton (1803–73), prolific novelist, short-story writer and poet.

5 (p. 49). *Mrs Gaskell*: Elizabeth Gaskell (1810–65), important novelist; author of *Cranford*, *North and South*, *Sylvia's Lovers* and *Life of Charlotte Brontë*.

6 (p. 50). *a writer on prophecy called Jukes*: Gosse seems to have had a particular loathing for Andrew John Jukes, the author of innumerable exegetical works on the Bible published from 1842 onwards. He is referred to again on pp. 73, 79 and 197.

7 (p. 50). *a publication called The Penny Cyclopaedia*: Gosse refers

again to this publication on pp. 67 and 88. *The Penny Encyclopedia* was published by the Society for the Diffusion of Useful Knowledge. It was completed in twenty-seven volumes in the spring of 1844. It had originally sold 75,000 weekly parts though by 1843 it had dropped to 20,000. It was the product of a period of cheap printing and a widespread desire for self-education.

8 (p. 52). *FRS*: Fellow of the Royal Society. Philip Gosse became a Fellow of the Royal Society on 4 June 1856.

9 (p. 52). *Charles Wesley*: Charles Wesley (1707–88), brother of John Wesley and a composer of many hymns.

10 (p. 52). *George Whitefield*: George Whitefield (1714–70) a follower of the Wesleys who later started his own group of Calvinistic Methodists.

11 (p. 54). *called 'The Guardsman of the Alma'*: in *The Life of Philip Henry Gosse FRS* (1890) Edmund Gosse writes: 'in the autumn of 1855 was published *The Young Guardsman of the Alma*, a Gospel Tract issued in leaflet form by the weekly Tract society.' Emily Gosse published forty-one such Tracts and they were published after her death in 1857 as a single volume.

12 (p. 55). *Princess Blanchefleur*: heroine of a medieval verse romance. Captured by pirates and sold as a slave, she was rescued by Floris who gained entrance to the harem in a basket of roses.

13 (p. 58). *Mrs Jellyby*: a character in Charles Dickens's *Bleak House* who neglects her own house as she labours for various charitable schemes.

14 (p. 60). *Great Globe in Leicester Square*: according to Edmund Gosse's diary this visit took place on 10 September 1857.

15 (p. 62). *in Donne's poem*: John Donne (1571–1631). Gosse is referring to the first stanza of 'The Primrose, being at Montgomery Castle, upon the hill, on which it is situate' published in his *Songs and Sonets*. Edmund Gosse published an important biography of John Donne in 1899 and was partly responsible for establishing his modern reputation.

16 (p. 63). *a packet of spilikins*: metaphor from the Victorian game made up of thin straws.

17 (p. 66). *excellent Irish peer*: Lord Congleton (1805–83) did missionary work with the Plymouth Brethren; his second wife was an Armenian.

18 (p. 67). *Penny Cyclopaedia*: see note above for p. 50.

1 (p. 69). *one of the most cruel maladies*: Cancer. Emily Gosse died on 9 February 1857 from cancer of the breast. Edmund Gosse gives a further account of this death, particularly from his father's viewpoint, in chapters 9 and 10 of his *Life of Philip Henry Gosse FRS*.

2 (p. 73). *Toplady*: Augustus Toplady (1740–78) hymn-writer, the author of 'Rock of Ages'.

3 (p. 74). *James Hyslop*: James Hyslop (1798–1827) Scottish poet, successively shepherd, schoolmaster and tutor on board ship.

4 (p. 74). *Robert Louis Stevenson*: Robert Louis Stevenson (1850–94), the novelist, was a close literary friend of Edmund Gosse. He also had had a strict Calvinistic background.

5 (p. 75). *Sir James Simpson*: James Simpson (1811–70) won in 1856 the French Academy of Sciences Monthyon prize for the development of anaesthesia.

6 (p. 77). *very effective Parthian shot*: a Parthian shot is one fired in retreat. The Parthian horsemen were trained to fire their missiles backwards while in real or feigned flight.

7 (p. 78). *Trimalchion's feast*: an episode described in Petronius' *Satyricon* in which the opulent Trimalchion entertains the hero of the book to a sumptuous meal. The incident came to symbolize gluttony.

8 (p. 78). *'the interpretation of prophecy'*: Philip Gosse published two volumes interpreting Biblical prophecy, *The Revelation: How it is to be Interpreted* (1866) and *The Prophetic Times* (1871). He argued that the prophecies told obscurely of contemporary events and he himself lived in permanent expectation of the Second Coming.

9 (p. 79). *Habershon and Jukes*: Matthew Habershon (1789–52) an architect who wrote works on prophecy. There is a direct account of Philip Gosse's response to Habershon's work in Appendix 2 of Edmund Gosse's *The Life of Philip Henry Gosse FRS*.

10 (p. 79). *the Horae Apocalypticae of a Mr Elliott*: Bishop Edward Elliott (1793–1875) published his chief work, *Horae Apocalypticae*, in 1844.

11 (p. 80). *my parents faced the awful hour*: Emily Gosse died on 9 February 1857. Philip Gosse gave his own account of the death of his wife in a pamphlet, circulated among friends, called *A Memorial of the Last Days on Earth of Emily Gosse* (1857).

12 (p. 81). *John Henry Newman*: Cardinal Newman (1801–90),

influential writer and convert to Catholicism, author of *Apologia pro Vita Sua* (1864), an autobiographical account of his spiritual history.

1 (p. 83). *kind but little known paternal cousin*: the cousin was Mrs Ann Morgan who had actually helped to nurse Emily Gosse during her fatal illness according to Philip Gosse's account in *Memorial*.

2 (p. 85). *eldritch scream*: eldritch; of Scottish origin: meaning 'weird', 'unnatural'.

3 (p. 85). *sealed in a Leyden jar*: a Leyden jar is an electrical condenser invented in the city of Leyden in Holland. Except for a conducting rod the jar is hermetically sealed off from the outside world.

4 (p. 88). *Penny Cyclopaedia*: see note above for p. 50.

5 (p. 91). *Charlotte Elliott*: Charlotte Elliott (1789–1871), hymn-writer and composer of religious poetry.

6 (p. 91). *James Montgomery*: James Montgomery (1771–1854), poet, clerk to the *Sheffield Register* and hymn-writer.

7 (p. 91). *Puseyite*: follower of Doctor Pusey (1800–82), one of the leaders of the Oxford Movement expounding the Anglo-Catholic position. He joined John Henry Newman and John Keble in the production of 'Tracts for the Times' (1833 onwards).

8 (p. 91). *The Christian Year*: the collection of religious poems published in 1827 by John Keble (1792–1866).

9 (p. 91). *Horatius Bonar*: Horatius Bonar (1808–89), Scottish divine and hymn-writer.

10 (p. 93). *'Line upon Line: Here a Little, and there a Little'*: a publication giving paraphrases of, and commentary on, passages in the Bible, written by F. L. Bevan and published during the 1830s.

11 (p. 94). *Lord Chesterfield*: Lord Chesterfield (1694–1773), best known for his *Letters* written from 1737 to his son, describing the education of a gentleman.

12 (p. 96). *Mrs Pipchin and Miss Sally Brass*: Mrs Pipchin, a Brighton boarding-house keeper, appears in Charles Dickens's novel *Dombey and Son* (1848) while Sally Brass appears in *The Old Curiosity Shop* (1841).

13 (p. 97). *The House of Rimmon*: Miss Marks bows to her Master's

God as Naaman does when he returns to Syria to worship Rimmon, the Assyrian divinity (see 2 Kings v, 18).

CHAPTER V

1 (p. 99). *Wordsworth . . . the 'Prelude'*: William Wordsworth (1770–1850) wrote his long autobiographical poem 'The Prelude' between 1799 and 1805.

2 (p. 99). *The village, on the outskirts*: St Marychurch which has now been absorbed into Babbacombe and is part of Torbay.

3 (p. 102). *Lyell*: Sir Charles Lyell (1797–1875), Professor of Geology at London University. He revolutionized the prevailing idea of the age of the earth by insisting upon the gradual process of natural laws.

4 (p. 102). *Darwin*: Charles Darwin (1809–82), author of *The Origin of Species by Means of Natural Selection*, published in 1859.

5 (p. 102). *Hooker and Wallace, Asa Gray and even Agassiz*: all of these scientists were coming close to the idea of natural selection as the principle of evolution. Alfred Wallace (1823–1913) came to the notion of natural selection independently of Darwin in 1858 and communicated his theory to Darwin. The outcome was a joint communication to the Linnaean Society (of which Asa Gray was a member) on the theory of evolution.

6 (p. 103). *Vestiges of Creation*: work by Robert Chambers published anonymously in 1844.

7 (p. 103). *Owen*: Sir Richard Owen (1804–92), Professor of Comparative Anatomy and Physiology at the Hunterian Museum. He was a leading opponent of the theory of evolution through natural selection.

8 (p. 103). *Carpenter*: Philip Carpenter (1819–77), naturalist and teacher.

9 (p. 104). *though Sir Thomas Browne denied it*: Sir Thomas Browne (1605–82) was author of a number of works including *Religio Medici* (1643), a confession of Christian faith. In *Omphalos* Philip Gosse takes issue with Sir Thomas Browne's view that Adam was created with a navel.

10 (p. 105). *This 'Omphalos' of his*: Philip Gosse's book published in the autumn of 1857 was titled *Omphalos* and subtitled: *An Attempt to*

Untie the Geological Knot. Its content is further described by Edmund Gosse in *The Life of Philip Henry Gosse F.R.S.*

11 (p. 105). *the youthful Huxley*: Thomas Henry Huxley (1825–95) eminent scientist and writer; also a discriminating supporter of Darwinism.

12 (p. 105). *Charles Kingsley*: Charles Kingsley (1819–75) the author of many books including *The Water Babies* (1863) and *Westward Ho!* (1855). A friend of Philip Gosse, with a strong interest in natural history.

13 (p. 109). *'the Carpet-bag Mystery'*: on 9 December 1857 a carpet-bag was found on Waterloo Bridge and inside was a hacked body without head and limbs. The murder was thought to be connected with a plot against the government of Napoleon III.

14 (p. 111). *assafoetida*: strongly smelling resin that used to be employed in medicine.

15 (p. 113). *Huxley*: see note above for p. 105.

CHAPTER VI

1 (p. 117). *the Nestor of our meeting*: Nestor was one of the wise counsellors of the Greeks during the Trojan Wars.

2 (p. 118). *affected with phthisis*: tuberculosis.

3 (p. 122). *in the very words of Shelley*: the lines quoted are the first six lines of the third stanza of Shelley's poem 'The Question', first published in 1822.

4 (p. 123). *affranchissant l'esprit et pesant les mondes sans haine, sans peur, sans pitié, sans amour et sans Dieu*: 'releasing the spirit and weighing up worlds without bitterness, without fear, without pity, without love and without God.' This description of the scientific mind was made by Gustav Flaubert (1821–80), the great French novelist.

5 (p. 124). *Keats' Grecian vase, 'a still unravished bride of quietness'*: The description is that used by John Keats (1795–1821) in his *Ode on a Grecian Urn* (1819).

6 (p. 126). *History of the British Sea-Anemones and Corals*: volume published by Philip Gosse in 1860.

7 (p. 127). *Actinologia Britannica*: this work of Philip Gosse was published in January 1860. For a commentary on the volume and other

works by Philip Gosse see Edmund Gosse's *The Life of Philip Henry Gosse FRS* (1890).

1 (p. 129). *a détraquée*: equivalent to English 'gone off the rails'.

2 (p. 129). *in which the philosopher expresses the hope*: John Collins (1724–1808), actor and poet; extract from the poem 'In the Downhill of Life'.

3 (p. 132). *bound hand and foot like Mazeppa*: Byron's poem 'Mazeppa' (1819) is the story of a Polish nobleman named Mazeppa who was bound for his misdeeds to a wild Ukranian horse.

4 (p. 136). *âme d'élite*: an elite or superior soul.

5 (p. 138). *we gained Pisgah-views*: Pisgah was the name of the mountain from which Moses viewed the Promised Land.

6 (p. 138). *hirsuta et horrida*: 'hairy and terrible'.

7 (p. 139). *Hypatia*: Charles Kingsley's novel published in 1853.

8 (p. 141). *what the French call entr' ouvert*: half-open.

9 (p. 142). *Like Aurora Leigh*: 'Aurora Leigh', a romance in blank verse by E. B. Browning published in 1856. The poem describes the life of the heroine, Aurora Leigh.

10 (p. 143). *Tityre, tu patulae recubans sub tegmine fagi,*

> 'Tityrus, you're lying under the awnings of a spread-
>   ing beech-tree'.

> *tu, Tityre, lentus in umbra*
> *Formosam resonare doces Amaryllida silvas.*
> 'Tityrus, reclining in shade
> you teach the wood to echo the beautiful Amaryllis'.

Both passages are from the first stanza of Virgil's *Eclogues*: lines 1 and lines 4 and 5.

1 (p. 148). *Papers read before the Linnaean Society*: society founded in

honour of Carl Linnaeus, the Swedish naturalist, to promote natural history.

2 (p. 153). *'another Infant Samuel'*: a child of God in the manner of Samuel as described in 1 Sam. i and ii.

3 (p. 158). *James Smith*: James Smith (1775–1839), co-author of *Rejected Addresses* (1812) and *Horace in London* (1813).

CHAPTER IX

1 (p. 165). *the church of Laodicea*: the church of Laodicea was rebuked for being lukewarm in religion and politics (Rev. iii, 15–16).

2 (p. 167). *no close time for souls*: a metaphor from game shooting: when the birds are breeding and rearing their young, it is close time and there can be no shooting.

3 (p. 167). *nunc dimittis*: the first words of the Song of Simeon upon seeing the infant Jesus in whom he recognized the Messiah: now let me depart (in peace). Luke ii, 29.

4 (p. 169). *Archbishop Leighton*: Robert Leighton, seventeenth-century archbishop of Glasgow, celebrated for his moderation and enlightenment in a time of persecution and fanaticism.

5 (p. 170) *Tom Cringle's Log*: written by Michael Scott (1789–1835) and published first in *Blackwoods Magazine* in 1829–33.

6 (p. 171). *most febrifugal story-book*: a book that would prevent any fever of excitement.

7 (p. 172). *shut up, like Fatima, in a tower*: Fatima, the last wife of Bluebeard in *Bluebeard*, a popular tale from the French of Perrault (1628–1703).

8 (p. 176). *James Sheridan Knowles*: James Sheridan Knowles (1784–1862). After trying the army, medicine and the stage, James Knowles became a writer by profession and wrote a number of popular tragedies and comedies.

CHAPTER X

1 (p. 181). *'don't tell me that she's a pedobaptist?'*: a pedobaptist is

one who believes, unlike the Plymouth Brethren, in child baptism.

2 (p. 182). *always a lodge in my garden of cucumbers*: the phrase derives from the Bible 'And the daughter of Zion is left as a cottage in a vineyard, as a lodge in a garden of cucumbers, as a besieged city.' (Isaiah i, 8).

3 (p. 183). *All the quidnuncs*: from the Latin meaning 'What now?'. Hence, busybodies.

4 (p. 185). *The Romance of Natural History*: this was published in two volumes in 1860 and 1861. Each chapter dealt with a different facet of nature in a poetic and anecdotal manner. In his *The Life of Philip Henry Gosse FRS*, Edmund Gosse wrote that this book preserved 'a charm which may never wholly evaporate. The editions of this book have been very numerous, and after a lapse of thirty years I believe that it is still in print, and enjoys a steady sale.'

5 (p. 186). *cette tromperie mutuelle*: 'mutual error'.

6 (p. 186). *Pascal*: Blaise Pascal (1623–62), the great seventeenth-century French mathematician and philosopher.

7 (p. 186). *Tartuffe*: *Tartuffe* is a comedy by the French playwright, Molière. Tartuffe assumes piety in order to gain entrance to the household of Orgon; having done so, he attempts to seduce the wife and, being repulsed, works to ruin the family.

8 (p. 189). *The Lady of the Lake*: the poem in six cantos by Walter Scott (1771–1832), published in 1810. All the references to Duncrannon, and Cambus-Kenneth, Fitzjames and Ellen's Isle are references to characters and situations in the narrative.

9 (p. 190). *The Lord of the Isles*: the poem by Walter Scott, published in 1815, describing the return of Robert Bruce to Scotland.

10 (p. 190). *Rob Roy*: the novel by Walter Scott, published in 1817, set in the period immediately preceding the Jacobite rising of 1715.

11 (p. 190). *Pickwick*: Charles Dickens's well-known novel, first published as a volume in 1837.

12 (p. 191). *Old Crome*: John Crome (1768–1821), one of the English landscape painters, founder of the Norwich school of painting.

13 (p. 191). *no less a person than Cotman*: John Sell Cotman (1782–1842), the landscape painter of Crome's Norwich School.

14 (p. 191). *Liber Studiorum*: John Sell Cotman's Book of Studies.

15 (p. 192). *Mr Holman Hunt's 'Finding of Christ in the Temple'*: Holman Hunt (1827–1910), one of the English Pre-Raphaelite painters, most famous for his painting 'The Light of the World'.

16 (p. 192). *phylacteries*: slips of parchment inserted with passages from the Scriptures.

17 (p. 192). *'Preraphaelite' treatment*: the Pre-Raphaelites sought to return to art forms as they supposed them to exist in European art before the time of Raphael. The movement, to which Edmund Gosse was greatly attracted, began about 1850 and was composed of such figures as Holman Hunt, John Millais and Dante Gabriel Rossetti.

18 (p. 192). *chiaroscuro*: pictorial representation in terms of light and shade.

CHAPTER XI

1 (p. 196). *Campbell was there, and Burns, and Keats and the 'Tales' of Byron*: Thomas Campbell (1777–1844), Robert Burns (1759–96) John Keats (1795–1821) and George Byron (1788–1824), probably a characteristic selection of poetry for an educated person around 1860. The 'Tales' refer to the long narrative poems of Byron.

2 (p. 196). *gloomy funereal poems*: poems written by Robert Blair (1699–1746) and Edward Young (1683–1765) and their followers. The group was known as the 'graveyard school of poetry'.

3 (p. 197). *autochthonous*: rooted deep in the earth.

4 (p. 197). *Jukes' On the Pentateuch*: see notes above for page 50. Pentateuch: the first five books of the Old Testament.

5 (p. 197). *The Javelin of Phineas*: strictly *The Javelin of Phinehas*, published in 1863 by William Lincoln.

6 (p. 198). *'The Last Day'*: poem of Edward Young (1683–1765), one of the funereal poets.

7 (p. 198). *sanctimonious rector of Welwyn*: namely Edward Young who became rector of Welwyn in 1730.

8 (p. 198). *Beilby Porteus*: English poet (1731–1808).

9 (p. 198). *its extravagant and preposterous author*: Samuel Boyse (1708–49) was the author of the popular work 'The Deity'. He was known for wearing home-made paper shirts and endlessly begging for money.

10 (p. 198). *Blair's 'Grave'*: see note above for p. 196.

11 (p. 200). *'Casabianca'*: poem by the popular poet Felicia Dorothea Hemans (1793–1835).

12 (p. 200). *We are Seven'*: one of the Lyrical Ballads, published by Wordsworth in 1798.

13 (p. 200). *Calverley*: Charles Stuart Calverley (1831–84), barrister and author.

14 (p. 202). *to parody the poet Gray*: the line parodied is from the 'Elegy' by Thomas Gray (1716–71). The original line reads: 'How jocund did they drive their team afield' (line 27).

15 (p. 202). *'Sandford and Merton'*: *The History of Sandford and Merton* by Thomas Day, the first volume of which was published in 1783 In the book, the rich and objectionable Merton is contrasted with the virtuous Sandford, a farmer's son.

16 (p. 204). *with foreign savants*: learned figures.

17 (p. 206). *If I had ever read 'Hellas'*: 'Hellas', a lyrical drama by Shelley, published in 1822. Shelley had written:

> Apollo, Pan and Love
> And even Olympian Jove
> Grew weak for killing Truth had glared at them.

(lines 232–4).

18 (p. 207). *S. T. Coleridge*: the Romantic poet Samuel Taylor Coleridge (1772–1834).

19 (p. 208).

> *Behold him how Hell's reek*
> *Has crisped his hair and singed his cheek!*

The lines are taken from the poem 'Dante at Verona' (published in 1870) by Dante Gabriel Rossetti (1828–82).

20 (p. 211). *in a neighbouring seaport town*: the town of Teignmouth

CHAPTER XII

1 (p. 212). *as Elkanah and Hannah had long ago taken Samuel*: for the full reference see 1 Sam. i and ii. Samuel is described as 'a child, girded with a linen ephod'.

2 (p. 213). *in custodiendo sermones Dei*: observing the word of God.

3 (p. 214). *I felt very much like Gehazi*: the covetous servant of Elisha

who was punished with leprosy for deceitfully obtaining a present from Maamen. (2 Kings v, 20–7).

4 (p. 216). *Montaigne*: Michel Montaigne (1533–92), the great French essayist.

5 (p. 216). *parceque c'était lui, parceque c'était moi*: Montaigne wrote about his friend Étienne de la Boëtie: 'If you press me to say why I love him, I can say no more than it was *because he was he and I was I*' (*Essays* XXVII).

6 (p. 217). *poor half-starved phthisic lad*: the boy was suffering from tuberculosis.

7 (p. 219). *like that chimerical flower, the Rose of Jericho*: a small rose, native to the deserts of Egypt and Syria. When it is dry, if it is exposed to moisture, the branches uncurl.

8 (p. 227). *Ben Jonson and Christopher Marlowe*: Ben Jonson (1572–1637) and Christopher Marlowe (1564–93), the Elizabethan dramatists.

9 (p. 227). *'Hero and Leander'*: the poem by Christopher Marlowe, published in 1598.

10 (p. 229). *the plethoric elders*: elders, the number of which was excessive.

11 (p. 230). *with Shelley whose 'Queen Mab'*: 'Queen Mab', a philosophical poem, was first published in 1821.

12 (p. 230). *The Golden Treasury*: Francis Palgrave's (1824–97) anthology of verse, first published in 1861.

13 (p. 231). *Unitarian (or 'Socinian', as he preferred to say)*: the Unitarians believed that God could only exist as one person. The Socinians denied the divinity of Christ. In *The Life of Philip Henry Gosse FRS*, Edmund records how his father refused to dine with a Socinian because he denied 'the Divinity of the Blessed Lord'.

14 (p. 232). *the stately Puginesque cathedral which Rome had just erected*: a cathedral built by the Roman Catholics in the Gothic style advocated by the writer and architect Augustus Pugin (1812–52).

15 (p. 233). *'Endymion'*: long narrative poem by John Keats, published in 1818.

16 (p. 234). *the great chorus which so marvellously portrays our double nature*: this is a reference to the chorus in Shelley's 'Hellas' (1822). The chorus culminates in a strange paradox about the loss secured by Christian Truth:

Apollo, Pan and Love
And even Olympian Jove
Grew weak for killing Truth had glared on them;
Our hills and seas and streams
Dispeopled of their dreams
Their waters turned to blood, their dew to tears,
Wailed for the golden years.

17 (p. 234). *I wrote a tragedy in pale imitation of Shakespeare*: according to Charteris, in his biography of Edmund Gosse, this tragedy was written in 1865 and was called *Jonathan: a lyric drama in three acts* and ran to 1,600 lines. Charteris writes: 'His Muse was spreading its wings in preparation for flight. Verse is now found scattered in diaries, on the back of accounts and on the fly-leaves of books.'

18 (p. 234). *'Prometheus Unbound'*: a lyrical drama in four acts by Shelley, published in 1820.

EPILOGUE

1 (p. 239). *in his uplifted Quixotism*: in his enthusiasm for visionary ideals characteristic of the literary hero Don Quixote, created by Cervantes (1547–1616).

2 (p. 240). *Bossuet*: Jacques Bossuet (1627–1704), French theologian and preacher.

3 (p. 240). *cri de misère a l'entour de nous, qui devrait nous fondre le coeur*: 'the cry of misery all around us which ought to open up the depths of the heart'.

4 (p. 240). *Jeremy Taylor*: Jeremy Taylor (1613–67), seventeenth-century bishop and author of *Holy Living* and *Holy Dying* (1650).

5 (p. 241). *a volume of Carlyle or Ruskin*: Thomas Carlyle (1795–1881) and John Ruskin (1819–1900) were the emerging prophetic voices of that time. Edmund Gosse was later to react against their intense moral convictions and establish a lighter, essentially amoral form of criticism.

6 (p. 242). *called The Continuity of Scripture*: this was a series of excerpts from the Bible published in 1867 and running through several editions. It was edited by William Page Wood (1801–81), a distinguished lawyer and writer.

7 (p. 242). *an old edition of Bunyan*: an edition of Bunyan's *Pilgrim's Progress*, first published in 1678.

8 (p. 243). *Elihu the Buzite, of the kindred of Ram*: In Job xxxii–xxxvii, Elihu asserts that God is not the petty and exacting Being that others claim him to be.

9 (p. 244). *in that intellectual Abdera*: Abdera is a Greek city whose inhabitants were proverbial for their stupidity.

10 (p. 244). *which Zedekiah, the Son of Chenaanah prepared for the encouragement of Ahab*: The source of this reference to Zedekiah's horns of iron can be found in 1 Kings xxii, 11.

11 (p. 245). *Claudite jam rivos, pueri: Sat prata biberunt*: 'Boys, close now the fountains; the meadows have drunk enough'. From Virgil's *Eclogue* 3 (line 111).

12 (p. 246). *The Wild Duck*: the play by Henrik Ibsen (1828–1906) written in 1884. Edmund Gosse's book on Henrik Ibsen was published in 1907, the same year as *Father and Son*.

SELECTED BIBLIOGRAPHY

ON AUTOBIOGRAPHY

Abbs, Peter, *Autobiography in Education* (Gryphon Press, 1974); Essay on autobiography in *The New Pelican Guide to English Literature*, Vol. 8 (Penguin Books, 1983).

Buckley, J. H., *The Turning Key* (Harvard University Press, 1984).

Fleishman, Avrom, *Figures and Autobiography* (University of California Press, 1983).

Jay, P., *Being in the Text* (Cornell University Press, 1984).

Landow, George, *Approaches to Victorian Autobiography* (Ohio University Press, 1979).

Morris, John, *Versions of the Self* (Basic Books, 1966).

Olney, James, *Metaphors of Self* (Princeton University Press, 1972); *Autobiography: Essays Theoretical and Critical* (Princeton University Press, 1980).

Pascal, Roy, *Design and Truth in Autobiography* (Routledge & Kegan Paul, 1960).

Pateman, Trevor, 'Autobiography and Education' (University of Sussex, Occasional Paper 13, 1986).

Peterson, Linda, *Victorian Autobiography: the Tradition of Self Interpretation* (Yale University Press, 1986).

Shumaker, Wayne, *English Autobiography* (University of California Press, 1954).

Weintraub, Karl, *The Value of the Individual: Self and Circumstance in Autobiography* (University of Chicago, 1978).

ON EDMUND GOSSE'S FATHER AND SON

Grylls, David, *Guardians and Angels* (Faber, 1978).

Nicolson, Harold, *The Development of English Biography* (Hogarth Press, 1927).

Pritchet, V. S., *The Living Novel* (Chatto and Windus, 1946).
Woolf, Virginia, *Collected Essays*, Vol. IV (Hogarth Press, 1967).

RELATED AUTOBIOGRAPHICAL LITERATURE

Butler, Samuel, *The Way of all Flesh* (1903).
Mill, John Stuart, *Autobiography* (1873).
Rutherford, Mark, *Autobiography* (1881).

OTHER RELEVANT BOOKS FOR
UNDERSTANDING BACKGROUND ETC.

Brugmans, Linette (ed.), *Correspondence of André Gide and Edmund Gosse* (Owen, 1960).

Charteris, Evan, *The Life and Letters of Sir Edmund Gosse* (Heinemann, 1931).

Ford, Boris (ed.), *The New Pelican Guide to English Literature, Vol. 6: From Dickens to Hardy* (Penguin Books, 1982).

Matthieson, P. and Millgate, M., *Transatlantic Dialogue: Selected American Correspondence of Edmund Gosse* (University of Texas Press, 1965).

Sampson, Ronald, *Equality and Power* (Heinemann, 1969).

Strachey, Lytton, *Eminent Victorians* (Penguin Books, 1981).

Thwaite, Anne, *Edmund Gosse: a Literary Landscape* (Secker & Warburg, 1984).

Woolf, James, *Sir Edmund Gosse* (Twayne Publishers, New York, 1972).

SELECTED WORKS BY EDMUND GOSSE

The Life of Philip Henry Gosse FRS (Kegan Paul, 1890).
Critical Kit-Kats (Heinemann, 1896).
Collected Poems (Heinemann, 1911).
The Life of Algernon Charles Swinburne (Heinemann, 1917).
Silhouettes (Heinemann, 1925).
Leaves and Fruit (Heinemann, 1927).